Agricultural Change and the Peasant

Economy of South China

Harvard East Asian Series 66
The East Asian Research Center at Harvard University administers research projects designed to further scholarly understanding of China, Japan, Korea, Vietnam, and adjacent areas.

AGRICULTURAL CHANGE AND THE PEASANT ECONOMY OF SOUTH CHINA

Evelyn Sakakida Rawski

Harvard University Press
Cambridge, Massachusetts
1972

Preparation of this volume has been aided by a grant
from the Ford Foundation.
Library of Congress Catalog Card Number 77–173407
SBN 674–01210–0
Printed in the United States of America

To E.T.S. and T.W.S.

Acknowledgments

The research for this study was originally conducted in 1964–65 with the aid of a Foreign Area Fellowship and was incorporated into a Ph.D. dissertation begun under Professor Yang Lien-sheng at Harvard University. Since then it has been revised extensively on the basis of further research in Japan, where the continued generosity of librarians at the National Diet Library, Tōyo Bunkō, Naikaku Bunko, and Sonkeikaku Bunko in Tokyo enabled me to use again the rare editions of local gazetteers and other Chinese sources which form the backbone of this book. My debt to these libraries is clear in the bibliography.

Like every student, I owe a great deal to the instruction and encouragement of my teachers: my first instructor in Chinese history, Professor Knight Biggerstaff, and Professors Yang Lien-sheng and John K. Fairbank. Professor Fairbank has been a constant source of advice and aid, material and intellectual; this manuscript owes much to his helping hand. Thomas G. Rawski and Professor Dwight H. Perkins exhorted, debated, and prodded the manuscript through every stage of its painful progress from the dissertation onward.

My thanks and appreciation go also to Mr. George Potter at the Harvard-Yenching Library, who has been so kind in his response to pleas for assistance; to Atsuko Hirai, who has struggled manfully to correct my Japanese; and to Thomas B. Wiens and Mi Chu Wiens for comments on the manuscript.

Acknowledgments

Contents

TABLES

MAPS

FIGURES

Agricultural Change and the Peasant

Economy of South China

MEASUREMENT UNITS

Capacity measure

10 ho = 1 sheng
10 sheng = 1 tou
10 tou = 1 shih
1 shih = 100 liters

Weight

1 catty = 1.1 lb., or 0.5 kilograms
100 catties = 1 tan, shih tan (picul) or 0.5 quintals

Length

1 li = 0.5 kilometer

Area

1 mou, shih mou = 0.1647 acre
15 mou = 1 hectare
100 mou = 1 ch'ing

These are modern standardized units; historical and regional variations are discussed in the text and notes as they occur. A detailed study of the subject is presented by Wu Ch'eng-lo, *Chung-kuo tu-liang-heng shih,* Chung-kuo wen-hua shih ts'ung-shu, vol. VII, Wang Yün-wu and Fu Wei-p'ing, eds. (Shanghai: Commercial Press, 1937).

Chapter One / INTRODUCTION

The economic landscape of Ming China is most commonly studied not for itself but as a reference point in larger interpretations of Chinese history. Modern preoccupations, in particular with the "failure" of China to respond as did Japan to Western "impact," have shaped the nature and content of research, so that much of the scholarship on Chinese economic history in the Ming and Ch'ing periods (1368–1911) reveals a Europo-centric bias in its focus on why China did not independently sustain an Industrial Revolution. The 1957 movement in mainland Chinese circles to uncover "sprouts of capitalism" in the sixteenth century remains as solidly welded to this orientation as does the work of non-Marxist historians elsewhere.[1] From this viewpoint, Ming and Ch'ing China were periods of economic stagnation: in the absence of self-sustaining industrialization, nothing of note occurred.

In a landscape which by and large shows no factory smokestacks, we believe that those scholars, both Chinese and Western, who have concentrated on proving or disproving that Ming China was or could be industrialized have posed what is at best a peripheral question.[2] China's economy was and still remains predominantly agrarian. The historical relationship between rural China and urban commercial development has been studied, primarily by Japanese scholars, but many basic questions remain unanswered, not for lack of materials so much as lack of interest. It is only recently that scholars have begun to ponder the question of precisely how a "stagnant" economy managed to accommodate the five- or six-fold population increase which occurred in this period and in so doing, emerged with a description of development and change in Chinese agriculture.[3]

Research on Chinese agriculture is important not simply for its own sake, but because it can provide insights into the influence of commerce on the Chinese economy. The chapters which follow are concerned with some of the changes stimulated by market expansion in certain parts of sixteenth century Fukien and eighteenth century Hunan provinces. In these and other areas, commercial developments had an impact which extended beyond urban artisan and mercantile worlds, into the rural household economy. This effect is illustrated in Fukien, where the expansion of foreign trade in the sixteenth century brought identifiable changes to both the urban and rural economy, described in Chapter Four. Because the historical materials on Chinese commerce are scanty and provide little basis for evaluating changes in either the quantity or quality of trade, study of Chinese agriculture can provide a useful measuring stick against which the largely descriptive evidence on markets can be judged. In comparison with commerce, materials on farming are rich, and it is possible to examine developments in agriculture in some detail. One paradoxical conclusion of this study is that significant changes in commerce can be best studied indirectly, by tracing their effect on agriculture. The interaction of trading and agricultural activity provides a focus of interest in the following chapters.

THE AGRICULTURAL CONTEXT

The Chinese agricultural system differed in several respects from those in pre-industrial Europe. For at least the last millennium, Chinese agriculture has been dominated by a large number of free, small-scale farmers, working under a system of private landownership. A Chinese peasant, if he did not own his land, aspired to eventually do so. Both tenants and landowning farmers were free to decide what to grow on their plots and to dispose of their own produce. This introduced great flexibility into the Chinese agricultural system, for there were no institutional barriers to the adoption of new crops or new agricultural methods. Nor were there bureaucratic obstacles to the propagation of knowledge concerning agriculture. Chinese rulers derived their revenues directly from a largely agrarian populace. Both ideologically and practically, agriculture, the "root" of Chinese society, was a matter of great concern to them. Chinese agriculture was thus open to change.

The direction of this change was influenced by several factors. Perhaps the most basic was population and its relationship to the available arable land. Throughout Chinese history, the trend toward increasing population density has exercised a major impact on agriculture. In eighteenth century Hunan, for example, we can clearly see the effect of population growth on tillage practices.

Each crop has specific technical requirements which exercise an important influence on the agriculture of a region: first, by eliminating the possibility of some crops for climatic and soil reasons; second, by determining the ways in which farmers can increase their harvest. In south China, the most important crop was rice. The characteristics of paddy rice culture affected not only the proportions of seed, labor, water, and fertilizer applied to the soil but also influenced rent and tenurial relationships. This will be discussed in detail in Chapter Two.

Nor can crops be studied in isolation. In reality, a whole range of alternatives was potentially under review when a farmer decided what to grow. These alternatives included rural handicrafts and other non-agricultural sources of income. The relative importance of each alternative open to the farmer was partly dependent on individual circumstance: the size of his farm, the number of available farmhands, and past experience, a category which included the response of his own plots to specific crops, expectations of rainfall and temperature conditions at crucial points in the growing cycle, and the other minute calculations meaningful to farmers the world over.

Market conditions influenced the farmer's decision on what to grow, in several ways: not simply and directly in terms of the price he could anticipate for a given crop but also in terms of the handicraft items and subsidiary products he could produce for sale. It is at this juncture, where natural soil and climatic conditions and market considerations intermingle, that geographical location was an important limiting factor.

Although the Chinese farmer was oriented to and had participated in a market economy for at least the last millennium, not all farmers lived in areas with favorable marketing opportunities. The key to the economic development of an area lay in the availability of cheap transportation. Into the nineteenth century, the existing technology made it prohibitively expensive to transport goods overland, with the result that land-based commerce remained, as it had been in the days of the Roman empire, a traffic in luxury goods. Before the advent of the railroad or truck, cheap transport was water-borne: this was as true for Europe as for China.[4]

Transportation was thus an important negative factor in urban location.[5] In general, it was too expensive to alter natural geographic conditions, so geography largely determined the location of China's largest commercial centers. Into the nineteenth century, the distribution of water routes in China was also an index of commercialization. Water routes were lacking in the largely unurbanized north China

MAP 1. CHINA IN THE CH'ING (1644–1911): KIANGSU, FUKIEN, AND HUNAN PROVINCES

plain, and densest in the Yangtze delta, whose cities were at the heart of the empire's domestic trade. Until the construction of railroads, the distribution of water routes guaranteed the continued dominance of the southeast in commerce.[6]

Availability of cheap water transportation played a similarly crucial role in determining the commercial potential of areas within a province. In Fukien, mountainous terrain, which isolated inland areas, contributed to increase the comparative advantage enjoyed by the coastal prefectures. In Hunan, localities which were not directly on Lake Tung-t'ing or the major river systems flowing into this lake were barred from participating in large-scale marketing.[7] It is in this sense that geographical location played an important role in the farmer's life. In a region without access to water transportation, the farmer was confined to small-scale marketing activities, with little prospect for expansion,[8] but in localities with trading outlets to the large cities of China or to overseas markets, the possibilities for rural ties to commerce were great. Chapters Four and Five examine the repercussions of these ties in Fukien and Hunan.

MARKETS AND COMMERCE

In Fukien and Hunan, agriculture in favored parts of the province fed directly into large-scale commerce. We have many descriptions of this trading activity: travelers to fifteenth and sixteenth century China wrote glowing accounts of its commercial prosperity. In the 1480's, the Korean Ch'oe Pu found that in the lower Yangtze region, "whether it is market town . . . village, or embankment post, sometimes for three or four li, sometimes for seven to eight li, sometimes for over ten li, and often for as much as ten li around them, village gates crowd the ground, markets line the roads, towers look out on other towers, and boats ply stern to stern."[9] In Tz'u-ch'i county (Chekiang), "on both banks of the river, markets and warships were gathered like clouds," while at Soochow, "shops and markets, one after another, lined both river banks, and merchant junks were gathered together."[10]

Long distance trade was not confined to the Yangtze. The sixteenth century Jesuit, Matteo Ricci, marveled at the trade headed for Canton at Mei-ling-shan: "A tremendous amount of merchandise is brought here from many provinces to be carried over the mountain and sent south, and likewise, from the other side (Canton) and over the mountain, to be sent in the opposite direction. Goods coming into Canton from foreign kingdoms are transferred over this same pass into the interior of the realm. Travellers cross on horseback or in palanquins and the merchandise is transported on beasts of burden or by carriers, who seem to be innumerable, and the procession is constant all day long and every day."[11] Although these descriptions, and studies of mercantile activity in Ming China[12] indicate that domestic commerce prospered in the fifteenth and sixteenth centuries, the size of this commerce cannot be ascertained from the available sources.[13] Studies of the rice trade, however, suggest that national markets were very small.

Rice has been an important commodity in long distance trade from the Sung period on. In average years during the sixteenth century, over three million piculs of rice were shipped to Peking by the Grand Canal.[14] Rice flows to private consumers living in the cities of the Yangtze delta were perhaps still larger in quantity. By the early eighteenth century, these totaled from seven to ten million piculs a year.[15] Nonetheless, the rice entering long distance trade was minuscule when compared with the grain produced and consumed by the entire population.[16]

Although long distance rice flows were negligible in comparison with China's total output, such an aggregate statement conceals tremendous regional variations. The national rice markets drew only on those rice producing areas with water links to the Yangtze River. In fact, the bulk of the commerce of pre-modern China was confined to a very few geographically favored regions. In these areas, there developed a highly commercialized agriculture. By the late Ming, subsidiary handicrafts had become as important as basic farming to the peasant economy of the Soochow plain, with sericulture and cotton growing occupying increasing shares of the farm routine.[17] The information in Chapter Four shows that Fukien provides a further example of commercially oriented agriculture.

Periodic markets provided the link between national markets and the farming household. For the farmer, the most important market was his own. Though he may not have sold his cash crops here, the periodic market was his source for agricultural tools, credit, and information about conditions in the larger markets lying outside his ken. As a feature of pre-industrial, agricultural economies, these markets have been studied in many parts of the world. The most conceptually useful study of Chinese periodic markets is G. William Skinner's, based in part on field work done in Szechwan province.[18] Although some of Skinner's assumptions are not applicable to our study,[19] his description of the process of intensification of rural marketing and his analysis of the alternative ways in which this intensification is accomplished are most useful for investigating the development of local markets.[20] In both Fukien and Hunan, expansion of long distance trade brought an increase in the number of periodic markets in the surrounding area. This is one indication of the transmission of commercial influence from the market city to the agricultural countryside.

The following chapters will discuss most of the points outlined above, using selected areas of sixteenth century Fukien and eighteenth century Hunan as case studies of economic change within a largely agricultural context. Population changes will not be treated further, despite the obvious importance of the topic. As Skinner points out, population growth stimulates expansion in marketing systems and is important in the study of commercial development. Population and productivity are also clearly interrelated, and the linkage is especially marked in rice cultivation. In the long run, population growth may bring about basic structural changes in the economy.[21] The appendix on Ming population statistics in Fukien is an attempt to explain why it is not possible to produce population totals on the county level with any usefulness for comparing regional population changes over time.

Chapter Two / CONDITIONS OF RICE CULTURE: LABOR REQUIREMENTS AND LAND TENURE

> The *Chou li* says that in Yang-chou the best (of the five grains) is rice; in Fukien, which falls under Yang-chou, the primary grain is rice.
>
> — *Min shu*, 150.1a.

The early agriculture of Europe and China was based on very different seed resources. Each crop exercised a distinct influence on the shape of the agricultural economy. Buckwheat and primitive wheat varieties dominated European agriculture for centuries. Buckwheat and wheat were also grown in China, but from very early times rice predominated in the agriculture of the southeast. By its very nature, rice cultivation is linked to factors which until recently were foreign to European agriculture: water supply, fertilizer, and careful tillage.

In Fukien and the rest of southeastern China, agriculture and rice cultivation have been fundamentally synonymous for a long time. Rice has been a major crop in the province since Sung, when Fukien was identified as one of the most productive rice growing areas in the empire.[1] A recent study estimates that in the 1930's rice continued to be grown on 59 per cent of the cultivated land in Fukien.[2]

Since rice was Fukien's major crop, the ecology of its cultivation, particularly its labor-intensive aspects, led to the development of tenure and rent conditions favorable to the tenant. As a result, the Fukienese cultivator, owner or tenant, could personally enjoy the fruits of increased output and had every incentive to raise his productivity.

CONDITIONS OF RICE CULTIVATION

Although some strains of rice are grown on dry land, rice in China has primarily meant paddy rice. Agriculturalists have noted that "rice can be grown successfully on marginal soils that will not support other crops";[3] this is due to the primary importance of water as a nurturant. Clifford Geertz notes that in paddy agriculture the supply of water is more important than the type of soil. In its timing, quality, and quantity, water is a major factor in successful cultivation.[4] The construction of complex irrigation systems to provide water is a prerequisite for rice cultivation in most areas. Even in water-rich Fukien, only a small portion of the coastal plain could dispense with irrigation.

Descriptions in Ming gazetteers reveal the importance of irrigation systems in Fukien. The extent of the role played by man-made works in some parts of the province is shown by a gazetteer describing and classifying land in Chang-chou prefecture into five grades according to fertility. Only part of the first grade land could have been planted successfully without much irrigation; this was located on the coastal alluvial plain and had direct access to water. The rest of the land was provided with a variety of irrigation works. In many cases, efforts in Fukien went far beyond supplying water from streams in the area. Reclamation projects along the coast created new land out of the sea. The conversion of "brackish land" into fertile rice paddy is recorded and eulogized in the gazetteers.[5] Other reports concern areas requiring irrigation: mountainous land to be terraced and watered; land formed by diking off parts of lakes and stream beds; and land reclaimed from the sea by dikes and drainage systems. The land in Chang-chou was very much the product of intensive human effort.[6]

Dikes and irrigation works were on too large a scale to be undertaken by the individual peasant. For one thing, the irrigation systems usually affected hundreds of mou of land. The Lung-ch'i Embankment, built in 1565, irrigated 3,000 mou of land, and was not unusually large.[7] Dikes also deteriorated rapidly: "When waterworks are constructed, each has its banks. As time goes on, some areas where the water current is strong, burst; there is siltage in areas with sandy soil; powerful local figures invade the system; or it is stopped up by careless peasants; thus in time of drought there is nothing with which to flood (the fields) and in floods, no spot that does not leak." [8] Dikes required frequent repair if they were to remain effective. In Hai-ch'eng hsien, for example, a dike was constructed in 1498 which improved the irrigation system in the hsien. Yet by 1510, only twelve years after it had been completed, the system had broken down and needed repair.[9] In Fukien as elsewhere, local gentry members played an important role in initiating and financing such repair and construction projects. In return, dikes were often named (or renamed) after the leading gentry sponsor.[10]

The provision of water through large-scale irrigation systems is only the first step in undertaking to grow rice. In most of the other phases, individual effort on the part of the farmer is the crucial determinant of the final yield. First the fields must be prepared, leveled so that the depth of the water will be uniform when the field is flooded. To accomplish this, the land is ploughed: first, after the harvest in order to turn over the rice roots; then several times before the field is harrowed; and yet again before the shoots are planted. The banks of the plot, which hold in the water, must be strengthened to prevent crumbling after the rice is put into the flooded field.[11]

The process of rice growing is labor-intensive, and yields are very sensitive to skill and additional effort on the part of the cultivator. In preparing the field for planting three ploughings are better than two. Then comes the transplanting of rice shoots into the paddy. Great care must be taken to space the shoots evenly, for "If the planting is too dense, the shoots will be small and fine like brush hairs, difficult to grow and make abundant, and the (resulting) rice will be scanty and small." [12] Variations in spacing depend on the general quality of the soil; in any case, transplanting is a painstaking process which must be accomplished within a fairly short time period when climatic and water conditions for the plot are optimal. This period may be as short as a week.[13]

After transplanting, the fields are weeded. This involves stamping the roots of the rice shoots more securely into the soil of the flooded field with the feet, as well as clearing it of weeds. Again, the more often the process is repeated, the better the harvest.

In this form of agriculture, the native fertility of the soil is far less important than careful tillage. This was recognized in a comparison of yields from several regions made by the Sung scholar-official, Ch'en Fu-liang (1137–1203). The reason Hunan's rich soils did not produce rice yields to match those of the "barren" lands of Fukien and Chekiang was because manpower was scarce in Hunan. Rice could not be grown with the same care found in the two densely populated Chiangnan provinces.[14]

In rice cultivation, then, the output can be "almost indefinitely increased" by more careful, fine-comb cultivation techniques;[15] as a sixteenth century tract encouraging farmers in Chang-chou promised, "If these methods of preparing the field, planting, and cultivation are followed, then the yield from one mou will match the profit of two or three mou." [16] Conversely, the carelessness of a cultivator can ruin the quality of a field. If the banks crumble, or the essential leveling work is omitted, or the fertility of the soil is not maintained with applications of fertilizer, the landlord is left with a field gravely depreciated in quality.[17]

The tiller thus occupies a more crucial position in rice culture than in the cultivation systems for other grains. This was recognized in the writing of the time. As put by a gazetteer of Ning-yang (Chang-chou prefecture), "These were formerly stony and barren lands; later, when people were densely settled on it, it was transformed into fertile soil." [18] On terraced paddy, the relationship between the tiller and successful farming was even stronger: not only did paddy building represent a considerable labor investment, but the areas without natural sources of water were supplied with water by the direct efforts of the cultivator. This was the reason the harvest on terraced land was attributed largely to human effort.[19] In Fukien, the contribution of the tiller was reflected in tenure and rent arrangements which were favorable to him.

TENANCY IN FUKIEN

Fukien is an especially auspicious focus for an investigation of tenancy, thanks to the work of Fu I-ling. In 1939, Fu discovered a box containing about 100 papers in a village in the interior called Huang-li hsiang (Yung-an hsien). In the box were land mortgage, sale, and tenancy contracts dating back to the sixteenth century. Fu published the full texts of eight tenancy contracts, ranging in date from 1770 to 1880. Further contracts were discovered in 1958, this time in the coastal county of Min-ch'ing (Fu-chou prefecture); six tenancy contracts from this discovery, ranging in date from 1714 to 1839, have been published by Fu.[20] No Ming tenancy contracts have been found, and therefore these Ch'ing contracts form the basis for much of the subsequent discussion.

There are several reasons for believing that tenancy conditions did not change very much from Ming to Ch'ing times. The first is the persistence of local practice, evident in the almost two centuries covered by the documents themselves and supported by studies of twentieth century conditions which found many of these practices still continuing. The second is the corroboration provided by information on rent and tenancy included in the three sales contracts of Ming date found and published by Fu.[21] Finally, there is the support of Ming contract forms presented by Niida Noboru.

Like other documents, tenancy contracts had a fairly standard format. The following, presented by Fu I-ling, is a contract made upon the taking of a new tenant:[22]

> To contract a tenant and settle a quota:
>
> To set up a contract: the tenant Kung Kwang-liu is a resident of the second tu in Min-ch'ing hsien (who) now, because he lacks land to till and plant, voluntarily wishes to draw up a document for the third parcel of civilian land in the second tu called *Ta-yang-o ch'i-chung lung-hou keng,* (literally, the fields behind the embankment of Ta-yang-o stream) belonging to the Wang "office" of Fu-chou city, bearing 0.55 tan of seed, and an annual rent of 11 tan (unhusked rice) in all; henceforth to plant and cultivate year after year, irrespective of loss in the

harvest to manage payment of good, pure white rice, to come and turn over the rent on the stipulated day without daring to delay payments or put sand, mud, or water into the rice; furthermore, without daring to shift the plot or illegally deliver the "bottom soil" rights to others; if there are instances (of the above) he will willingly report and bear investigation.

If this land is let to another tenant, Kwang-liu will not dare oppose his occupation. (We) set up this tenancy on the above terms. The annual rent of unhusked grain, 815 catties by local measure, is reiterated (plus a droppage charge of 1.3 tan).

Paying husked white rice, 66 tou	Guaranteeing the tenant Tenant Kung Kwang-liu (imprint)
August 10, 1714	Representative Fang Wei-te (imprint)

Annual field sacrifice, 11 catties unhusked grain
"Broom fee," 1 ho
Potatoes, 8 catties

The form of this contract agrees with the others presented by Fu, as well as the "typical" Ming tenancy contract form synthesized by Niida Noboru from the forms found in Ming "encyclopedia of daily use."[23] A tenant, identified by name and residence, contracts to cultivate a piece of land, whose name and location appear in the contract. In all the Fukien contracts, acreage was denoted by the amount of seed planted on the plot rather than in terms of the official areal unit, the mou. This seems to have been general practice; the Ming contract forms cited by Niida also used this method of defining the size of a plot.[24]

It is difficult to determine from the contracts what the acreage of the plots in mou was, since the amount of seed customarily sown on a mou of land depended on local practice, which varied from region to region. Some Ming agricultural handbooks recommended sowing over 1 tou of seed per mou of land, but even in the Chekiang region, one of the most progressive and productive rice growing areas in Ming China, instances of sowing as little as 0.7–0.8 tou are recorded.[25] On the level of actual practice, aside from the injunctions of agricultural guides, little information exists, but the available data show that the range was considerable. Ming Fukien records of seed quantities range from 0.5 to 1.4 tou per mou.[26] Sowing practices could differ even between contiguous hsien. In Chang-p'u county (Chang-chou prefecture), for example, a gazetteer records 1.475 tou of seed per mou were used, while in Hai-ch'eng, its neighbor to the east, a figure of 1.2 tou of seed per mou is noted.[27]

A similar emphasis on localism appears in the rent stipulations, which usually converted official measures of grain into local equivalents. In northeastern Fukien, the local measure was the *lo;* in the central and coastal parts of the province, the *hu* or the *p'ing*. In the contract cited above, the local catty must have been quite large, since the official rent measure of 11 tan was converted to 815 instead of 1,100 catties.[28]

In all the contracts available from Fukien, rents were defined in set quantities and not as percentages of the yield. This seems to have been common practice throughout the rice growing region, while share renting, whereby the farmer and landlord shared the risk of a poor harvest, was more characteristic of the wheat growing region of north China.[29] It is clear from the repeated injunctions in the tenancy contracts that Fukienese landlords had no intention of sharing risks with the tenant. On the contrary, all the contracts emphasize the tenant's obligation to pay the rent on the stipulated date, regardless of the vicissitudes of the harvest. Most contracts named the period after the autumn harvest as the deadline for rent payments, but some specified payment after the winter harvest.

From the landlord's perspective, land thus represented an investment with assured annual income. The Fukienese landlord, unlike his north Chinese counterpart, did not generally provide either tools or seed to the cultivator. He did not participate in the farming process, and his only link with the land was the rent received from the tenant.

This emphasis on a fixed rent had two potential meanings for the tenant. In a bad year, it posed the prospect of genuine hardship, the worry that the grain left over after payment of the rent might not suffice for seed and subsistence. On the other hand, since the landlord received only the amount set in the contract, the gains of a good harvest or increasing productivity accrued to the peasant, at least throughout the length of the contract. None of the contracts contained clauses regarding the landlord's rights in renegotiating the amount of the rent. Again, this condition seems a more general characteristic of the southeast rice cropping area; in the twentieth century, D. K. Lieu observed that fixed rents here were generally inflexible upward, although they could be reduced.[30]

Fixed rents provided tenants with incentive to increase yields, because these increases would be theirs and not the landlord's to enjoy. The landlord, however, could theoretically raise rents when a contract came up for renewal. The length of tenure covered by a contract was therefore of great interest to the tenant. In Ming Fukien, some areas practiced a special kind of permanent tenancy which was ideal from the tenant's point of view. This was the *i-t'ien liang-chu* or *i-t'ien san-chu* system, which recognized two or three ownership claims to a plot of land.

PERMANENT TENANCY

The high percentage of Chinese cultivators tilling the soil as tenants has been noted by many observers of twentieth century China. Although there have been some attempts to investigate the relationship between tenancy and agricultural productivity,[31] the available evidence permits no clear conclusions on this fundamental subject. A common expectation, however, has been that productivity is depressed under conditions of tenancy; the cultivator is "exploited" by the landlord and has no incentive to increase yields. The systems of two or more levels of land ownership, which existed in certain regions of China from the sixteenth century into the twentieth, provide a striking illustration of the conditions under which, contrary to expectation, tenancy did not interfere with the cultivator's incentive to raise productivity.[32]

The origins of the system of two levels of land ownership are unclear. By the sixteenth century, when it is first described in the gazetteers of Fukien, it had become customary practice. The occurrence of this system within the boundaries of the rice growing area, and Niida Noboru's investigations into its origins, suggest that the stimulus may have been the necessity for tremendous investments of labor in preparing fields for wet-rice cultivation.[33] In some cases, security of tenure was the inducement used to attract new tenants into lands which had been abandoned and left untilled in times of civil strife. Elsewhere, as in Kiangsu, it represented recognition of the tenant's contribution in creating new land out of sand banks, or in clearing hillsides, as in Kiangsi.[34] Whatever its origins, by the sixteenth century, security of tenure could be obtained in Fukien by paying a fee, the "manured field silver" (*fen-t'u yin*).[35] In exchange, the tenant received transferable and negotiable cultivation rights over the land, which could be passed on to his heirs. In Fukien this was called *t'ien mien* or *t'ien p'i,* the topsoil right.[36]

Unlike his European counterpart, the Chinese cultivator under this system was free to subrent or sell his cultivation right without the consent of the subsoil owner or landlord. The two rights were essentially held autonomously, in the sense that sale of one did not affect the continuance of the dual ownership.[37]

A further aspect of the permanent tenancy system was a strong limitation on the landlord's prerogatives. The subsoil owner was entitled to receive rent, but he did not generally have the right to evict the tenant, even when rent payments were in arrears.[38] Although the tenancy contract from Min-ch'ing, presented earlier, stipulated that the tenant would not stand in the way if the landlord negotiated a new tenancy agreement with someone else, custom was on the side of the tenant and not the landlord. Moreover, the fact that most subsoil owners were absentee landlords meant that the tenant's position was strengthened even further, because the subsoil owners often did not know the location of the plots.[39] This led to a fear that the tenant would simply cut off his obligations to the subsoil owner, reflected in the contract injunctions that the tenant must not move the location of the plot or sell the subsoil rights to someone else.

The system of two or more lords to a field was a special development of a more general form of permanent tenancy common in the Ming period. The contract forms found by Niida Noboru in "encyclopedia of daily use" of Ming date are very informative on this point. Many of these tenancy contract forms placed no time restriction on the contract.[40] In Ming Fukien, permanent tenancy which did not have all the attributes of the two lords to a field system seems to have existed. Under this type of tenancy, the cultivator enjoyed security of tenure but did not have a separate topsoil right. A tenancy contract in a Ming encyclopedia compiled and published in Fukien states that the tenant, who was granted permission to till the fields "forever," must return the field to the landlord should he want to stop farming it; he was not permitted to transfer the tenancy to others.[41] From the perspective of the cultivator, the two lords to a field system was therefore an advance on the more general practice of permanent tenancy.

The two lords to a field system brought a further separation of the tax burden from the land. Tenants paid rent but no tax: that was always the landlord's responsibility. When the landlord lived in the same village as the tenant, it was easy for the tax collector to identify him and press for payment. A system of multiple landownership, which permitted the subsoil and cultivation rights to be sold separately, confused the tax records. Moreover, the government found it difficult to collect taxes from absentee landlords, who frequently lived in urban areas at a distance from their properties. These collection difficulties multiplied under the three lords to a field system practiced in Chang-chou prefecture, where the tax burden was farmed out to a third party.[42] As a result, officials consistently opposed and tried to abolish the system of multiple landownership. We owe most of our information on the system to records of official actions against it. These reflect the government's preoccupation with tax evasion and blur the fact that the practice represented a real gain for the tenant in his relationship with the landlord.

The terms topsoil right and subsoil right (*t'ien ku, t'ien ken*) appear in the school and sacrificial land records of Yu-ch'i and Nan-p'ing hsien, counties in Yen-p'ing fu. They also appear in subsequent local records for Chien-ning, T'ing-chou, Fu-chou, and Fu-ning chou.[43] In the northeastern prefecture of Chien-ning, documents discovered by Fu I-ling show the existence of a further variant of the two lords to a field system. These are the *p'ei t'ien* contracts, which introduced an intermediary between the cultivator and absentee landlord, the *p'ei chu* or second landlord.[44] In this system as in the others, the tenant held negotiable and transferable cultivation rights.

It is possible that the two lords to a field system was more widespread in Fukien than the written records which have been found. Although the tenancy contract from Min-ch'ing hsien, presented earlier, spelled out the bottom soil rights of the landlord, the system generally remained outside the written agreements on land, in the realm of customary rights. From the materials that are presently available, it is possible to conclude that permanent tenancy of the more general kind, and the two lords to a field system, were enjoyed by Ming peasants in many areas of coastal and interior Fukien. In modern times, the system was also found in parts of Anhwei, Chekiang, Kiangsu, Kwangsi, Hunan, and Hupei provinces.[45] As noted earlier, it was confined to rice growing regions.

Even in areas which did not practice permanent tenancy,

the conditions of rice cultivation won special privileges for the farmer. Recognition of the tiller's contribution in rent arrangements is most strikingly revealed in some studies of rent in twentieth century Kwangtung and Kiangsu.[46] Here, when rent was calculated in terms of the annual yield of the plot, it was discovered that the best grade of land was actually assigned a lower rent than land of medium quality. The most expensive land was therefore the middle grade and not the best land. Ch'en Han-seng provided an explanation for this paradox: "The share rent does not . . . depend on the fertility of the soil alone but largely on the respective amount of labor power and fertilizer which the tenant puts into the land. In this particular district, the tenant of good land often supplies more means of production per mow than other tenants because such an investment is certain to pay. Improving the soil, he is actually in a better position to bargain with the landlord who cannot afford to lease his good land to tenants who cannot or will not keep up the fertility of the soil. It is for this reason that the landlord gets less rent from the tenant of the best land, paradoxical as this may seem, than he gets from the tenant of medium grade land."[47]

Though the Fukien materials do not include such clear linkages between rice cultivation conditions and tenure arrangements, a suggestive contrast is supplied in two contracts for limited tenure of land in Yung-an hsien. The first is a contract for rice paddy land, dated 1877; the second, a 1788 contract for mountain land, on which tea and t'ung nuts were grown.[48] The term of tenure in the rice paddy contract was ten years. The contract was written on a woodblock printed form, with blank spaces left for pertinent details. Since the ten year term was printed on the form and not written in, this was probably a fairly common time limit on tenancy contracts in the area. None of the paddy land contracts had a term shorter than ten years, but the 1788 contract for tea and t'ung nut land had only a six year tenure. This contract differed from those for rice paddy in that the landlord also stipulated that no trees could be cultivated for the market, because these would disturb the *feng-shui*. The contract for tea and t'ung nut land imposed limitations on the cultivator which were absent from the rice paddy land contracts. These limitations suggest again that it was rice growing which accounted for the favorable position of the Fukien peasant in Ming times. The paucity of documents on the subject does not permit further exploration of this theme.

OTHER IMPOSITIONS ON CULTIVATORS

The conclusion of this survey of tenancy conditions is that the peasant in Ming Fukien was favored by fixed rents and long or permanent tenancy. Since both owner-farmers and tenants could retain the fruits of increased productivity, the industrious peasant could benefit more from these conditions than his less energetic neighbor. Before leaving this topic, however, we must consider the significance of payments imposed on tenants in addition to rent. Most of the research on these extra payments has concentrated on explaining them from the viewpoint of the "exploitation" of the peasant,[49] but the fees themselves, when studied, turn out to be negligible. Many were once-only collections; others were customary and fixed annual payments which represented less than 4 per cent of the primary rent payment. If these fees represented landlord efforts to appropriate productivity gains for themselves, they illustrate the limitations rather than the extent of landlord power in rural Fukien.

Once-only Collections

By the sixteenth century, permanent tenure could be purchased for a fee, called the "manured field silver" (*fen-t'u yin*). A similar payment was the tenant guarantee fee, the *pao-tien yin,* or the *tien-t'ou yin.*[50] All these were payments made at the beginning of a new tenancy.

Annual Payments

Several fees which appear as annual payments in Fukien contracts seem to have common origins. The *tung-hsi* (winter sacrifice) appears in contracts from Yung-an hsien, and seems to have also been levied in parts of Fu-chou, Ch'üan-chou, and T'ing-chou in Ming times.[51] A similar levy, the *shih-hsi* (food sacrifice) also appears in Yung-an contracts, and in Min-ch'ing tenancy contracts as *hsi-t'un* (feast provisions) and *t'ien-hsi* (field sacrifice). These were all subsidiary rents, paid in kind, and written into the contract as an obligation of the tenant.

The *tung-hsi* probably began as a contribution to an annual feast, given for the landlord when he came to collect rents.[52] It was often paid in ducks and chickens but could at times be phrased in terms of grain, beans, or cash. In Yung-an tenancy and sales contracts, *tung-hsi* was paid in livestock;[53] in Min-ch'ing hsien the *t'ien-hsi* and *sao-chou* (broom) fees were paid in rice or livestock.[54] The amount and kind of payment required was written into the contract. By Ming times, these had become part of the fixed income from land and were included in mortgage and land sale contracts along with the rent payments.[55]

The sums involved in these subsidiary fees were negligible. In the Min-ch'ing contracts where they were paid in grain, the fees amounted to only 1 to 2 per cent of the rent grain.[56] In no case did they reach 4 per cent of the primary rent payment.[57] The subsidiary fees may have been an attempt by the landlord to increase his share of the yield; Fu I-ling suggests that the *tung-hsi,* for example, was found in contracts dealing with land of better quality.[58] Not only were these impositions minor, but, like fixed rents, they seem to have been inflexible upward.

Rents

In two successive editions of a gazetteer for Yu-ch'i hsien (Yen-p'ing prefecture), Fu I-ling discovered rent records for identical plots of land, whose revenues were used to support an academy in the region. These figures are presented in Table 1.[59] In both records, the rent was given first in catties of unhusked rice, then in copper cash. In both 1770 and 1823, the rice rents were identical for each plot of land listed, but the 1823 money rents were about 40 per cent higher than those of 1770, even when the 1823 copper cash totals are assumed to include the *tung-hsi* fees which in 1770 were itemized separately. As Table 2 shows, however, the 1770–1823 period was one of strong inflation. Table 2 presents the price of rice in terms of copper cash. From 1770 to 1823 rice prices increased by over 60 per cent. The upward trend in the price of rice was greater than the rise of money rents in the Yu-ch'i records, and the 40 per cent increase in Yu-ch'i rents was a rather unsuccessful attempt to keep up with the inflationary trend, instead of a real rent increase. Constancy of the rice rents supports this conclusion. Since the period covered by the Yu-ch'i records is 53 years, the time-span in which farmers could keep the fruits of their

TABLE 1. RENTS IN YU-CH'I HSIEN, 1770–1823

Plot name	1770[a] Rice[b] (catties)	1770[a] Money (copper wen)	1823 Rice[b] (catties)	1823 Money (copper wen)	Per cent increase in money rent
Tung pien, Ma wan ke	2,200	10,040	2,200	14,080	40
Hsi pien	1,600	7,307	1,600	10,240	39
Wo t'ou, Chi lung	300	1,378	300	1,920	39
Ssu men shou yen ch'eng	200	913	200	1,280	41
Hai k'e lung, Ch'ang ho	700	3,188	700	4,480	40
Shui chien ke, Huo kuan lung	700	3,197	700	4,480	39
Shui chien (keng) ke	300	1,370	300	1,920	39

Source: Fu I-ling, *Ming Ch'ing nung-ts'un she-hui ching-chi* (Peking: San-lien shu-tien, 1961), pp. 36–38.

[a] The money column in the 1770 rent is a total of the primary rent and *tung-hsi* levies.

[b] Unhusked rice.

labor for themselves was probably very long, indeed. It was more than one peasant's working lifetime.[60]

Absentee landlordship was one of the factors which promoted favorable conditions for the tenant. Ming contracts usually stipulated that tenants should deliver rent rice to the landlord's warehouses, which were often located in the walled city. The rent receipt from Min-ch'ing hsien published by Fu is the result of such a delivery to a landlord's

TABLE 2. RICE PRICES IN TERMS OF COPPER CASH, 1770–1850

Date	Rice price copper cash/*kung tan*[a]	Price index 1761–1770 = 100
1761–1770	1,513	100
1771–1780	1,347	89
1781–1790	1,465	97
1791–1800	2,750	182
1801–1810	3,262	216
1811–1820	3,330	220
1821–1830	2,524	167
1831–1840	3,548	234
1841–1850	3,871	256

Source: P'eng Hsin-wei, *Chung-kuo huo-pi shih* (Shanghai, Jen-min ch'u-pan she, 1954), II, 531, 542.

[a] The copper cash calculations are in *chih-ch'ien*, or standard cash, the system used in Fukien. See Frank H. H. King, *Money and Monetary Policy in China* (Cambridge: Harvard University Press, 1965), p. 246, for further elucidation.

granary.[61] In Min-ch'ing, there were so many absentee landlords collecting their rents in the hsien city that a part of the town was still linked in the Ch'ing gazetteer with the warehouses which had originally stood there.[62] Other areas in Ming times with large numbers of absentee landlords were Shang-hang (T'ing-chou), Nan-ching (Chang-chou), Chin-chiang, An-ch'i, Nan-an (all three in Ch'üan-chou prefecture), and Chien-yang (Chien-ning prefecture).[63] The prefecture of Chang-chou, where the system of three lords to a field was common, had what amounted to absentee landlordship as well. Separated from contact and acquaintance with the soil, landlords were ignorant of the condition of the fields and the annual harvests. Local histories record the anxiety that tenants held the upper hand: "If the tenant flees, then the rent disappears, and the landlord does not know the location of the land." [64]

The common factor in all the situations of absentee ownership in Fukien was the landlord's decision to settle for a stable fixed income with fairly low risk, rather than to invest capital with the tenant and participate in the increased yields which might result. As will be shown in Chapter Four, the income which could be derived from owning farm land was very small when compared with alternative investments in commerce. Only noneconomic motives for holding land can explain why urban dwellers continued to bid up the price of rural land despite the fact that it generally became increasingly unprofitable for them as an investment. The process of land accumulation in absentee ownership occurs in the context of a commercialized economy.

It was commerce which provided the profits plowed into land purchases. Landlord participation in farming in north China suggests a paucity of nonagricultural investment opportunities in that area. This was not the case in Ming Fukien, where commercial opportunities provided prospects of high profits. In the Fukienese context, land, which because of its social prestige represented a form of investment desirable from other than purely economic points of view, did not attract capital seeking high returns. The existence of market outlets for investment may have been indirectly linked to the favorable conditions enjoyed by the Fukien tenant. Because the landlord could and did obtain higher returns elsewhere, he did not have to squeeze agricultural profits as did the north China landlord. For the tenant, land was a question of life or death. For the absentee landlord in the southeast, it was one of a number of investments, and was held for prestige and security rather than profit.

This survey of tenancy conditions shows that there were no institutional barriers to profit-maximizing responses by peasants. We have no information on the extent of tenancy in sixteenth century Fukien, although the documentary evidence suggests it was fairly widespread. Whether he owned his own land or rented it, however, the Fukien peasant enjoyed favorable tenure and rent conditions. Permanent tenancy and fixed rent, arrangements which allowed the peasant who rented land to retain increases in productivity, derived in part from the particular conditions of rice cultivation, which emphasized the cultivator's role in determining final yields.

Favorable tenancy conditions did not of themselves stimulate large productivity gains. These occurred only under appropriate market conditions. In the next chapter, we shall examine the linkages between rice cultivation and market activity in some detail.

Chapter Three / FACTORS IN RICE CULTIVATION

Although the work of Theodore Shultz has transformed the traditional peasant into an economically rational being, the Chinese peasant remains a largely unreconstructed figure in the secondary literature, too ignorant to know how to improve his lot, and too oppressed by poverty to have the means, even had he the knowledge, to do so. The historical evidence contradicts this image: Chinese peasants responded quickly to opportunities for improving their economic position.[1] Nor were they self-sufficient; as Tawney observed, Chinese peasants relied on market exchanges even for basic needs.[2] In this respect, European agricultural history, with its model of a self-sufficient peasantry, is very different from China's. Chinese agriculture was sensitive to market changes because it was tied to a market economy, not divorced from it.

Market conditions weighed heavily in determining the cropping pattern for whole regions. They were important, for example, in shaping double cropping patterns in Fukien. The following detailed study of important elements in rice growing illustrates the complexity of the calculations required of the cultivator and highlights the importance of market factors in the decision-making of individual peasants. Market conditions were equally important in choosing between rice and other commercial crops, or between farming and rural handicrafts. The farm economy was thus inextricably bound to the market.

DOUBLE CROPPING PATTERNS

A significant feature of cropping patterns in Fukien is the distinction between areas with double cropping of rice and those growing one crop of rice with another winter crop. These areal differences are presented in Table 3.

A double crop of rice was preferable to one crop of rice and another grain. "The two crops (of rice) a year are prized," writes a sixteenth century gazetteer.[3] The grain yield from one crop of rice was greater than the yield from other grains.[4] Two crops of rice were preferable to an alternation of rice with some other grain, for the same reason. According to a modern estimate,[5] changing from single cropping to double cropping can raise yields by 70 to 80 per cent. If double cropping produced such superior results, why was it not universally adopted? Water shortages, topography, climate, and labor shortages figure prominently in the explanations that have been offered.

In modern times, rice has been double cropped only in the southern part of Fukien.[6] Buck drew a line through the province dividing this region from the area further north, which he called the "rice–tea" area. The rice–tea region, which began at Fu-chou, was predominantly an area growing one crop of rice with a second crop of wheat, barley, or rapeseed.[7]

Water shortages, which could prevent adoption of double cropping, cannot explain why northern Fukien failed to double crop rice. In fact, the region was richer in irrigation works than southern Fukien: 78 per cent of the cultivated land in the rice–tea area was irrigated, as opposed to only

TABLE 3. RICE CROPPING IN FUKIEN[a]

Area	Single cropping	Double cropping	Sources
Coastal			
Fu-chou fu	x	x	*Min shu* 150.1a; *FC* 1596 ed., 8.1a; 1613 ed., 37.1a.
Fu-ch'ing	x	x	*HC* 2.2a–8b.
Ch'üan-chou fu	x	x	*FC*, 1612 ed., 3.38b–40b.
Chang-chou fu	x	x	*FC*, 1573 ed., 13.9ab, 19.6a, 21.6a, 23.6a, 25.5a, 27.5a, 28.4a, 29.5b, 30.7a, 31.3b; 1628 ed., 27.1a–2a.
Chang-p'u	x	x	*HC*, 1700 ed., 4.1ab.
Lung-yen	x	x	*HC*, 1558 ed., 2.60a; 1689 ed., 3.31a.
Hai-ch'eng	x	x	*HC*, 1633 ed., 11.10a–11a.
Hsing-hua fu	x	x	*FC*, 1503 ed., 13.2a; 1575 ed., 1.51a.
Ch'ien-yu	x	x	*HC*, 1558 ed., 1.67a.
Fu-ning chou	x	x	*CC*, 1593 ed., 1.43a; 1616 ed., 7.31a.
Ning-te	x	–	*HC*, 1591 ed., 2.6b.
Fu-an	x	x	*HC*, 1597 ed., 1.19a.
Interior			
Chien-ning	x	–	*FC*, 1541 ed., 13.1a–2a.
P'u-ch'eng	x	?	*HC*, 1650 ed., 4.8a.
Chien-yang	x	–	*HC*, 1607 ed., 3.26a–27a.
Sung-ch'i	x	–	*HC*, 1700 ed., 6.1b.
Ch'ung-an	x	–	*HC*, 1670 ed., 1.20a–21a.
Shou-ning	x	–	*HC*, 1637 ed., 1.43a.
T'ing-chou	x	x	*FC*, 1637 ed., 4.8a.
Kuei-hua	x	x	*HC*, 1614 ed., 1.18ab.
Yen-p'ing fu	x	–	*FC*, 1660 ed., 4.1a.
Chiang-lo	x	–	*HC*, 1585 ed., 1.31b.
Yu-ch'i	x	x	*HC*, 1636 ed., 4.7a–8a.
Yung-an	x	–	*HC*, 1594 ed., 4.27a; 1723 ed., 5.1b.
Shao-wu fu	x	–	*FC*, 1623 ed., 8.1ab.

[a] This table includes all the prefectural and chou units in Fukien. Only hsien for which information was available were included.

69 per cent of the cultivated land in the double cropped part of the province.[8]

Another explanation stresses topography and soil as determinants of paddy field construction.[9] The need to lift water to the fields limited the extent to which hills could profitably be converted to terraced paddy. C. K. Yang comments on the same problem in modern Kwangtung.[10] Rice cultivation may have been relatively difficult in the hills of Fukien but flourished on the rich Min River drainage of Fu-chou. Topography does not explain why this area did not double crop rice.

Buck himself stressed climate: "The amount of double-cropping is primarily influenced by climatic factors, such as length of the growing season and whether or not a winter crop can be grown. Size of farm has little to do with the amount of double-cropping, since all farms within a given locality have the same climate, and it is chiefly climate that is the determining factor in the amount of double-cropping."[11] Historical records, however, show that double cropping was practiced in Fu-chou and other regions within Buck's rice–tea area. These areas had reverted to single cropping by the twentieth century, but climate could not have been the stimulus for this cropping change.

Double cropping was practiced in Fu-chou during the Sung period, when the twelfth century gazetteer, *San shan chih* records that Min, Hou-kuan, and Huai-an hsien were able to produce two rice harvests a year. These areas were located next to the administrative center of Fu-chou. The Fukienese had developed a late ripening variety from the Champa rice seeds and used both early ripening and late ripening seeds in a double cropping cycle.[12] During Ming times, Fu-chou and Fu-ning chou, the coastal region to its north, continued to double crop rice. Double cropping may also have been practiced in some parts of Chien-ning prefecture, in the northwest corner of Fukien. Certainly the seeds which enable two successive harvests of rice were known and used in the region. A gazetteer from P'u-ch'eng hsien lists not only the early ripening seeds, which were planted in the third lunar month and harvested during the summer, but also includes a large number of varieties harvested in the ninth to eleventh lunar months, the ripening period for a second crop of rice.[13] The feasibility of growing two rice crops in this part of Fukien has been reiterated in Communist Chinese publications.[14] Climate is definitely not a barrier to double cropping in the area.

The labor shortage explanation stresses the heavy overhead labor investment involved in rice paddy cultivation and from this concludes that a certain minimum population density is necessary before rice can be grown.[15] Since double cropping involves duplication of labor effort, the manpower required is very large, but the argument that labor shortages prevented double cropping in some areas of Fukien is suspect for several reasons. The most obvious is that Fu-chou, Fu-ning chou, and Chien-ning represent cases of reversion from double cropping to a less intensive cropping pattern, in which there is no evidence that population declined. Population densities throughout Fukien probably rose without interruption until the nineteenth century. Subsequent emigration may have slowed down the rate of population increase,[16] but it is highly unlikely that population actually declined and it is difficult to see how it could have sunk below Sung levels in any period under discussion.

Another reason for suspecting the validity of a labor shortage explanation is that there was always free movement of population within Fukien. Even in Ming times, there are some hints that population pressures on the coast prompted a movement of workers into the interior; these are the *p'eng min* referred to by Fu I-ling.[17] These men hired themselves out for farm work, and the abundance of contract forms in Ming "encyclopedia of daily use" suggests that the practice was not unusual. Such population movements helped distribute manpower more evenly within Fukien.

The issue of population densities can also be examined by comparing statistics for areas which practiced double cropping and others which did not. As noted earlier, Fu-chou grew two crops of rice in Ming times, while Chien-ning, with the possible exception of P'u-ch'eng hsien, grew only one crop of rice a year. If labor shortages were the reason for Chien-ning's failure to adopt double cropping, this shortage should have affected the population–land ratio for the prefecture and should be reflected in its per capita acreage figures. The figures comparing Fu-chou and Chien-ning's population–land ratios are presented in Table 4. Both the

TABLE 4. PER CAPITA ACREAGE, FU-CHOU AND CHIEN-NING PREFECTURES

Item	Fu-chou	Chien-ning
1491 acreage (mou)[a]	2,481,385	2,653,227
Officially recorded population, 1491	282,573	433,585
Unadjusted per capita acreage (mou)	8.75	6.12
Adjusted population, 1491	633,800	712,700
Adjusted per capita acreage (mou)	3.7	3.7

Source: Pa Min t'ung-chih, 20.2a–6a for population, 21.12a–16a for acreage. For information on the derivation of the adjusted population figures, see Appendix.

[a] All the acreage figures are for land under cultivation.

adjusted and unadjusted figures indicate that population densities in Chien-ning were as high, if not higher, than those in Fu-chou. Labor shortage does not satisfactorily explain double cropping patterns in Fukien.

Katō Shigeshi and Amano Motonosuke, who found instances of reversion to single cropping in southern Kiangsu, proposed an institutional explanation for this change. They suggested that farmers switch from double cropping rice to a single crop of rice with a winter crop of wheat because the wheat crop, unlike rice, was exempt from rent. Farmers could keep all the wheat harvest for themselves. According to Katō, the same phenomenon occurred in Japan.[18] Neither scholar based his explanation on direct evidence from contracts.

Whether the same rent arrangements existed in Fukien is difficult to determine with the available evidence. Of the contracts printed by Fu I-ling, those from Min-ch'ing hsien bear directly on this question, because Min-ch'ing (under Fu-chou prefecture) was a region where double cropping was both feasible and practiced. In only one of the five contracts from this hsien was there a winter rent as well as rent from the first rice crop.[19] Since we have no information on whether or not the other four contracts concerned double cropped fields, it is impossible to draw any conclusions from this finding.

The other contracts discovered in Fukien by Fu I-ling also fail to reveal clear linkages between rentals and double cropping. Among the one hundred-odd contracts found by Fu in Yung-an hsien (Yen-p'ing prefecture), there were two Ming land sale contracts. One plot collected a winter and autumn rent, and the other collected only one rice rent a year.[20] In none of the other contracts printed by Fu was there another instance of a double rent on rice.[21] Nor, in the double cropped area of Chang-chou, do we find any evidence that double cropping brought double rents — at least in the direct sense. The interaction of increased productivity, rising demand for land, and rents depended on market forces much more than on rent arrangements such as those observed by Katō and Amano. Indeed, the reversion to single cropping in southern Kiangsu is also more forcefully explained by the growth and development of a market oriented peasant economy, as described later in this chapter and in Chapter Six. Rent arrangements are but one part of the complex framework within which the individual peasant decided how best to earn his livelihood. Cropping patterns can be best explained in the context of peasant incomes. In southern Kiangsu as in coastal Fukien, peasant incomes were heavily dependent on market conditions.

Climate and labor supply are necessary but not sufficient conditions for double cropping of rice. When both conditions are satisfied, double cropping may, but need not, occur. In northern Fukien, the factors that worked for double cropping were predominant in the sixteenth century but not in the twentieth. The importance of marketing and market conditions, both of which are absent from previous discussions of double cropping, seems obvious. The Ming sources describe a complex agriculture, highly sensitive to market conditions and strongly tied to the market. The cultivation of rice, which was grown for market as well as for home consumption, illustrates some of the issues involved.

RICE TECHNOLOGY

Improvements in rice cultivation during the Ming period were less dramatic than those of the Sung. Amano Motonosuke, a leading historian of Chinese agriculture, suggests that Ming improvements stemmed from a modification and diffusion of already known techniques, rather than from innovational break-throughs in technology. There were no dramatic changes in agricultural implements, but there was a steady diffusion of tools which had earlier been confined to the Chekiang region.[22] Since most of the agricultural handbooks written in China originated in the Chekiang-Kiangsu region, they are useless for a study of this diffusion of agricultural tools and farming practice. The researcher must rely instead on occasional references in local gazetteers or essays by local citizens, and the topic has therefore not yet been adequately investigated. In Chapters Four and Five, information on different levels of technology in Fukien and Hunan show that agricultural practice diverged greatly from the models presented in the handbooks. Knowledge and actual practice did not march hand in hand. The topic is an important one and deserves more attention than it has received.

A combination of new seed strains, improved tillage, and more fertilizers brought productivity gains to Ming Fukien. Whereas the top yield of good land in Sung times seems to have been three piculs of unhusked rice per mou, some areas in sixteenth century Fukien enjoyed yields nearly twice this figure.[23] Although increasing yields was a goal shared by many cultivators, there were potential conflicts between increasing yields and maximizing income. These conflicts were resolved through the agency of the market.

SEED VARIETIES

Perhaps the most startling aspect of a study of seeds is the profundity of localism revealed in the exclusiveness and number of specific seeds grown in a province. Ming gazetteers for Fukien list more than 150 different seeds, more than two thirds of which are to be found in only one part of the province.[24] The number and particularism of the seeds represent an adaptation of basic seeds to the soil and climate of each locality. That this process involved a steady and constant change in seed types is revealed by the newness of most seeds in Ming sources. Only seven out of 150 had survived from Sung times. The others were modifications of basic seeds known in the Sung.

Because seed developments involved a pragmatic selection of seeds on the basis of performance, certain regional differences emerge from an analysis of seeds listed in local histories. The coastal areas were rich in special kinds of double cropping seeds: the *Chin-chou, T'u-lun, Huang-mang,* and *Fen-ch'ih tsao* were found only in Fu-chou and Fu-ning chou.[25] The interior part of the province developed many different strains of Champa seeds, both early and late ripening varieties, suited to a wide range of soils. About half the seeds found in the interior were in the Champa category.[26] The hardier Champa strain may have initially possessed advantages in farming the hilly interior, where conditions were rougher than on the coastal plains. And, by Ming times, development of the Champa had gone far towards removing many initial disadvantages noted in Sung records.

The importation of early ripening or Champa rice into China in the eleventh century enabled modifications of rice culture along two dimensions, time and soil. With early ripening rice, it was possible to develop a system of double cropping in the southern provinces, and Fukien had done so. Champa rice also had drought resistant qualities that enabled it to be grown on poorer land than was possible with earlier seed varieties. On the other hand, Champa was not as high in quality as the late ripening rice, called *keng t'ao*. It had smaller kernels and could not be stored as long. As a result, the Southern Sung seems to have discriminated against Champa by requiring that taxes and rents be paid in *keng t'ao*. When Champa rice was used, a 10 per cent penalty surcharge was often imposed. *Keng* was the expensive rice, a luxury consumption good, while Champa was the cheaper and more plentiful grain.[27]

By Ming times, seed improvements seem to have erased this earlier distinction in quality. Unlike Southern Sung chronicles which carefully distinguished between *keng* and the early ripening strains, Ming gazetteers and essays grouped rice into other categories: early, late, and glutinous rice (used to make wine). Because late ripening varieties of Champa were used, the early-late distinction did not continue the Sung division of *keng* from Champa. In the government regulations on payment of the autumn rice tax, no preference for *keng* was stated, and though occasional memorials by Board of Revenue officials report rotting rice in government granaries, the blame is not laid on particular rice strains.[28] As one Ming writer put it, "Keng, hsien, Champa, early-ripening rice, these are all different names for the same thing."[29]

Another indication of improvement in Champa quality is found in the displacement of *keng* from the most fertile fields. In Sung times, Champa was grown on the poorer, marginal lands, and *keng* dominated the most fertile paddies. Now many of the seeds specified for fertile fields were offshoots of the Champa strain: the Straight-necked Early (*So-ching tsao*) or the Yellow Bamboo Early (*Huang-chu tsao*) show in their names their descent from the original *tsao* seeds which were Champa varieties.[30] Late ripening Champa seeds recommended for fertile paddies included the *Huang ho* (Yellow grain) and the *Su-chou* White.[31]

Improved quality was accompanied by the development of seeds with shorter growing periods. The original Champa took 100 days to mature after transplanting. By the early seventeenth century, Ch'üan-chou prefecture was planting a seed which took slightly over fifty days to mature after it had been transplanted. The fifty day variety was unusual in this period, and a sixty day seed was much more common.[32]

Seeds were also developed which could produce rice on lands heretofore marginal to rice growing. In the prefecture of Chien-ning, for example, a half dozen seed varieties suited to poor land are cited. In some cases, the specific soil conditions for which they were adapted was indicated in the name, as in the Soft Mud early ripening rice, or the Barren Land variety, grown in the mountainous terrain of Chien-yang hsien.[33] Champa (*Chan-ch'eng*) rice was still grown in dry-land plots, but a new seed is mentioned in the coastal prefectures of Ch'üan-chou, Chang-chou, and Hsing-hua. This was the Barbarian (*She-t'ao*) seed, used in mountainous areas where land was still farmed on older principles of slash-and-burn agriculture.[34]

New seed developments also pushed cultivation toward the ocean. The development of a salt resistant seed which could be planted in brackish soil was an innovation in Ming Fukien. Called the Black Awn (*Wu-mang*), it was found in Hui-an hsien, Ch'üan-chou prefecture.[35] Fukienese peasants also adapted seeds to meet different climatic conditions. Some seeds were chosen for their resistance to cold: the Frost Seed (*T'ien-hsiang tsao*) and the Great Winter (*Ta-*

tung) were two. Other seeds gave good returns in warmer areas: the Two Crop (*Erh-shou*) found in Yen-p'ing is an example.[36] Farmers thus had a variety of seeds from which to select those best suited to the condition of their individual plots. As a gazetteer explained, "Generally the early and late ripening rice seeds have special characteristics, some being best for excessive rain, others best for drier fields. What is best depends on the fields." [37]

Most of the seeds described helped extend the geographical and climatic boundaries for rice growing and improved the quality of the final product. The development of a seed which permitted interplanting introduced a new, innovational element into rice cultivation. This was the Lodger (*Ch'i-chung*) seed. Planted with the first crop of rice, it did not ripen until the tenth lunar month.[38]

In the sixteenth century, seed varieties in Fukien permitted both interplanting and successive planting methods of double cropping rice, but farmers did not always select yields over quality. This is illustrated by the growing of the *Ta-tung* seed. The primary advantage of the *Ta-tung* was its large rice grains. Though it yielded 2 tan per mou more than the late ripening varieties,[39] it could not compete against a double cropping cycle in terms of yield. Yet in Hsing-hua, one of the more prosperous agricultural regions of Fukien, an early sixteenth century gazetteer reported that because the quality of the rice from a two crop cycle was inferior to the *Ta-tung,* the farmers of the region chose quality over quantity and grew one crop of *Ta-tung* on the heavily fertilized paddies.[40]

As new seeds permitted rice cultivation in areas which had not previously been committed to paddy, they had an obvious effect on the cropping pattern. In the interior, rice advanced into lands which were already being tilled, generally with cash crops grown under conditions of extensive agriculture. In the hills and in the newly reclaimed lands on the coast, conversion to paddy required a heavy investment of labor. Development of seeds enabled rice cultivation to expand into new areas, but the motivation to devote the resources necessary for rice growing must surely have been profit. In rice-deficit Fukien, population growth had necessitated imports of rice from other regions since Sung times.[41] In the Ming period, increased population was already pressing upon the position of rice as a common staple food. Although a seventeenth century gazetteer in Chien-ning asserts that rice was eaten three times a day, the poorest peasants no longer consumed rice, but flour products, and slightly later, sweet potatoes. As rice prices continued to rise, these became the staple for the poorer elements of the population.[42]

FERTILIZER AND TILLAGE

Ming developments in fertilizer were expansions and elaborations of practices already found in the Sung. Many of these originated in Chekiang and only later spread to other rice producing areas. Others were new fertilizers. For regions outside the Yangtze delta, the Ming period saw improvement and expansion in fertilizer use. Although a full description of these developments awaits further research, the extent of the improvement can be seen by comparing the wealth of fertilizers described by the Kiangsi author, Sung Ying-hsing, in the Ming compendium, *T'ien-kung k'ai-wu,* with the dried stalks which had been the common fertilizer used in this province in Sung times. Many vegetable products joined animal and human manure on the lists in Ming records. Among these, the best, according to Sung, was sesame cakes, followed by rape seeds and t'ung seeds.[43] Some of the new fertilizers were waste products, such as the liquid residue left when green lentil flour was made. Others were edible vegetables such as radishes, soybeans, and other legumes.

As in seed developments, heavy emphasis was placed on local products. In the coastal areas of Fukien, crushed oyster shells were used to enrich the land.[44] In An-ch'i, a mountainous region in Ch'üan-chou prefecture, cattle and horse bones were reduced to ash and then used.[45] In Chang-chou prefecture, a magistrate of the sixteenth century recommended hog bristles. These were chopped to bits, mixed with ashes, soybeans, and other legumes, then soaked for several days before application. If pig bristles were not available, the writer recommended human or animal manure or fertilizers such as sesame oil cakes and animal bone ash.[46] These were applied to the soil before planting and again when the shoots were transplanted. In fields of poor quality, the process was repeated at the time of the first weeding. Fertilizer was highly beneficial to crops in a good year and was recommended even in years of bad weather. "The shoots obtaining fertilizer will be nourished, the sprouts will be rich and large, and the rice resulting from this abundant and full." [47]

Though the application of fertilizers increased the yield, fertilizers were an expensive investment. When human manure was purchased in areas close to cities, the expense was phrased directly in money terms. Growing legumes or edible vegetables for fertilizer meant sacrificing potential income from alternative uses of the land. The sharpest example of competition for land arising from increased use of fertilizer is reported by Sung Ying-hsing: "There are those who plant 'fertilizer wheat' in the southern rice fields; that is, no crop is expected from the wheat, but in the spring, when the wheat and barley plants are good and green, they are ploughed under in the field, and this always doubles the autumn yield of rice." [48] The cost of forsaking a crop of winter barley or wheat in exchange for a doubling of the next rice crop was as real as the cost of buying manure from the city.

The issue of competing and alternative uses of land brings us to a central issue in the peasant world: the choice between often conflicting means of expending available time and resources. Maximization of yields was achievable through several means. The Ming peasant, through his own efforts, could raise the quality of his land and his yield through careful seed selection, increased fertilization, and painstaking cultivation of the crop. In all instances, potential gains had to be weighed against costs, not only in money terms but in bypassing alternative uses of land and energy. To increase yields was not always the surest way of maximizing personal income. We have already noted that in some cases, peasants rejected higher yields in favor of grain quality. There are earlier historical examples which suggest that in doing so, they responded to the higher prices offered for quality grain.[49] There were similar potential conflicts between yield and increases in income where labor effort was concerned. Once alternatives outside agriculture were open to the peasant, labor cost could become as important a factor as yield.

For much of southeastern China, the Ming period saw a development of rural handicrafts, and in particular, weaving.[50] In Fukien, the existence of markets for textiles provided a concrete measure of the income forsaken by putting women to work in the fields rather than at the looms. While silk seems to have been a city based industry, ramie and cotton cloth production were both handicraft enterprises peopled by peasant women throughout the province. Some of the cloth was produced for trade outside Fukien. Cloth merchants from Chekiang flocked to Chang-chou to buy materials, and textiles of various kinds were the most important commercial good produced in Hsing-hua.[51] According to an early sixteenth century gazetteer, a skilled woman weaver in Hsing-hua could weave a bolt of cotton cloth every four or five days, which would fetch a picul of unhusked rice in the market at Hsien-yu.[52] Since this represented one sixth the annual harvest from a mou of excellent land, the incentives for keeping women at the loom in this area were high, and the profits from intensive cultivation had to be considerable before it was profitable to put these women to work in the fields. One solution was represented in Te-hua hsien, Ch'üan-chou, where all the women were kept at weaving; one crop of rice was grown, and the flooded paddies were used as fish ponds for additional income in the winter.[53]

Handicraft industries were a market linked alternative to agriculture which had considerable influence on the labor supply available for farming, but the other factors which we have discussed were also dependent on the market. The price of fertilizer, crop prices, and land rents were equally influenced by market conditions. Cultivation conditions imposed tensions similar to those described above, which affected the choice among various cash crops competing for space.

OTHER CASH CROPS

The rice paid to absentee landlords was the most important, but not the only source of the nonglutinous rice sold in local markets. Coastal Fukien was consistently a rice-deficit area, so there was no lack of demand. Rice moved quite routinely from one hsien to the next. Te-hua, a county in Ch'üan-chou prefecture, had a twenty day lag in crops behind its neighbor to the south, Yung-ch'un. Since the rice price is highest just before harvest, Yung-ch'un's farmers saw an opportunity to profit from the time difference in harvests and took Yung-ch'un's first cropped rice to Te-hua to gain the profit afforded.[54]

Even in the interior, where transportation was more difficult and costly, rice flowed from areas of plenty to areas of shortage. An early seventeenth century gazetteer describes how the rice of one interior district was carried to neighboring areas undergoing famine on the light boats of the salt merchants, which could navigate the rapids. As a result of rice shipments to more profitable famine markets, the local price of rice had also risen.[55]

Glutinous rice, used to make wine, was a commercial crop. Seed developments in glutinous rice had also produced numerous varieties which represented adaptations to local conditions. In areas like Min-ch'ing hsien (Fu-chou), glutinous rice seems to have been more important than staple rice in the local cropping pattern.[56]

Other contenders for the best land in Fukien were sugar cane and tobacco. Sugar cane had been growing in Fukien as long as rice. By Sung times, the coastal prefectures of Ch'üan-chou and Fu-chou were prominent sugar producers.[57] By Ming times, sugar from Fukien was sold in Southeast Asia as well as in domestic Chinese markets. A 1503 gazetteer in Hsing-hua, one of the centers of sugar production, notes that traveling merchants thronged to the prefecture in the ninth lunar month to trade in sugar.[58] In this area, sugar had ousted rice from many paddy plots: "The (citizens of) P'u-t'ien who pursue profit plant much of it." [59] Sugar cane cultivation moved inland, too, and by Ming times was supplanting rice in landlocked areas such as Yu-ch'i hsien.[60]

Tobacco, introduced into Fukien in the late sixteenth century, had an almost immediate impact on cropping. In the coastal areas the introduction of tobacco intensified the competition for land. Even in the interior, tobacco changed the pattern of agricultural economy. A gazetteer of Yung-an hsien records that peasants had abandoned terraced rice cultivation in favor of planting sugar cane or tobacco on the fertile valley plots, because the profits from either were twice those from rice.[61]

Cultivation requirements for both sugar cane and tobacco resembled those of rice. Water was important. In sugar cane culture, irrigation systems were beneficial in draining off water at the proper point in the growing cycle. Fertilizer was required for both crops, and harvests were improved with careful tillage. Tobacco was especially sensitive to soil fertility and to careful tending. A Lung-yen gazetteer notes that tobacco crops could be increased several-fold through irrigation, weeding, and fertilizing.[62] The same painstaking methods were recommended for sugar cane.[63]

Because the labor, water, and fertilizer requirements for tobacco and sugar were similar to those for rice cultivation, the most important factor in choosing among these crops was the relative market price of the three. The farmer who chose tobacco or sugar could vary the intensity of tillage and fertilizer use as market valuations altered the cost of cultivation. The market, then, was involved not only in the initial decision to supplant rice with a more profitable cash crop but in subsequent decisions on fertilizer and tillage.

Nor were market influences confined to the most fertile and expensive paddy plots. They extended to utilization of marginal soils. As noted earlier, Ming seeds expanded the boundaries of rice growing. The implications of these seed developments on agriculture in general were many-sided. In addition to competing with tobacco and sugar for space in fertile lowland paddies, rice growing in the hills of Fukien was challenged by indigo, tea, and ramie, all of which fed into trade extending beyond the province. Still further competitors on the poorest lands were other cash crops: t'ung nut, and timber, a product for which Fukien was famous. These were only the most important cash crops. A multiplicity of more specialized products, such as lacquer, plaintain fiber cloth, and purple dye are noted in local records.[64] Together, these crops drew even more marginal lands into direct relationships with the market.

The extensive cultivation conditions which characterized these cash crops, grown on marginal lands, represented an advantage against which labor-expensive rice had to compete. Unlike rice, these crops did not have to be planted every year and did not require much care once they were planted. A single planting of ramie, for example, lasted several years and provided four cuttings a year.[65] Indigo plants, whose leaves provided dye, could be "harvested" two to four times a year from the first year they were grown.[66] Tea bushes, found on the hills throughout Fukien, produced three crops a year for the market,[67] and although t'ung nut trees did not begin to bear nuts until three to six years after planting, twenty to fifty pounds of nuts could be harvested every year thereafter.[68]

We have already noted that a steady increase in rice prices provided incentives to supplant these extensive cash crops with rice and to push these crops onto yet more marginal lands. An eighteenth century gazetteer states: "Formerly (we) tilled fields, now (we) till mountains. Formerly we planted only rice, panicled millet, beans and wheat; now what is planted on the mountains is melon, or tea, t'ung nuts, pine, cedar or bamboo: all of these can supply daily needs." [69]

Cropping trends on fertile lands probably encouraged further conversion of land into paddy and stimulated land reclamation. As cash crops such as sugar and tobacco supplanted rice on many first-grade paddies, the resulting decline in local rice production increased the upward pressure on the price of rice. This encouraged expansion of rice cultivation into new lands. The result was an increase in local rice supplies which restrained the rise in rice prices, thus encouraging the trend toward growing cash crops on the best paddy lands by enhancing the profitability of sugar and tobacco relative to rice. The cultivation of sweet potatoes had a similar effect: by providing a substitute food crop for poorer peasants, who sold their rice and ate sweet potatoes instead, the demand for rice was checked, and rice prices were moderated. Barley, wheat, and most of the dryland grains grown as supplementary crops in Fukien were also significant as alternative staples to rice, with similar implications for the local rice market.[70]

The pattern of land use thus represented a delicate balance among numerous and complex market relationships.

This was especially the case because of the development of rural handicrafts in China. Unlike premodern Europe, there was no clear distinction between an urban handicraft sector and the rural peasant economy. Handicraft production for the market was common to farm and town in Fukien, and many regions along the lower Yangtze. This meant that changes in the relative price of agricultural and craft products, especially textiles, affected the distribution of rural labor between farming and crafts, rather than the distribution of income between urban artisans and farmers. The Fukienese farmer had a choice between farming and devoting more effort to a variety of crafts: wine making, lacquer production, weaving.

The best illustration of the process described above is found in Ming Soochow. As shown in Map 2, Soochow is located in the heart of the Yangtze delta, where urbanization and agricultural development went hand in hand. Transportation was no problem here: southern Kiangsu enjoys the greatest river density in China.[71] With an excellent network of streams and canals, nearby peasants enjoyed easy access to the city markets of Soochow, and beyond them to the cities in the lower Yangtze.[72] It is therefore not surprising that market considerations were very important in determining the pattern of peasant economy. In the Sung period, when early ripening strains of rice first made double cropping feasible, Soochow peasants continued to specialize in growing older *keng* varieties. This was because the Champa at that time was considered an inferior grain: the *keng* rice could only be grown on the most fertile soils, was expensive, and was preferred by those who could afford it. Soochow farmers chose to grow the more expensive rice for sale in nearby cities.[73] In Ming times, peasants in this area intensi-

MAP 2. KIANGSU PROVINCE, WITH SELECTED POINTS OF INTEREST

fied the care with which they tilled the soil but did not change to a double cropping pattern. Since they expended extra labor in transplanting wheat and vegetable crops,[74] it is not likely that a labor shortage was the cause of their adherence to a single cropping cycle for rice. A more profitable outlet for peasant labor existed in rural handicrafts and supplementary farm activities.

Thanks to two agricultural handbooks of the period, it is possible to describe the alternatives open to a seventeenth century Soochow peasant in some detail.[75] The *Shen-shih nung-shu* (1643) by Shen Ch'i and Chang Lü-hsiang's *Pu nung shu* (1658) give comprehensive descriptions of a highly commercialized peasant economy. In addition to rice and a supplementary crop of wheat, beans, or oil plants, farmers could grow mulberry leaves to sell to silkworm producers, cultivate silkworms, raise livestock for sale to urban meat markets, make rice wine or soybean products, or weave textiles. The two books present detailed information on market prices for various crops and cost calculations for each.

In Shen Ch'i's model of the peasant economy, rice continued to be the primary crop. He calculated that at the market price of one liang of silver for a picul of rice, a peasant with eight mou of land could afford to hire a helper, farm all eight mou, and emerge with a profit after paying rent of one liang of silver per mou.[76] But, as Chang Lü-hsiang pointed out, a normal year's harvest yielded only three piculs of rice a mou, but the same land, if devoted to sericulture, could produce enough mulberry leaves for over ten baskets of silkworms.[77] When rice prices are low and silk prices high, a basket of silkworms "matched the profit" of a mou planted to rice.[78] Both authors advocated planting one crop of rice and cultivating silkworms as part of the annual farming cycle.[79]

Weaving was also an important source of peasant income. Shen Ch'i presents a detailed calculation comparing the costs involved in setting two women to work at weaving with the potential market price of the finished goods, and concluded that two women could make an annual profit of 30 liang of silver.[80] Profits from silk weaving were almost four times the profits obtainable from growing rice: this was because silk weaving was a highly skilled occupation. More commonly, farm women spun silk thread for sale to urban weavers. From the late Ming period on, they also purchased cotton thread and wove cloth.[81]

In Soochow we can see in concrete form the reasons why a farmer might reject increasing yields in favor of other activities which would augment his income. Despite an urban demand for rice strong enough to attract grain from provinces as distant as Szechwan, there were simply more profitable alternatives to a second crop of rice in Soochow.[82] In Shen Ch'i's accounts, the model farmer received only 40 per cent of his total income from rice; in Chang Lü-hsiang's version, this was lowered to 18 per cent, and the farmer's major source of income came from growing mulberry leaves.[83]

His wife could earn almost as much as he did. In a year, she could weave sixty rolls of cloth for a total income of sixty silver liang. Even after the cost of raw materials was deducted, her contribution to the family income was twenty liang a year.[84] It was clearly to the family's advantage to keep her at home, since a hired laborer cost only thirteen liang a year.

By removing the women from the fields, high textile prices halved the available supply of labor for agriculture. Diverse marketing opportunities further restricted the labor allocated to rice cultivation: the period before and after one crop of rice was more profitably spent growing mulberry leaves than in tending another crop of rice.

Emphasis on market conditions as determinants of cropping patterns is relevant to understanding the pattern of coastal rice deficits and interior self-sufficiency noted in Fukien from Sung to Ch'ing times. Most scholars noting this pattern have attributed it to the larger populations of the coastal region,[85] but one of the outstanding characteristics of rice cultivation is its ability to absorb almost indefinite increases in labor and respond with increases in yield. A more likely explanation, based on our study of the close linkage between market factors and cropping decisions, is that from an early period, peasants in the coastal area found it more profitable to grow alternative cash crops, ship them to other markets, and import rice. The coast enjoyed the advantages of cheap water transport, which made it possible to export lychee, oranges, plums, and timber as well as textiles, iron, and wine from Sung times.[86] Profit motives stimulated specialization in cash crops from an early point in Fukien's history.

The prices of various crops, rents of various grades of land, cost of fertilizers, and income available from nonagricultural employment all influenced the choice of crops and cultivation methods in Fukien. In an economy in which price factors entered every phase of agricultural decision making, changing market conditions were bound to affect the pattern of farming and not just the commercial sector.

Chapter Four / MARKET STIMULUS AND ECONOMIC CHANGE: THE CASE OF FUKIEN

> The Province of Fukien abounds with everything that grows in most other Provinces of the Empire, the Commerce which the Inhabitants have with Japan, Camboya, Siam, etc. renders it extremely rich; they have Steel, and all sorts of Utensils wrought to the greatest Perfection; and they import from other Countries Cloves, Cinnamon, Pepper, Sandalwood, Amber, Coral, and many other Commodities of this Nature: Its Mountains are Covered with Trees fit for building of Ships: they have Mines of Lead and Iron; 'tis supposed they have also Gold and Silver, but it is forbidden to dig for these under Pain of Death.
>
> —J. B. du Halde, *Description Geographique,* I, 163.

This chapter is concerned with the repercussions of location on the economies of two regions in Fukien, the interior northwest prefecture of Chien-ning, and Chang-chou, a prefecture on the south Fukien coast.[1] By far the greatest advantage enjoyed by Chang-chou was its access to cheap sea transportation and to overseas markets. In the sixteenth century, Chang-chou participated in the expanding foreign trade stimulated by Portuguese and Spanish ships, while Chien-ning's markets stagnated. The effect of these differences in opportunity was felt in virtually every segment of the economies of both regions. The comparison of these two prefectures reveals not only the actual and potential dynamism of commerce but also its limited role in the context of Ming and Ch'ing China.

GEOGRAPHY

Fukien is a coastal province in southeastern China, bounded to the north by the province of Chekiang, to the

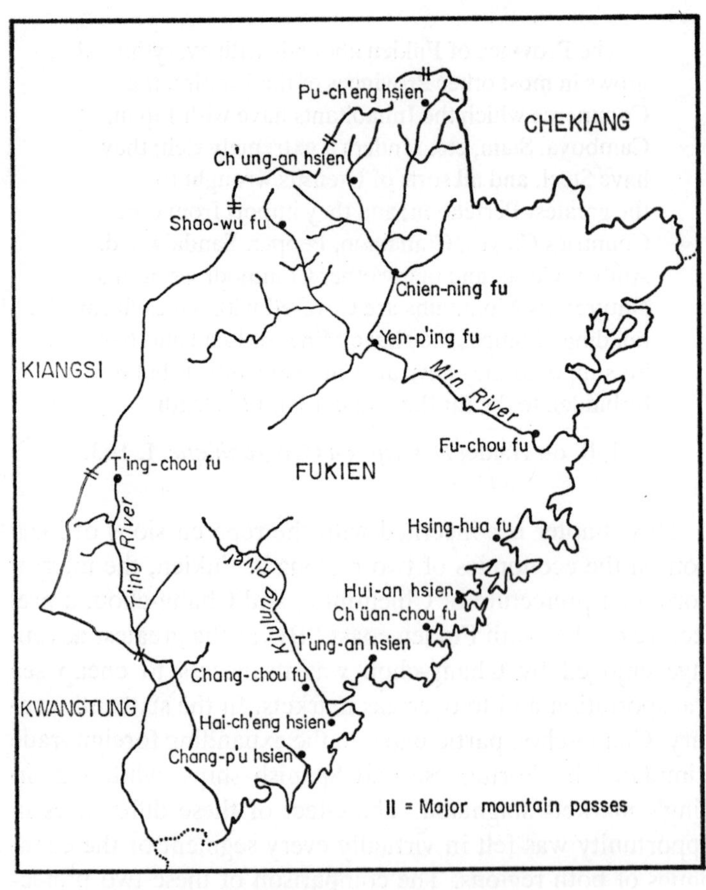

MAP 3. FUKIEN PROVINCE, WITH PREFECTURAL CAPITALS AND IMPORTANT HSIEN

west by Kiangsi, and to the south by Kwangtung. Geography, the most important historical determinant in Fukien, has for the most part played a negative role. Enclosed by mountain ranges to the north and west, and divided by mountains into a relatively isolated hinterland and coast, Fukien has been far less unified than its status as a single administrative unit suggests. To a twentieth century observer, Fukien was "one of the most completely isolated provinces of China," [2] whose numerous dialects testified to a long history of limited social contact.[3]

Rugged terrain restricted travel and communication between interior Fukien and neighboring provinces to three routes. The most important, and the oldest, connected Fukien with Chekiang at P'u-ch'eng hsien, Chien-ning prefecture. From this point travelers could also move into Kiangsi province, at Ch'ung-an hsien in the same prefecture. Another important route from Kiangsi passed into Fukien at Kuang-tse hsien, Shao-wu prefecture. The third allowed travel from southeastern Kiangsi to Ch'ang-t'ing hsien, in T'ing-chou prefecture, and thence into Ch'ao-chou, Kwangtung. Most of these routes combined water and overland travel.[4]

Several major river systems cut through the mountains in the interior and allow communication between the hinterland and coast. Of these the most important were the Min River system, which flows from Chien-ning prefecture in northwestern Fukien to the sea, and the Kiulung River, which drains one fifth of the southeastern part of the province.[5] Wherever such waterways existed, they were used for transport. The many narrow and fast flowing streams in these river systems stimulated the development of boats which were adapted to highly specific conditions: the "rat boats" on the Min-ch'ing, a tributary of the Min River, and the shallow draught boats on the Yen-p'ing River are examples. A seventeenth century description of junks mentions two types, the *ch'ing-liu* and the *shao-p'eng*, which, starting out at Kuang-tse hsien (west Fukien) and Ch'ung-an hsien (in the northwest) respectively, sailed regularly down the Min River to Fu-chou. The *ch'ing-liu* junk was used by traveling merchants to convey goods, and the *shao-p'eng* was patronized by traveling officials and wealthy families.[6] With these specially adapted junks, most of the streams in Fukien were navigable to their sources.[7] The difference in transport cost between overland and water travel strongly encouraged their use, as illustrated by an available estimate of the cost differentials of shipping tea in the nineteenth century.

There were two alternative routes for transporting tea from northwest Fukien, where it was grown, to Canton. The overland part of the journey via Kiangsi, though only one seventh of the total distance, accounted for more than one third of the total transport cost, which was itself equal to one third of the initial cost of the tea at the point of origin. If the tea were sent to Fu-chou and then shipped to Canton, the distance was greater, but because transportation was entirely by water, the cost was only one fifth that of the first route.[8]

Yet, despite the great savings possible through water transport, the interior of Fukien tended to remain primarily oriented to commerce with Kiangsi and Chekiang rather than with the coast. When Robert Fortune visited the tea country of northwest Fukien, he found tea still being shipped by overland routes to Canton.[9] For its part, traffic along the coast tended to move in a north-south direction, whether by land or by sea.[10]

There has been a tendency for Fukien to divide into at

least three parts: the coast, the northwest corner of the province, Fukien's major inland link with Chekiang and Kiangsi, and the southwest corner of the province, which enjoys trade contacts with Kiangsi and Kwangtung provinces. The dialectal patterns in Fukien correspond to these three regional demarcations. The Fuchou dialect of northern Fukien is supplanted by dialects which tie southern Fukien to the Swatow region in Kwangtung province, and a form of Mandarin is spoken in both northwest Fukien and the contiguous Kiangsi region.[11]

CHIEN-NING AND CHANG-CHOU

In the sixteenth century, two areas within Fukien were important in long distance trade. One was the interior northwest prefecture of Chien-ning, situated astride the province's oldest inland transportation route, linking Fukien with its neighbor to the north, Chekiang. This route, involving a combination of overland and water travel, had achieved importance by the tenth or eleventh century. It was used by Marco Polo at a slightly later date and continued to be the major route into Fukien in the nineteenth century.[12]

Chien-ning's commerce was based on locational advantage, its geographical access to Chekiang and Kiangsi. But it was not simply an entrepot. By Ming times, it had developed an array of rural as well as urban handicrafts feeding into commerce and produced cash crops for long distance trade.

Tea was undoubtedly Chien-ning's most famous cash crop. The Bohea Hills (Wu-i-shan) had provided tea for Imperial tables in the tenth century,[13] and Ming tea connoisseurs continued to praise it most highly. Tea was grown on the hilly slopes just above the paddy fields. On the higher slopes, timber and bamboo were also grown as commercial

MAP 4. CHIEN-NING PREFECTURE, FROM A 1693 PREFECTURAL GAZETEER

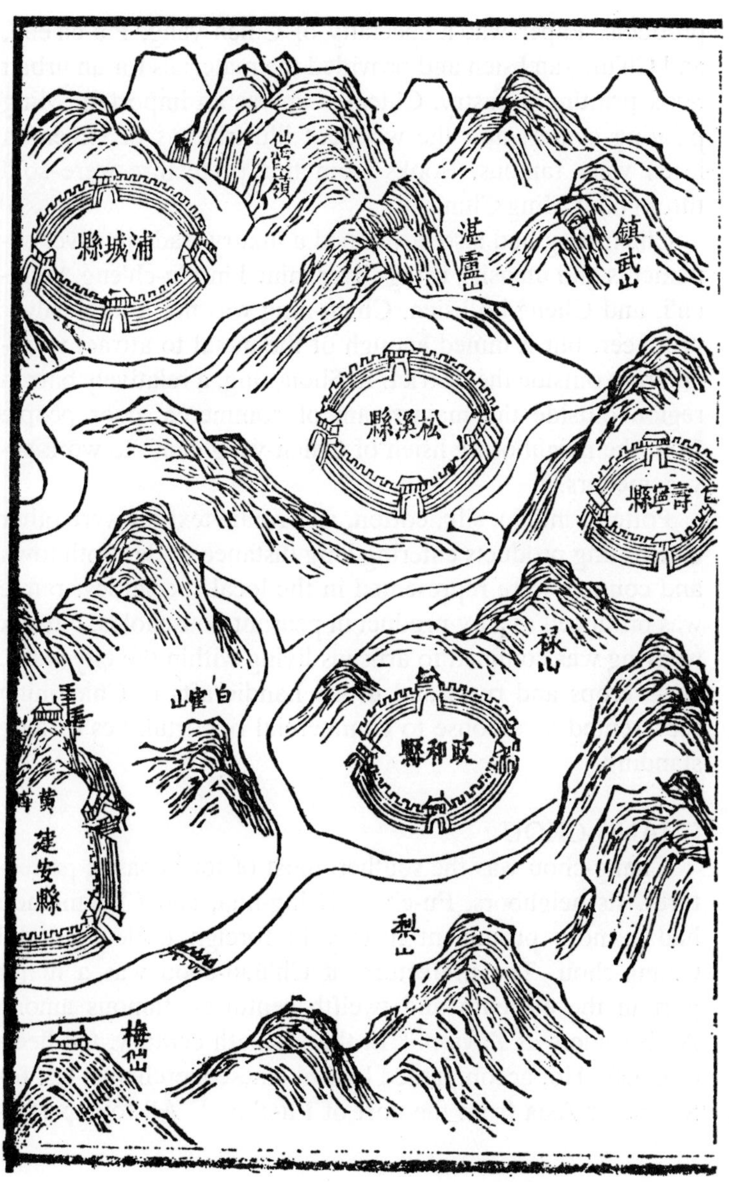
仙霞嶺
浦城縣
湛盧山
鎮武山
松溪縣
壽寧縣
政和縣
建安縣
梨山
梅仙山

products. Paper was a specialty of Chien-yang, P'u-ch'eng, and Ch'ung-an hsien and provided the materials for an urban book printing industry. Chien-yang was an important Ming printing center, and the woodcut illustrations of Chien-an hsien were famous. Books from this prefecture were sold throughout Ming China.[14]

Chien-ning had also developed a luxury trade in silver ornaments and utensils, using silver mined in P'u-ch'eng, Sung-ch'i, and Cheng-ho hsien. Chien-ning was not a large silver producer, but it mined enough of the metal to attract workers from outside the district. In Shou-ning, a relatively barren region outside the mainstream of commerce, poor people from the neighboring hsien of Chien-yang came to work silver smelters.[15]

Pottery, indigo, silk, cotton, and ramie textiles were other Chien-ning products entering long distance trade. Both town and country were represented in the local specialties: ramie was produced as a by-product in peasant households, but silk weaving was confined to artisans living within the city walls. Cash crops and rural and urban handicrafts in Chien-ning represented a response to commercial opportunities of long standing.

CHANG-CHOU

Chang-chou was the southernmost of four coastal prefectures. Its neighbors, Fu-chou, Hsing-hua, and Ch'üan-chou had a more prominent history in foreign trade than did Chang-chou. The prefecture of Ch'üan-chou was a major port in the eleventh and twelfth centuries, famous among Arab traders as Zayton.[16] In the fifteenth century, the fleets of Cheng Ho, accompanied by Fukienese merchants, left for Southeast Asia from the port of Fu-chou.[17] All four prefec-

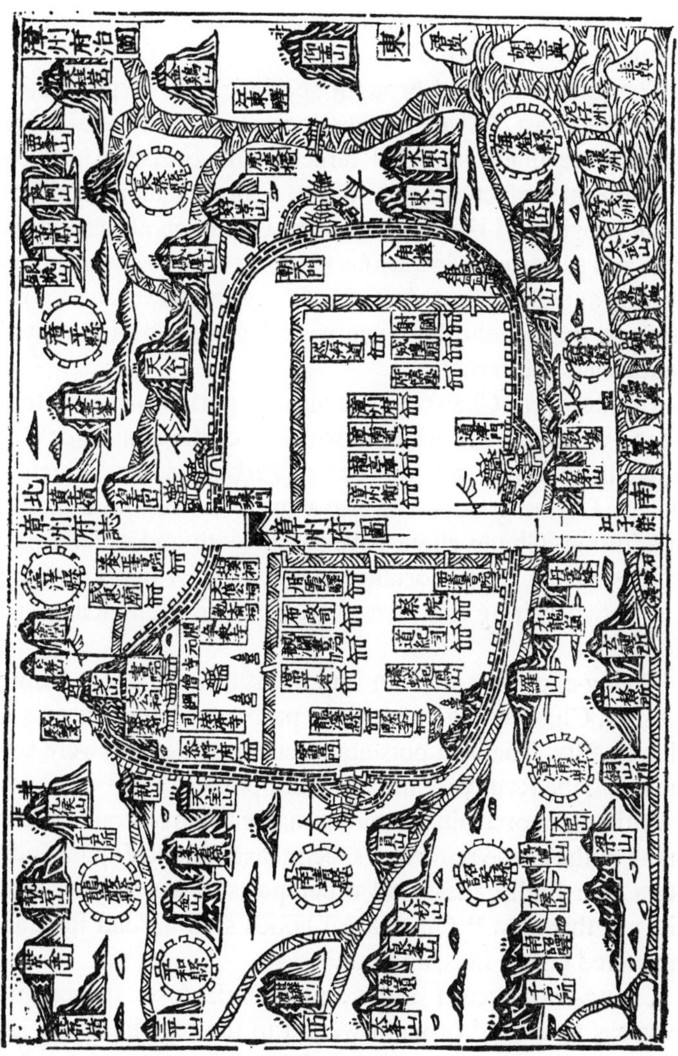

MAP 5. CHANG-CHOU PREFECTURE, FROM A 1573 PREFECTURAL GAZETTEER

tures sent junks to other Asian markets in a trade which was centuries old by 1500.

The junk trade had brought specialization to production along the coast. Sugar, textiles, porcelain, and metal wares which were made here fed directly into overseas markets. The coastal prefectures were one of China's major sugar producing regions. Like its neighbors, Chang-chou grew sugar cane and exported it in various stages of refinement to Japan, Luzon, and Southeast Asia. Fruit was preserved and sold: oranges, lychee, and lung-yen were regional specialties with established markets.[18]

Textiles were Chang-chou's most important manufacture. Chang-chou silk was well known: one of the names for Chinese silk in Japan was *hokken* or *Fukien* in the Fukienese dialect. Cotton goods were also woven and sold in quantity. In addition, Chang-chou wove ramie cloth and other coarse textiles. Given the importance of weaving for the prefecture, it is not surprising that dyes were another Chang-chou specialty.[19]

Chang-chou was also an important iron producer. Lung-yen and Chang-p'ing counties in particular had iron ores of high quality. The iron pots and utensils made here were sold in Japan, the Ryukyus, and the Philippines.[20]

Although porcelain was not a major Chang-chou product, many of the crude porcelain specimens found in Japan, Indonesia, the Philippines, and other parts of Asia came from kilns in this area.[21] Other local goods sold abroad included lacquered boxes, fans, and salt.[22]

Chang-chou's cash crops and manufactures flowed into overseas trade and brought wealth to the region. In the late fifteenth century, the prefectural city was sufficiently prosperous to be called a "little Soochow." [23] Comparison with the largest commercial center in China may have stemmed from exaggerated local pride, but contemporary documents show that Chang-chou, like Chien-ning, had a commercially oriented economy of long standing.

In 1500, Chang-chou and Chien-ning were each part of an extensive market economy. The coastal region was oriented to overseas trade, and the interior prefecture of Chien-ning to domestic markets. In the commercialization of their economies, there were no discernible new developments of recent date: many of the local products had been regional specialties for four or five centuries. During the sixteenth century, however, while Chien-ning's markets continued unchanged, Chang-chou became the center of an expanding illegal trade,[24] first with the Portuguese and Japanese, and later with the Spanish at Manila.

THE NEW TRADE

When the Portuguese moved to the coast of Fukien and Chekiang after their expulsion from Canton in 1521–1522, they found a ready response among local merchants. Through the twenties and into the forties the Portuguese and Chinese held markets on off-shore islands close to Ning-po and Chang-chou. The Portuguese Gaspar da Cruz's account of this illegal commerce is echoed by reports in the *Shih-lu* and is described by Chinese contemporaries.[25] Trade, which was expanded into a triangular exchange of goods after the Portuguese discovery of Japan in 1542, flourished until the appointment of Chu Wan as Viceroy of Chekiang and Fukien in 1547. Chu was given a special commission to abolish the Portuguese–Japanese–Chinese "piracy," and his campaigns against the traders in 1548–1549 were successful in routing the Portuguese.[26] Although the Portuguese were driven back to more southern waters, where they operated in the 1550's, the Japanese trade with Fukien continued. Meanwhile, an expanded commerce with the Philippines developed.

When the Spaniards sailed to Luzon in the early sixteenth century, they reported finding Chinese traders there and in villages in Mindanao and the Ladrones. The volume of this traditional junk trade was small: only two junks a year were reported in Mindanao.[27] The founding of Manila in 1571 and the initiation of shipments of Mexican silver to this settlement spurred Chinese trade with this Spanish colony. Chinese merchants acted as middlemen between the Spaniards and natives, providing the latter with Chinese goods and making an annual profit of about two million silver pesos from the three-way exchange.[28]

From 1522 on, the coastal prefectures of Fukien participated in a rapidly increasing trade with the Portuguese and the Philippines. Although the volumes of trade with the Portuguese are not known, over twenty Portuguese vessels a year journeyed to China in the 1560's.[29] The development of the Manila trade caused another large increase in coastal Fukien's commercial activity. Figures on the number of ships permitted to participate in the legalized Hai-ch'eng trade with the Philippines show this expansion. A 1589 ruling had limited the Hai-ch'eng trade to 88 junks a year. Later this was increased to 110.[30] The enormity of this increase can be seen by noting that only ten to twenty junks had been involved in the pre-Spanish commerce with the Philippines.

THE IMPACT

From the second decade of the sixteenth century, the coastal prefectures of Fukien were direct participants in a sudden and rapid increase in commerce. Though the traditional junk trade continued, the Portuguese and Spanish presence introduced a new level of marketing activity. This increased trade continued to expand in the course of the century and especially affected the economy of southern Fukien. According to Chu Wan, the majority of the Chinese who were collaborating with the *Fo-lang-chi* (Portuguese) were from Chang-chou and Ch'üan-chou, the coastal prefecture to its north. Fukienese from these prefectures were also active participants in the Manila trade.[31]

How did Chang-chou react to this rapid and sustained expansion of overseas markets? Information from contemporary gazetteers points to changes on several levels, ranging from the introduction of new products to a broader impact on the pattern of land use and the structure of land values.

MARKETS

The immediate effect of trade expansion is shown by the growth of periodic markets. Increases in the numbers of markets reflected growing commercial involvement of rural localities, and not just of merchants in the walled towns.

The expansion of periodic markets in Chang-chou from 1491 to 1628, shown in Table 5,[32] must be evaluated with full recognition of the potential market growth attributable to a natural increase in population. Even so, it is clear that the pace of market expansion in this prefecture far exceeded the rate of natural population increase. The actual population records remaining from this period give a growth rate averaging 0.15 per cent a year from 1491 to 1573: this figure may well underestimate the growth which occurred. Yet the use of a higher figure of 0.5 per cent a year[33] to estimate population increases under normal conditions of peace and

TABLE 5. GROWTH OF PERIODIC MARKETS BY COUNTY, CHANG-CHOU PREFECTURE, 1491–1628

County	1491 (a)	1573 (b)	1628 (c)	Percentage change 1491–1573	1573–1628	1491–1628
Lung-ch'i	8	11	15	37.5	114	88
Chang-p'u	1	5	10	400	100	900
Lung-yen	0	4	4	–	0	–
Nan-ching	0	1	5	–	400	–
Ch'ang-t'ai	1	5	7	600	40	600
Chang-p'ing	1	5	5	400	0	400
Chao-an[a]	–	0	1	–	–	–
Hai-ch'eng[a]	–	4	7	–	75	–
Ning-yang[a]	–	0	2	–	–	–
P'ing-ho[a]	–	3	9	–	200	–
Total	11	38	65	245	71	491

Sources: (a) 1491 ed., *Pa Min t'ung-chih*, 14.14b–15b. (b) 1573 ed., *Chang-chou FC*, 2.15b, 12.27b, 19.12b, 21.12a, 23.13b, 25.8b, 27.8a, 29.9a, 30.11a, 31.5b. (c) 1628 ed., *Chang-chou FC*, 29.9a–10b.

[a] These counties were all created in the sixteenth century and therefore do not exist in the source for Column *a*. (P'ing-ho was established in 1517; Chao-an, 1530; Ning-yang, 1565; and Hai-ch'eng, 1567.)

prosperity does not alter our conclusion that population growth was not the major cause of market expansion in Chang-chou. At 0.5 per cent a year, the population would have increased by 50 per cent (1491–1573) and by 32 per cent from 1573 to 1628. As shown in Table 5, markets increased by 245 per cent from 1491–1573, and by 71 per cent in the subsequent period. From 1491 to 1628, market expansion far outpaced population, and we must look to commerce for the driving force behind this growth.

A direct link between the expansion of foreign trade and

periodic market growth is provided by historical records which identify Chang-p'u and Lung-ch'i counties as the coastal areas most active in the illegal trade. Table 5 shows that Chang-p'u had the most remarkable (900 per cent) expansion of markets in the prefecture. It was to Yüeh-kang, initially located in Lung-ch'i county, that the Portuguese and Japanese came in largest numbers. In 1567, the sites which were most active in trading were isolated from Chang-p'u and Lung-ch'i and combined to form the new county of Hai-ch'eng, in an unsuccessful government effort to suppress the illicit commerce.[34] These three counties differed from most others in Chang-chou by having markets located outside the walled city which was the county seat. Moreover, increases in these "nonurban" markets occurred within a few specific areas, tied to foreign trade. In Lung-ch'i, for example, three fourths of these new markets were located in two subdistricts directly on the coast. In Chang-p'u, two thirds of the new markets were on the coast, and in Hai-ch'eng, five sixths of the markets, new and old, bordered a creek leading to the ocean and Wu-hsü Island, where the Portuguese and Japanese ships gathered.[35]

The establishment of new markets in Chang-chou to cater to the expanded trade serves only to establish the fact that there was a response to new trading opportunities. What was the nature of this response? Again, artisans in cities and peasants in rural areas were affected.

NEW PRODUCTS

Products introduced into China were sometimes taken up by local artisans and copied. A 1633 hsien gazetteer describes a "self-chiming clock" which automatically cried out the hour and was brought to China by the European traders.

At first, these cuckoo clocks were made of iron, but later ones coming from the "Great West" were made of copper. The manufacture of these clocks required considerable skill, and the Chang-chou artisans who tried to produce imitations had not succeeded in equalling the quality of the originals.[36]

Foreign trade thus brought technical change in the form of new manufactures. This was also true in textiles, where Ming artisans in the prefecture had learned to weave "Japanese satin."[37] Another material which was previously imported but now woven locally, was a velvety fabric called swansdown.[38] In silver metallurgy, the adoption of the liquation process, probably from Japan, was yet another instance in which technical change resulted from the trade expansion of the sixteenth century.

The liquation process, said to have been developed in Saxony about 1450, appeared in Japan by 1580. It was a method by which copper and silver could be separated from ores containing the two metals, and in both Europe and Japan it had had a significant impact on silver production.[39] Historical records do not cite any such improvement in silver extraction techniques for the Ming period. The liquation process is not recorded in the seventeenth century compendium on technology, *T'ien-kung k'ai-wu.* Although this work states that lead is the only ore from which silver could be extracted (indicating a pre-liquation technique), it also notes that Chang-chou merchants were able to refine argentiferous copper and separate out the two metals. The liquation process, though unknown in other parts of China, was thus familiar to people in Chang-chou, who had probably learned it from the Japanese. Indeed, *T'ien-kung k'ai-wu* records that Japanese copper-silver ingots were imported and the two metals were separated in Chang-chou.[40]

The introduction of new food and cash crops was another result of new trade contacts. It was through Chang-chou that the peanut, the sweet potato, and tobacco were introduced into China. The first two crops were grown on heretofore uncultivated hills and used to supplement staple grains, but the impact of tobacco, which was planted on fertile plots, was quite different.

Tobacco smoking seems to have caught on fairly quickly among the Chinese population. A seventeenth century work records the spread of smoking practices: "In the latter part of the sixteenth century (when it was first introduced) only soldiers and border peoples used it, but since the T'ien-ch'i and Ch'ung-chen reign periods (1621 on), everyone uses it." [41]

As a domestic demand for tobacco developed, areas in Chang-chou quickly began growing the plant. According to the 1628 prefectural gazetteer, tobacco (*tan pa ku*) was already much planted in Chang-chou.[42] In Ning-yang hsien, a 1692 gazetteer described the plant, known locally as "smoke grass" (*hsün ts'ao*), which had spread over fields in the area because "cultivators grab its profit." [43] Tobacco became a major cash crop along the Fukien coast in the seventeenth century, and Chang-chou seems to have been especially noted for its tobacco product.[44]

In addition to introducing new products, market expansion moved Chang-chou toward increased specialization in manufactures. There was an increase in the luxury trade, which used materials bought in Southeast Asia such as tortoise shell, ivory, bone, and sandalwood, to make combs, cups, and other items for the domestic market. This was a means by which "in addition to the foreign treasure, one can obtain profit" from the increased overseas trade.[45]

The textile industry in Chang-chou also processed imported materials which were subsequently shipped elsewhere for sale. The increased demand for Chinese fabrics probably accentuated the re-export trade. Sixteenth century cotton and silk merchants imported raw materials for weaving in Chang-chou. Because Fukien was ill-suited to cotton cultivation, it imported most of its cotton from the Sung-chiang and T'ai-ts'ang areas of Chekiang province. A sixteenth century source describes Fukienese merchants sailing in large numbers to T'ai-ts'ang with boatloads of sugar, which they exchanged for return cargoes of cotton.[46] Cotton merchants went as far as Luzon, where they exchanged finished cotton goods for raw cotton.[47]

Although some native silk was used for weaving, the quality of local silk thread was inferior to Chekiang silk, and the fabrics woven for long distance trade did not use Chang-chou silk. According to a 1573 prefectural gazetteer, the different silks for which Chang-chou was noted were woven using imported Hu-chou raw silk. From these, skilled urban weavers produced fabrics "renowned throughout the empire."[48]

The indirect effects of expanded trade on the peasant economy of Chang-chou are more difficult to trace, because the local histories of the period have left no detailed comments on this topic. There was probably an increase in the production of sugar cane and fruits, since both were sold in the new markets. The thriving textile industry may also have stimulated an increase in the manufacture of textile dyes. The 1573 prefectural gazetteer lists red, purple, black, and indigo dyes among the commercial products of the region.[49] As cotton fabrics flourished, there was even a gradual increase in local cultivation of cotton. The 1573 prefectural gazetteer describes the inferior quality of Chang-chou raw cotton, but by 1700, cotton seems to have become a common plant in the orchards and gardens of many counties in the prefecture.[50]

New products, and a booming market for old and new goods, enlarged the profitable alternatives open to both artisan and peasant in Chang-chou. Yet another major factor in changing the Chang-chou economy was the silver that flowed into the prefecture as a result of its expanded trade. In addition to providing fortunes for a lucky few, this new wealth affected agriculture through land prices, land rents, and productivity.

SILVER

The newly enlarged trade brought an influx of silver into Fukien throughout the sixteenth century. Silver was imported in coined form: the *huang-pi-shih* (Spanish peso), *t'u-ch'un* (testao), *lo-liao-li* (Portuguese 50 reis piece), and the *huang-liao-li* (Portuguese 20 reis piece) were all familiar to residents of Chang-chou.[51] According to a 1633 gazetteer, these coins had been brought from Luzon by the *Fo-lang-chi.*[52] There was also a flow of uncoined silver from Japan.

Monetary metals were not the only commodities exchanged between China and Japan: finished iron products, porcelain, and silk from China were in high demand on the Japanese market.[53] Nevertheless, copper and silver were important items in the commerce between the two countries. Japanese copper ore was exported to China, and Chinese copper coins imported into Japan.

At least one scholar has tried to explain the movements of Chinese copper cash and Japanese silver in terms of differential market price ratios.[54] Available price information supports his point. For the late sixteenth century, Cheng Jo-ts'eng noted that a string (1,000 wen) of copper cash brought four ounces of silver in Japan, and a string of illegally minted Fukien coins brought 1.2 ounces of silver.[55] Since the legal string of copper cash was valued at about 1.4 ounces of silver in China at this time, there was a strong profit incentive for Fukienese traders to ship not only the legal cash but to produce their own money for export to Japan. In return, they received uncoined Japanese silver.

How large were the silver importations from Japan? We have only one item of information on this question, derived from the capture of three merchant ships in 1542.[56] The ships, which were on their way to Ch'üan-chou from Japan, carried 80,000 ounces of silver. With perhaps ten to twenty ships plying the Japan–China trade during this period, silver imports into Chekiang and Fukien may have been as much as 530,000 ounces a year.[57] Perhaps there was more fact than fiction in Pinto's report that since the discovery of Japan by the Portuguese, the quantity of silver in Liampo (Ning-po) had increased three or four-fold.[58]

The flow of silver from Japan increased through the sixteenth century. By 1600, about 200,000 kilograms a year may have been imported to China. At the same time, the flow of Mexican silver reaching China from the Philippines was a minimum of 3 million pesos a year, or 8 million kilograms of silver.[59]

The inflow of silver helped to further stimulate silver monetization in southeast China. Chang-chou and Ch'üan-chou were direct recipients of much of this inflow. Not only had these prefectures been prominent in the illegal trade with the Portuguese which we have described, but the legalization of the Manila trade (in 1567) had granted the port of Hai-ch'eng in Chang-chou a monopoly of this market.[60] Chang-chou was thus the recipient of large quantities of silver through most of the sixteenth century.

LAND PRICES, AGRICULTURAL PRODUCTIVITY, AND RENTS

One of the consequences of the profitable foreign trade was a boom in Chang-chou land values, as the wealthy sought in land a safe and prestigious investment. Land prices in Chang-chou reflected the competition for land. According to a 1572 report, land was selling for 8 liang of silver per mou, and the rich temple lands in Hai-ch'eng brought from 7 to 10 liang per mou.[61] Land prices in Chien-ning during the same period ranged from 2 to 4 liang per mou,[62] about a third of the Chang-chou prices. Nor does this discrepancy in land prices reflect a premium attached to all coastal lands; in Ku-t'ien, a county under the coastal prefecture of Fu-chou, land was also selling for 2 to 3 liang per mou at the turn of the century.[63]

The land boom had several effects. Combined with the increased profitability of cash crops, rising land prices stimulated land reclamation and improvement. As a gazetteer from Ch'üan-chou put it: "In recent years, land prices have skyrocketed. The people struggle for the profit of a minuscule bit of land. Recently idle lands have been opened up for cultivation; [people have] razed mountains, filled in and leveled ditches and banks, and extended plot boundaries to touch neighboring ones and bring about mutual disputes. Land which was previously waterlogged or blocked with sand, which had landlords who did not reclaim them, has been taken over by others." [64]

In Chang-chou, the intense competition for land was concentrated on building up arable land from enclosed river and ocean areas. According to a district magistrate's report, "Those who aim at profit rush to compete here." [65] The importance of land reclamation for agriculture in Chang-chou is clear from a gazetteer which described and classified land in the prefecture into five grades according to fertility. Of the five categories three were varieties of reclaimed land: alluvial fields (*chou-t'ien*), which included upper and middle grade land; dammed land (*tai-t'ien*), of the middle grade; and low grade "sea land" (*hai-t'ien*).[66]

Chapter Three discussed the cumulative effects of expanding cash crops. As these claimed fertile paddies which were formerly planted in rice, it became profitable to convert more land into rice paddy. New seeds permitted heretofore marginal land to be used for rice cultivation. At the extensive margin of cultivation, rising crop prices enhanced the profitability of building new paddy fields under successively more difficult conditions. On the most fertile paddy plots, the expansion of acreage planted in cash crops also enhanced the profitability of rice, as it diminished the locally grown rice supply. At the intensive margin of cultivation, the peasant responded to rising crop prices by increasing the quantity of fertilizer, labor, and water which he applied to the land. The result was increased productivity.

When rice yields in Chien-ning are compared with similar figures for Chang-chou, we find that Chang-chou's lands were significantly more productive. Estimates of rice yields in Chien-ning, presented in Table 6, rest on information for school lands maintained by the prefectural and county governments. Yields ranged from 1.22 to 3.00 shih of unhusked rice per mou.[67]

TABLE 6. DERIVED YIELDS OF RICE IN CHIEN-NING PREFECTURE[a]

Administrative unit	Date	Rice yield (unhusked rice; shih/mou)
1. P'u-ch'eng hsien	1567–1572	1.22
2. Cheng-ho hsien	1573–1620	1.48
3. Chien-yang hsien	1596	3.0[b]
4. Chien-yang hsien	1598	3.0[b]

Sources: 1 and 2 are from school lands section, *Chien-ning FC*, 1693 ed., 9.6a–24b. Chien-yang figures from *Chien-yang HC*, 1929 ed., 6.27a–28b.

[a] General procedure by which yield estimates were derived: the school lands section presented figures on rent in kind. In the absence of information on the proportion of total yield represented by the rent, a 50–50 split between landlord and tenant was assumed. Rents in husked rice were converted at the rate of 2 shih unhusked rice = 1 shih husked rice. On tenant–landlord shares of the crop, see Fu I-ling, "Fu-chien tien-nung ching-chi shih ts'ung-k'ao," *Fu-chien hsieh-ho ta-hsüeh wen shih ts'ung-k'an*, 2: p. 7 (1944).

[b] The *lo* was a local measure which seems to have been equivalent to a shih. See the figures in *Chien-yang HC*, 1929 ed., 6.26a.

Similar information for Chang-chou plots is presented in Table 7. The yields reported in local histories ranged from 4 to over 7 shih (unhusked rice) per mou. Chang-chou's lowest yields were higher than the highest yields obtained in Chien-ning, and over three times Chien-ning's lowest yields.

Chang-chou practiced double cropping, but Chien-ning produced only one crop of rice a year.[68] Twentieth century figures estimate that conversion to double cropping can produce a 70 to 80 per cent increase in yields,[69] and this crop-

TABLE 7. RICE YIELDS IN CHANG-CHOU PREFECTURE

County	Date	Rice yield (unhusked rice; shih/mou)
1. Lung-ch'i, Nan-ching, P'ing-ho	1572	5[a]
2. Hai-ch'eng	1572	3.20–6.40[a]
3. Ch'ang-t'ai	1572	4
4. P'ing-ho	1578	7.54
5. Ch'ang-t'ai	1593	4
6. Hai-ch'eng	1605	6.16
7. Chang-p'u	1609	5.00–6.25

Sources:

1. *Chang-chou FC*, 1573 ed., 5.7a.

2. *Ibid.*, 5.53a. According to the gazetteer, the local volume measure was sometimes 70 to 80 per cent of the official one, and at other times 40 to 50 per cent of the official standard. If these equivalents are used against the 8 shih recorded in the text, the yield for this plot was only 3.2 to 6.4 official shih.

3. *Chang-chou FC*, 1628 ed., 5.27a. The same record appears in the 1877–1878 edition of the prefectural gazetteer, 7.38ab, with the character for "unhusked rice" (ku) replaced by a character which can mean "grain" (su) but can also refer to millet. The existence of two records for the same plot, with the first phrased in terms of *ku* and the second in *su* suggests that these were used interchangeably in this region.

4. *Chang-chou FC*, 1877–1878 ed., 7.39b. Phrased in *su*; see previous note.

5. *Chang-chou FC*, 1628 ed., 5.23a.

6. *Hai-ch'eng HC*, 1693 ed., 2.11b.

7. *Chang-p'u HC*, 1700 ed., 9.11b. This school land rent was the *ta-tsu* share of the *i-t'ien san-chu* system (see Chapter 2), but if we calculate total yield on the basis of information in *Chang-chou FC*, 1573 ed., 5.7a, the *ta-tsu* share is only 20 per cent of the crop, and the resulting estimate, 12.5 shih/mou, is unacceptably high. The figures above represent an estimate assuming, first, that rent was half of the crop, and second, that it was 40 per cent of the crop (the *hsiao-tsu's* share according to the 1573 prefectural gazetteer).

[a] These are direct citations and are not estimated from rent figures.

ping difference explains most of the discrepancy between the two areas. Another way of looking at this discrepancy is to examine the factors which promoted changes in productivity, including intensification of cropping, in Chang-chou. For even among areas which grew two crops of rice a year, the yields found in coastal parts of Chang-chou were unusually high.

In areas double-cropping rice, a yield of 3.64 shih[70] per mou had already been achieved in the twelfth and thirteenth centuries. Some of the yields found in Ming Fukien were much less than this. In Ku-t'ien hsien, part of Fu-chou prefecture, school land records for 1594 and 1600 indicate yields of only 2 shih per mou.[71] Even in fertile Ch'ien-yu hsien (Hsing-hua prefecture), derived yields were only 3.6 shih per mou (about 1558), just equal to Sung levels.[72] These yields are very similar to those found in Chien-ning, and they illustrate the point that double cropping per se did not bring about the productivity increases found in Chang-chou.

When two crops of rice a year are grown instead of one, the cultivator must increase not just his labor efforts but must also provide the extra water and fertilizer required if the second harvest is to be made worth his while. As noted earlier, rising crop prices in Chang-chou and prospects of profit induced Chang-chou farmers to invest more heavily in fertilizer and irrigation, and to expend extra labor to ensure abundant harvests. It was in these areas that a striking disparity between Chien-ning and Chang-chou agriculture appeared.

The recommended fertilizer in Chang-chou in the 1570's was a mixture of hog bristles, human fertilizer, ashes, and urine. In addition sesame cakes, animal bone ash, and oyster shells were suggested for use.[73] Into the early seventeenth century, fertilizers recommended in Chien-ning were much inferior to those used in Chang-chou. A 1637 gazetteer of the region suggested roasting firewood and using these and other plant ashes to enrich the soil. When these materials were not available, bamboo leaves or bracken leaves were recommended.[74] These fertilizers were not much better than those commonly used in China from much earlier periods.

In addition to the large scale public works which required a combination of forces which an individual cultivator was powerless to effect,[75] there are indications that the use of irrigation tools was more advanced in Chang-chou. By the early 1570's, the most fertile fields in Chang-chou were equipped with water wheels to bring water from the irrigation ditches into the plots. Even in mountain fields, some areas had systems of reservoirs to ensure an adequate water supply.[76] Chien-ning lagged far behind. Into the late seventeenth century, water storage ponds and well sweeps for transporting dike water into fields were unheard of in Ch'ung-an, one of the more prosperous regions of Chien-ning.[77] Crops thus depended entirely on rain water and mountain streams, and harvests were bad when the supply of water failed. Another local source from the early sixteenth century corroborates the impression that little was done to alter the natural flow of water from mountain streams.[78]

Peasants in Chang-chou and Chien-ning responded to different market opportunities with divergent patterns of fertilizer use and irrigation. The extra investment represented by these factors in Chang-chou was reflected in its more intensive cultivation of the soil and its more abundant harvests. In Chien-ning, failure to adopt double cropping was accompanied by agricultural practices reflecting a more primitive state of husbandry. It is this divergence in agricultural technique, rather than double cropping per se, that is responsible for the different levels of productivity in the two areas. The fact that double cropping presupposes increased inputs of water, fertilizer, and labor masks the wide range of yields still existing within areas which grow two crops of rice a year. Analysis of productivity differences should therefore properly rest on variations in inputs rather than on the cropping pattern itself.

The prosperity from market expansion pushed land prices in Chang-chou upward to levels which were not found elsewhere in Fukien. What was the effect of rising land prices on rents?

There were several kinds of rent arrangements in Fukien. The most common involved the payment of a fixed rent in kind: these were the heart of the tenancy contracts studied in Chapter Two. The yield figures presented in Tables 6 and 7 were largely derived from information on fixed rents. If they are divided in half, the resulting numbers represent fixed rents in Chien-ning and Chang-chou. The tenant farmer in Chien-ning during the last part of the sixteenth century paid from 0.6 to 1.8 shih of rice for each mou of land rented, and his counterpart in Chang-chou paid from 2 to 4 shih of rice for the same amount of land. The Chang-chou peasant thus paid rents over twice what was prevalent in the interior prefecture, but he also retained more rice for the same plot.[79] Having begun with a larger crop, he was by no means worse off for paying a higher rent.

Another form of rent arrangement was sharecropping. An indirect source of information on this subject comes from Fu I-ling. When fixed rents are calculated in terms of the total harvest, the Chang-chou peasant is found to have kept a higher percentage of his crops than did peasants in inland areas.[80] Modern studies suggest that the same sort of variance existed in sharecropping rent shares.[81] Chang-chou cultivators retained a larger share of a bigger crop than their counterparts in Chien-ning.

The third form of rent was payment in silver. The available information on silver rents for Chang-chou and Chien-ning, presented in Tables 8 and 9, is too scanty to permit

TABLE 8. SILVER RENTS IN CHANG-CHOU

Date	County	Acreage (mou)	Silver rent (liang)	Rent/mou (liang)
1. 1558	Lung-yen	120	14.5275	0.121[a]
2. 1609	Chang-p'u	8	5.0	0.625[a]
3. 1611	Chang-p'u	2.6	1.625	0.625[a]
4. 1628	Ch'ang-t'ai	4		0.2
1628	Ch'ang-t'ai	7		0.2
1628	Ch'ang-t'ai	29		0.07

Sources: 1. *Lung-yen HC,* 1558 ed., 4.14b. 2. *Chang-chou FC,* 1628 ed., 5.26a; also in *Chang-p'u HC,* 1700 ed., 9.11b-12a. 3. *Ibid.* 4. *Chang-chou FC,* 1628 ed., 5.27a.

[a] Calculated from data in the sources.

analysis of possible trends. In both regions, rents varied widely. Since the highest rents in Chang-chou exceeded the maximum rents found in Chien-ning, it is possible that average silver rents for Chang-chou were higher than those for Chien-ning, but the difference was probably not great.

From the landlord's viewpoint, higher rents did not enhance the profitability of landholding in Chang-chou. Information on rents as a percentage of the purchase price

TABLE 9. SILVER RENTS IN CHIEN-NING

Unit	Date	Acreage (mou)	Silver rent (liang)	Silver rent/mou (liang)[a]
1. Prefecture	1610	63.746	19.84	0.31
2. Prefecture	1573–1620	10	3+	0.3+
3. Prefecture	1573–1620	3	0.55	0.18
4. Prefecture	1573–1620	4	1.44	0.36
5. Chien-an hsien	1567–1572	10	3.32	0.33
6. Chien-an hsien	1565–1568	80	19.2	0.24
7. Chien-an hsien	1612	21	6.35	0.30
8. O-ning hsien	1567–1572	9.23	4.666	0.50
9. O-ning hsien	1573–1620	15.99	5.4	0.34
10. O-ning hsien	1573–1620	1.75	0.8	0.46
11. O-ning hsien	1573–1620	19.75	5.7	0.29
12. Ch'ung-an hsien	1522–1566	200	42.3	0.21
13. P'u-ch'eng hsien	1567–1572	200	12.2	0.06
14. Sung-ch'i hsien	1573–1620	68.5	18.4	0.27
15. Cheng-ho hsien	1572	43.9	8.2	0.19
16. Shou-ning hsien	1572	5	2	0.40
17. Shou-ning hsien	1573	2.2	0.88	0.40
18. Shou-ning hsien	1574	16	3.2	0.20
19. Shou-ning hsien	1575	6.4	1.8	0.28
20. Shou-ning hsien	1581	9.4	2.0	0.21

Sources: With few exceptions, the items above were listed in *Chien-ning FC*, 1693 ed., 9.6a-24b. The exceptions are 9, found in *O-ning HC*, 1694 ed., 4.9b, and 18, found in *Shou-ning HC*, 1686 ed., 2.5b-6a. The other entries for these hsien were checked against the prefectural gazetteer records, and when there was a discrepancy, the information in the earlier edition was used. Complete duplicate lists existed for O-ning hsien, Shou-ning hsien, Chien-an hsien (*Chien-an HC*, 1713 ed., 3.10a), and Cheng-ho hsien (*Cheng-ho HC*, 1832 ed., 4.38ab).

[a] Calculated from acreage and rent data.

paid for the land is presented in Table 10. The slightly higher returns enjoyed by the Chang-chou landlord were trivial in comparison with the profits obtainable from alternative investments in moneylending and commerce.

TABLE 10. RETURNS TO LAND INVESTMENT IN CHIEN-NING AND CHANG-CHOU

Area	Date	Land purchase price (silver[a])	Land rent (silver[a])	Rent as a percentage of the purchase price
Chien-ning				
1. Shou-ning hsien	1572	20	2	10
2. O-ning hsien	1628–1644	160	16	10
Chang-chou				
1. Chang-p'u hsien	1609	40	5	12.5
2. Chang-p'u hsien	1611	15	1.62	10.8

Sources: Chien-ning: 1. *Shou-ning HC*, 1686 ed., 2.5b. 2. *O-ning HC*, 1694 ed., 4.9b. Chang-chou: 1 and 2 are in *Chang-p'u HC*, 1700 ed., 9.11b-12b. Also in *Chang-chou FC*, 1877–1878 ed., 7.37ab.

[a] In *liang* (ounces).

The demand for land stimulated by commercially acquired wealth differed from peasant "land hunger" in that few of the purchasers wished to actually farm their plots. One effect of market expansion was thus an increase in absentee landholding. Absentee landlords did not invest in land for profit so much as to ensure a stable income and reaffirm a deep cultural value in owning land. Opportunities for accumulating wealth were much higher in activities such as moneylending and overseas trade. As noted in Table 10, silver rents represented only 10 to 12 per cent of the purchase price in Chang-chou. A man investing 100 liang of silver in land could thus anticipate an annual return of 10 to 12 liang of silver on his investment. By contrast, had he put the same amount into moneylending, he would have accumulated 43 to 80 liang a year as interest on the loan. The same sum invested in overseas commerce could produce a profit of 900 liang in a single voyage.[82] Commerce offered the possibility of ten-fold profits, which agriculture could never hope to match. Instead land was chosen for its relative security. Ships might sink, but land was a tangible and enduring asset. Because landholding stemmed from a desire for security rather than profit, the Chang-chou absentee landlord had no interest in actively participating in agriculture. Unlike the north Chinese landlord, he did not provide seeds, tools, or any other necessities for cultivation. His only tie with the land was the annual rent received from it.

Increases in land prices in Chang-chou probably made it difficult for peasants to purchase land, especially good paddy land.[83] The increase in absentee landowning which resulted was by no means to the disadvantage of the cultivator-tenant, however. In Hai-ch'eng hsien, and elsewhere in Chang-chou, the tenant enjoyed security of tenure under the system of three lords to a field. Rents, whether in money or in kind, were fixed and inflexible over long periods of time. The higher rent levels in Chang-chou absorbed only a small part of the greater productivity of the region and left the Chang-chou cultivator-tenant with a considerably higher income per mou than his Chien-ning counterpart.

In the preceding pages, we have traced the repercussions of an expansion of markets on Chang-chou in some detail.

Expanding foreign trade had an impact on almost every aspect of Chang-chou's economy. It led to greater peasant involvement in marketing, as revealed in rapidly growing numbers of periodic markets. In manufactures, some new technology was imported from abroad, and there was greater specialization in the production of textiles, including the processing and re-export of imported raw materials. Agriculture was deeply influenced, first by the introduction of new food and cash crops but more generally and profoundly by the rising opportunity costs of previous agricultural methods resulting from expanding markets. Nor did the change stop in the economic sphere. The prosperity brought by the new markets also gave Chang-chou marked success in the academic field.

DEGREE WINNING

As a province, Fukien had a long history of academic and bureaucratic prominence. As early as the eleventh century, it was the third largest source of high officials for government service;[84] in Ming times, Fukien continued to be an important academic and bureaucratic region. Through the Ming dynasty, Fukien had the highest numbers of *chin-shih* winners with respect to its population size,[85] as well as the highest numbers of official positions.[86]

Until the mid-sixteenth century, success in the *chin-shih* examinations was concentrated in the coastal prefectures of Fu-chou, Ch'üan-chou, and Hsing-hua. These three areas were among the ten most prominent producers of *chin-shih* in Ming China.[87] During this earlier period, Chang-chou did not share in the bounty enjoyed by its neighbors. In the latter half of the century, however, the number of successful Chang-chou candidates rose swiftly.

The emergence of Chang-chou as a prominent degree winning region in the second half of the sixteenth century is illustrated in Table 11 which presents the prefectural totals of *chin-shih* winners for the first and second half of the century. From producing only 3 per cent of the total number of *chin-shih* in 1513–1541, Chang-chou leapt to producing 22 per cent of all Fukien *chin-shih* in 1544–1601. Chang-chou climbed from fourth to second place ranking among the prefectures in the province.

TABLE 11. *CHIN-SHIH* WINNERS BY PREFECTURE IN FUKIEN

Prefectures, ranked	Period I Number of *chin-shih*, 1513–1541	Prefectures, ranked	Period II Number of *chin-shih*, 1549–1601
Fu-chou	112	Ch'üan-chou	237
Hsing-hua	111	Chang-chou	137
Ch'üan-chou	65	Fu-chou	103
Chang-chou	11	Hsing-hua	90
Chien-ning	8	Chien-ning	27
Yen-p'ing	5	Yen-p'ing	6
Fu-ning chou	3	Fu-ning chou	5
Shao-wu	2	T'ing-chou	5
T'ing-chou	2	Shao-wu	2
Total	319	Total	612

Sources: Data for *chin-shih* winners, 1513, 1517, 1520, 1522, 1529, 1532, from *Huang Ming kung-chü k'ao*, chüan 6, held by Naikaku bunko, Tokyo. Examination data for 1535 are from *Chia-ching shih-ssu-nien chin-shih teng-k'o lu*, held by Naikaku bunko, Tokyo. Data for 1538, 1541, 1544, 1547, 1550, 1553, 1556, 1559, 1562, 1565, 1568, 1571, 1574, 1577, 1580, 1583, 1586, 1589, 1595, 1598, and 1601 examinations from *Fu-chien t'ung-chih*, 1943 ed., 5.13a-19b.

The linkage of this sudden spurt in academic success with the prosperity resulting from foreign trade stems not only from the timing and consistency of Chang-chou's rise in *chin-shih* winners but also from the success of Ch'üan-chou over Fu-chou and Hsing-hua. In the second half of the sixteenth century Ch'üan-chou also rose to a commanding position in this regard, and its new prominence may also be ascribed to extensive participation both in the illegal trade of the 1520's to 1540's and in the activity which continued thereafter.

When *chin-shih* winners are listed by hsien, the success of the particular counties involved in foreign trade becomes clearer. The lists presented in Table 12 show that the most important change in the second half of the sixteenth century was the increased success enjoyed by Lung-ch'i and Chang-p'u counties in Chang-chou. These were the regions most closely connected to the foreign trade. Hai-ch'eng, created in 1567 expressly because of its illegal trade activities, was also a successful academic region. It had eleven *chin-shih* in the late sixteenth century.[88] This record is even more striking when one considers that almost half the hsien in Fukien had none or only one *chin-shih* winner in the century.

Hai-ch'eng's success was echoed in T'ung-an and Hui-an hsien, counties under Ch'üan-chou which were active in foreign trading.[89] The examination records suggest that there was a direct translation of wealth acquired from expanded commerce into academic success. One of the first uses to which profits were put was the hiring of tutors and acquisition of the expensive education needed to win a *chin-shih* degree. The records show a time lag of almost twenty years between the beginning of market expansion in the

1520's and the rise of Chang-chou in the *chin-shih* lists. An education was not acquired overnight, but the continuing prosperity of Chang-chou through the rest of the century ensured that once begun, the system of training potential officials was increasingly successful.

One of the reasons why wealth and degree winning were so closely correlated is that education in Ming times was still very much a private affair. Several school systems existed on the local level. A state-sponsored hierarchy of schools from the hsien level on up to the National Academies (*kuo-tzu-chien*) at the two capitals[90] was supplemented in some areas by a system of elementary schools (*she-hsüeh*) at the village level. The state schools, which set entrance examinations for admittance to student (*sheng-yüan*) status,[91] were significant not as educational institutions but for their official and institutional recognition of a literate elite. They were too advanced to count for essential elementary education, and the *she-hsüeh,* which were run voluntarily, had largely disappeared by the sixteenth century.

It was therefore privately financed education which was primarily responsible for preparing aspiring candidates for the academic degrees. A wealthy household hired private tutors for its sons. This was undoubtedly the way in which Chang-chou families spent some of their newly acquired wealth. Through *i-hsüeh,* the clan and charitable schools begun by private citizens for the poor,[92] the benefits of commerce were extended to talented students of the region. Private assistance through clan organizations extended to poor relatives and included grants of traveling funds for the necessary trip to the examination halls in the capital.[93] In Fukien, a region with strong clans, clan schools and travel funds

TABLE 12. DISTRIBUTION OF *CHIN-SHIH* WINNERS BY COUNTY, 1513–1601[a]

Unit	1513–1526	1529–1541	1544–1556	1559–1571	1574–1586	1589–1601	Total
Fu-chou							
Min	18	24	15	10	5	4	76
Hou-kuan	6	10	2	4	5	4	31
Huai-an	5	4	4	4	1	0	18
Ch'ang-lo	15	13	8	6	3	1	46
Lien-chiang	2	3	2	0	0	0	7
Fu-ch'ing	2	10	6	5	5	4	32
Ku-t'ien	0	0	0	0	0	1	1
Yung-fu	0	0	0	1	0	0	1
Min-ch'ing	0	0	0	0	1	0	1
Lo-yüan	0	0	0	0	1	0	1
Chien-ning							
Chien-ning	1	0	4	2	0	2	9
O-ning	1	1	1	3	3	0	9
P'u-ch'eng	0	2	1	3	1	2	9
Chien-yang	0	1	0	0	1	0	2
Sung-ch'i	2	0	0	0	0	0	2
Ch'ung-an	0	0	1	0	0	0	1
Cheng-ho	0	0	0	0	0	0	0
Shou-ning	0	0	0	0	0	0	0
Ch'üan-chou							
Chin-chiang	16	25	26	47	48	32	194
Nan-an	6	3	1	6	7	6	29
T'ung-an	3	7	5	10	5	11	41
Te-hua	0	0	0	0	0	1	1
Yung-ch'un	0	0	0	1	2	1	4
An-ch'i	0	0	0	2	1	1	4
Hui-an	1	4	12	2	3	6	28
Chang-chou							
Lung-ch'i	2	0	9	5	10	5	31
Chang-p'u	2	5	11	13	15	11	57
Lung-yen	0	0	0	1	1	0	2
Ch'ang-t'ai	1	0	3	1	1	4	10
Nan-ching	0	0	0	0	1	0	1
Chang-p'ing	0	1	0	1	3	0	5
T'ing-chou							
Ch'ang-t'ing	0	0	0	0	0	1	1
Ning-hua	0	0	0	0	0	0	0

TABLE 12 (Continued)

Unit	1513–1526	1529–1541	1544–1556	1559–1571	1574–1586	1589–1601	Total
T'ing-chou (cont.)							
Shang-hang	1	0	0	0	0	0	1
Wu-p'ing	0	0	0	0	0	0	0
Ch'ing-liu	0	0	2	1	1	0	4
Lien-ch'eng	0	0	0	0	0	0	0
Kuei-hua	0	0	0	0	0	0	0
Yung-ting	0	1	0	1	0	0	2
Yen-p'ing							
Nan-p'ing	2	2	0	0	1	0	5
Chiang-lo	0	0	1	0	0	0	1
Yu-ch'i	1	0	0	0	0	0	1
Sha	0	0	0	0	0	0	0
Shun-ch'ang	0	0	1	0	0	0	1
Yung-an	0	0	0	0	0	0	0
Shao-wu							
Shao-wu	0	1	2	0	0	1	4
T'ai-ning	0	0	0	0	0	0	0
Chien-ning	0	1	0	0	0	0	1
Kuang-tse	0	0	0	0	0	0	0
Hsing-hua							
P'u-t'ien	61	48	30	19	28	11	197
Ch'ien-yu	2	0	0	1	1	0	4
Fu-ning chou							
Fu-ning	1	0	1	0	1	0	3
Ning-te	2	0	1	0	1	0	4
Fu-an	0	0	1	0	0	0	1

Sources: 1513–1532 figures from *Huang Ming kung-chü k'ao*, chüan 6, held by Naikaku bunko, Tokyo. 1535 figures from *Chia-ching shih-ssu-nien chin-shih teng-k'o lu*, held by Naikaku bunko, Tokyo. 1538–1601 data from *Fu-chien t'ung-chih*, 1943 ed., 5.13a-19b.

[a] Each time interval except for 1589–1601 included the results of five examinations. 1589–1601 included only four. In the sixteenth century, four new hsien were created in Chang-chou: P'ing-ho hsien in 1517, Chao-an, 1530, Ning-yang, 1565, and Hai-ch'eng, 1567. In the years 1513–1601, P'ing-ho hsien had 3 *chin-shih* winners, Chao-an hsien had 4, Ning-yang hsien had none, and Hai-ch'eng hsien had 11 *chin-shih*. Yen-p'ing prefecture also added a new hsien, Ta-t'ien, which had two *chin-shih* winners in the period.

were one of the ways in which profits from trade benefited a large part of the population.

The conclusion of this survey of the impact of expanded commerce on Chang-chou is that the changes resulting from market growth were very broad, reaching beyond the economy to affect Chang-chou's access to power through bureaucratic representation. The Chang-chou example is a study of the potentials inherent in a dynamic economic situation. But Chang-chou was an unusual area. A more typical example of a commercialized economy in Ming times was the prefecture of Chien-ning.

CHIEN-NING

In the sixteenth century, Chien-ning enjoyed a considerable domestic trade. We have no direct information on the quantities involved in this commerce, but a hint of its possible size is provided by information on one of the other interprovincial trade routes. In Shang-hang hsien, on the Fukien–Kwangtung border, a tax was instituted on the salt which passed through the county on its way from Ch'ao-chou prefecture in Kwangtung to T'ing-chou in Fukien. Tolls were set at 0.28 liang of silver per salt boat, and 0.115 liang of silver per commercial boat. In this instance revenues were not fixed by quota but depended on the number of boats using the route. Under these circumstances, the annual revenue of 4,000 to 5,000 liang of silver reported by the hsien represented a minimum of over 14,000 boats.[94]

In Chien-ning, located on the most popular road between Fukien and Chekiang to the north and Kiangsi to the west, domestic trade must have been sizable. Chien-ning was Fukien's interior link to the markets of the lower Yangtze, described by Ch'oe Pu. To contemporary observers such as

Wang Shih-mao (1536–1588), Chien-ning appeared very prosperous: "There is not a single day that the silk fabrics of Fu-chou, the gauze of Chang-chou, the indigo of Ch'üan-chou, the iron wares of Fu-chou and Yen-p'ing, the oranges of Fu-chou and Chang-chou, the lichee nuts of Fu-chou and Hsing-hua, the cane sugar of Ch'üan-chou, and the paper products of Shun-ch'ang are not shipped along the watershed of P'u-ch'eng and Hsiao-kuan (in Chien-ning) to Kiangsu and Chekiang like running water."[95] Despite coastal shipping, on which Wang also comments, Chien-ning's position in long distance trade was strong.

But, compared to Chang-chou, Chien-ning was standing still. In the course of the sixteenth century, while Chang-chou experienced an economic boom, Chien-ning stagnated. Its periodic markets, as shown in Table 13, did not even keep

TABLE 13. PERIODIC MARKETS IN CHIEN-NING PREFECTURE, 1491–1541 (BY COUNTY)

County	1491	1541	Percentage change
Chien-an	4	4	0
O-ning	6	6	0
P'u-ch'eng	4	0	−100
Chien-yang	6	6	0
Sung-ch'i	3	5	+67
Ch'ung-an	6	10	+67
Cheng-ho	5	1	−80
Shou-ning	0	0	0
Total	34	32	−6

Sources: Figures for 1491 are from *Pa Min t'ung-chih*, 14.5b-10b. Figures for 1541 are from 1541 ed., *Chien-ning FC*, chüan 10.

pace with the natural population growth which occurred.[96] From 1491 to 1541 markets in Chien-ning actually declined.

The same impression of stagnation appears in Chien-ning's agriculture. Chien-ning's rice yields fell short of yields in Chang-chou. In examining fertilizer and irrigation investments, it was seen that in Chien-ning these important determinants of agricultural productivity were still relatively backward. There was no significant change in this respect in subsequent periods: the practice of burning vegetation to fertilize the soil was still reported in an early nineteenth century gazetteer of the region.[97] In the twentieth century, while Chang-chou adopted chemical fertilizers, one third of the fields in northwest Fukien, where Chien-ning is located, were not fertilized at all.[98] The academic success record of Chien-ning echoed this same lack of change. Chang-chou and Ch'üan-chou showed a sharp increase in *chin-shih* winners during the sixteenth century, but Chien-ning remained in a modest fifth place, as shown in Table 11.

CONCLUSION

One of the conclusions of this study of Fukien is that the rate of market expansion, and not the mere existence of market activity, is crucial to the impact of commerce on an economy. When markets expanded sharply over a short period, as in Chang-chou, they brought changes throughout the economy: handicrafts, cropping patterns, land value, productivity, all were affected. Since increased prosperity led to a marked increase in Chang-chou's academic success, the growth of commerce had repercussions in the political sphere as well. Conversely, when markets grew slowly or not at all, as in Chien-ning, we find no sign of the economic transformations which are so strikingly evident in Chang-chou during this period.

The case of Chien-ning suggests that as a rule, domestic commerce grew too slowly to stimulate changes in areas which were already commercialized. Chien-ning had reached a plateau of development in Sung times;[99] subsequent growth required increased levels of market activity which domestic commerce failed to generate. After the sixteenth century, documents concerning Chien-ning attest to its continued prosperity in trade,[100] yet in spite of this, there was no great improvement in the economy of the region. Certainly the pattern of the peasant economy remained unchanged. Rice continued to be confined to one crop a year,[101] and information on yields shows that into the nineteenth and twentieth centuries Chien-ning had still not matched the level of productivity achieved in Ming Chang-chou.[102]

The case of Chien-ning holds implications for Chinese economic history extending far beyond its own borders. As an inland district, Chien-ning was a far more typical area in Ming China than was Chang-chou. Its agricultural practices, including the resulting yields, were similar to those found elsewhere in Fukien and in other parts of southeast China. By Chinese standards, its markets were prosperous. It was Chang-chou that was an exception.

Transport technology was a major factor limiting domestic commerce in inland areas. We have already commented on the high cost of overland transportation. Even though Chien-ning was located on the Min River system, a combination of overland and water routes was needed to move goods into Kiangsi or Chekiang. In China, as in Europe, expansion overseas was easier to accomplish than market expansion in the interior of the continent.[103] There were substantial barriers to a rapid expansion of domestic commerce before the twentieth century, when railroad construction began to change the whole system of transportation in China. Under the technological conditions of Ming and Ch'ing China, most commercial centers in the interior were earthbound, in the most literal sense. The result was little or no change in basic economic conditions, and a stagnancy which was noted by Western observers in the nineteenth century.

This comparison of Chang-chou and Chien-ning is not meant to imply that foreign trade was the only factor which provided opportunities for rapid market expansion. If private domestic demand was inadequate, there are several examples of government action on a scale large enough to produce significant economic change. Future research may show that the movement of the capital from Nanking to Peking in 1421 had such an effect on the market economy of Pei Chih-li, the northern metropolitan province; the economic potential of inherently political decisions such as this has been amply demonstrated by Robert Hartwell's research on the metropolitan market for iron in an earlier period.[104]

Military considerations could also result in government policies with economic repercussions resulting from rapid expansion of demand, which occurred in the fifteenth century garrison areas of the north.

The northern borders were a vital defense perimeter for the Chinese government, which established a system of commanderies there to guard against the Mongols. The campaigns of the early Ming emperors brought peace to this border, but the period after 1449 saw a renewal of nomadic raids on China. For the next 120 years, the Ming government devoted increased attention and funds to its northern defenses. By the mid-sixteenth century, silver shipments to support these garrisons were never less than two million taels a year, and were often twice this sum.[105] The development of a market economy in this region as a result of the demand created by government defense needs has been studied in detail by Terada Takanobu.[106] As in coastal Fukien, demand, increasing rapidly and over a short period of time, brought palpable changes to the border economy.

Implicit in the examples of Chang-chou and the northern borders is the conclusion that there were no factors inherent in Chinese politics or culture which barred the Chinese economy from responding swiftly to economic stimuli. The nature of Chinese government, Chinese disesteem of manual labor, the Chinese antipathy to commerce — these were not insuperable barriers to dynamic economic growth in instances of rapid market expansion. The result of these generalizations is a tendency to emphasize the demand side of the economic equation for the failure of China to experience more sustained growth and development. Because Chienning was a more typical commercial region than was Changchou, the economy as a whole remained fairly unchanged from the twelfth to the nineteenth centuries.

On the other hand, it is clear that the decisive hindrance to increased marketing activity in China was the absence of radical break-throughs in transport technology. Into the twentieth century, much of China was enclosed in a system of small, fairly autonomous market areas. Government policies had important economic effects on specific regions, but the immensity of China would have forestalled overall change, even if the government had been so inclined. China remained landlocked. In Europe, the expansion of overseas markets may have been a precursor of the Industrial Revolution. For most of China, participation in expanding markets was not a possibility. It was left to Europe to pose the final irony when, in the nineteenth century, its merchants came to China seeking the mythical market of 400 million customers.

Chapter Five / REGIONAL DIVERSITY IN THE DEVELOPMENT OF HUNAN

The response of coastal Fukien to market expansion during the sixteenth century has a parallel in the Ch'ing development of Hunan.[1] This development was closely linked to Hunan's participation in the rice markets that fed the major urban centers of China. As in Fukien, the effects of increased trade spread throughout the economy, causing a rise in the number of periodic markets, increases in agricultural productivity, and stimulating the spread of cash crops.

In its history of periodic devastation and consequent economic recovery, Hunan's development differed from the pattern seen in Fukien. There, and in much of the lower Yangtze delta, the course of development from late T'ang and Sung times was fairly smooth and continuous. This meant that many of the dramatic changes involved in the commercialization of agriculture had taken place centuries before the Ming dynasty. By the Ch'ing, these more stable provinces were densely populated regions with relatively fixed patterns of marketing and land use. By contrast, Hunan in the same period was beginning yet another cycle of resettlement.

Although Hunan had long been a part of settled China, its history was punctuated by war. A frontier area in Sung times,[2] it was a battleground in the Mongol take-over. In the early Ming, Hunan was a sparsely populated province, attracting settlers from neighboring areas to its untilled lands.[3] Ming settlement was interrupted in the mid-seventeenth century, when the rebellions of Li Tzu-ch'eng, Chang Hsien-chung, and Wu San-kuei razed much of the area around Lake Tung-t'ing.[4] The negative effects of these military incursions were reflected in Hunan's agriculture; not until the late eighteenth century did the province regain the yield levels achieved in the sixteenth century. By the early Ch'ing period, Hunan was again a relatively underdeveloped region, and the government promoted efforts to resettle its abandoned lands.[5]

CH'ANG-SHA PREFECTURE

The prefecture of Ch'ang-sha best exemplifies the Ch'ing development of Hunan. Situated on either bank of the Hsiang River, Hunan's major north-south waterway, Ch'ang-sha fu lies in the region directly south of Lake Tung-t'ing. In the battles attending the civil disorder at the end of the Ming dynasty, troops on various sides destroyed the offices of ten of its twelve administrative subunits, the majority in 1643–1644.[6] The early Ch'ing was thus a period of rehabilitation and reconstruction in Ch'ang-sha.

One of the most important aspects of the reconstruction program involved resettlement of formerly cultivated lands. In Hsiang-t'an hsien, peasants could assert ownership of unclaimed land by planting bamboo branches on it and agreeing to pay the land tax. This was the *piao-ch'an* (marker) program.[7] In other areas, such as I-yang hsien, temporary tax exemptions were given as enticements for resettlement. This policy had succeeded by the early eighteenth century as the officially registered cultivated land more than doubled from 1685 to 1724.[8] The government could then turn its attention from the problem of resettlement to the problem

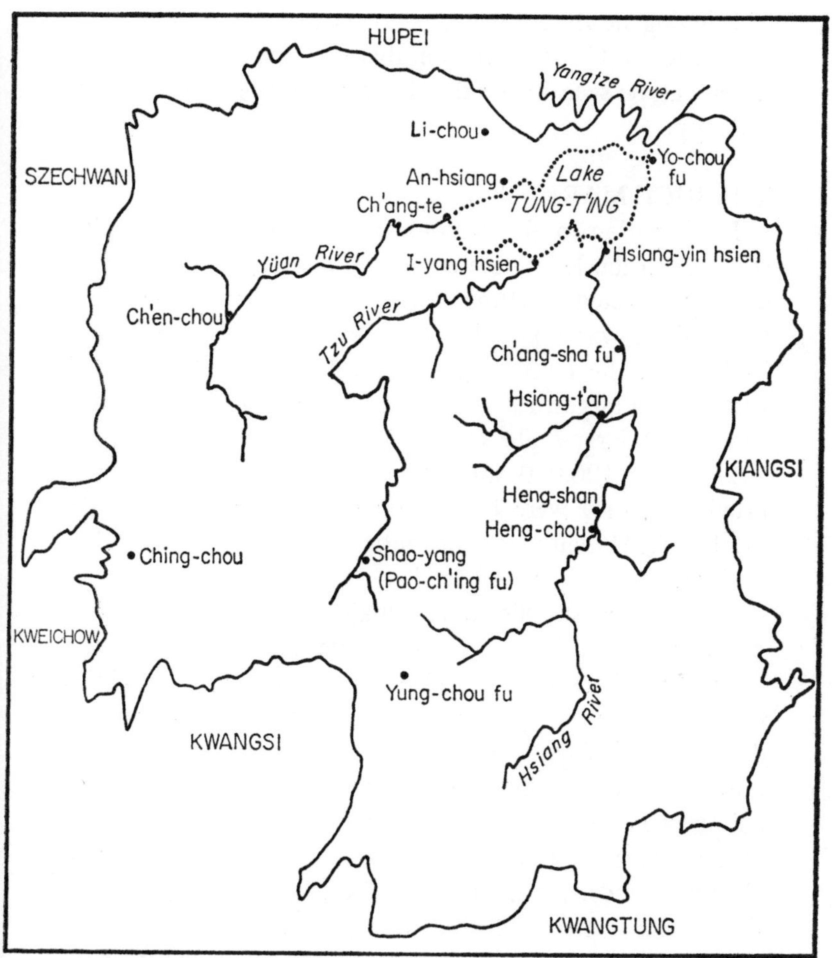

MAP 6. HUNAN PROVINCE. THE DOTTED LINES ATTEMPT TO SHOW THE ACTUAL SIZE OF LAKE TUNG-T'ING IN THE SEVENTEENTH CENTURY

of bringing newly cultivated lands onto the tax rolls.[9] The emergence of Ch'ang-sha from this early period of rehabilitation can be seen in the development of rice as a commercial crop.

THE RICE MARKET

Participation in the national rice markets was a major stimulus to the Hunanese economy, and rehabilitation was quickly reflected in Hunan's rice surplus. From late Ming times, there was a popular saying, "When Hukwang reaps its harvest, the empire has no want." [10] Although Hunan was not the largest rice producer in Ch'ing China, it was a source for large-scale interregional grain flows. Thus in 1724, when 100,000 shih of grain were needed for troop provisions, they were bought on the Hunan market.[11] By the 1730's, Hunan was contributing one to two million shih of rice to long distance trade.[12]

Because rice supplies were a major concern of a stability-conscious central government, more information on the state of markets exists for rice than for other commodities in China. The first part of the eighteenth century saw the development of specialized markets to handle rice. Rice was not transported to the central rice market at Hankow (Hupei province) by the same merchants who first purchased it in the country towns of Hunan. At various points, the rice changed hands. An example of the complexity inherent in this system is provided by a twentieth century study of the rice market in Anhwei, where rice passed through over 60 hands in its shipment from the producer (in Anhwei) to the consumer in Shanghai, only one province away.[13] In Hunan, special reports dating from the 1720's, the last years of the K'ang-hsi reign, and 1753 show a rapid increase in the number of markets which acted as central collection points for rice on its way to Hankow. In the space of about three decades, these markets increased from nine to sixteen; they are listed in Table 14.

Because grain shipments relied on water transportation,

TABLE 14. SPECIALIZED RICE MARKETS IN HUNAN, 1720–1753

Administrative unit[a]	1720	1753
Ch'ang-sha prefecture		
Ch'ang-sha hsien	x	x
Shan-hua hsien	x	x
Hsiang-yin hsien	x	x
Hsiang-t'an hsien	x	x
I-yang hsien	–	x
Hsiang-hsiang hsien	–	x
Heng-chou prefecture		
Heng-yang hsien	x	x
Heng-shan hsien	x	x
Yo-chou prefecture		
Pa-ling hsien	x	x
Lin-hsiang hsien	–	x
Hua-jung hsien	–	x
Ch'ang-te prefecture		
Wu-ling hsien	x	x
T'ao-yüan hsien	x	x
Yüan-chiang hsien	–	x
Lung-yang hsien	–	x
Li-chou		
An-hsiang hsien	–	x

Source: Shigeta Atsushi, "Shin-sho ni okeru Konan kome shijō no ichi kōsatsu," *Tōyō bunka kenkyū-jo kiyō,* 10: 441–442 (1956), for K'ang-hsi markets, pp. 445–451 for 1753 markets.

[a] Only hsien with central markets are listed.

geography was an important factor in distinguishing the response of different areas of Hunan to this rapid expansion of rice markets. In Fukien the most dramatic contrast lay between the coastal and landlocked areas. In Hunan, the most important factor in determining the commercial growth potential of an area was its access to water. All the central markets were located on one of two rivers, the Yüan or the Hsiang. Rice from western Hunan moved down the Yüan River eastward to Lake Tung-t'ing and thence out of the province. The major artery for central Hunan was the Hsiang River, which flowed on a north-south axis through the province.

The result of geographical location was that whereas the prefectures of Heng-chou, Ch'ang-sha, Ch'ang-te, and Li-chou thrived,[14] other prefectures in Hunan were blocked from access to the profits of the rice trade. In the southern prefectures of Pao-ch'ing and Yung-chou and the western and southwestern prefectures of Ch'en-chou and Ching-chou, transport barriers hindered development of rice as a commercial crop. Without easy access to water transport, these areas not only failed to participate in the "rice boom," but were often recipients of rice from areas on the river systems. Thus the granary stores in Ch'en-chou were purchased from Ch'ang-te markets; in Yung-chou as in Pao-ch'ing, rice was shipped into local markets by traveling merchants.[15] In describing the development of Hunan during this period, the fact that not all areas enjoyed access to the national rice market should be stressed. In actuality, the benefits of commercial expansion were limited to only part of Hunan.

Ch'ang-sha prefecture was fortunately situated on the Hsiang River. Not only did many of its county seats develop into central rice markets (see Table 14), but one of them, Hsiang-t'an, was the largest rice market of the province. It was to Hsiang-t'an that the merchants from Hankow came to buy rice.[16]

Hsiang-t'an benefited from its natural advantages as a port[17] and grew with the expanding rice trade. By the late eighteenth century, Hsiang-t'an had moved outside the confines of its city walls. There, in the tenth through the nineteenth *tsung* were major business streets linked with the river wharves (*ma-t'ou*) where merchants from outside Hunan and local rice brokers who acted as their compradores dealt with the "cloud-like" profusion of goods piled on the wharves. The markets of Hsiang-t'an were said to extend for some 20 li.[18] In the commercial districts, merchants from Soochow, Hui-chou (Anhwei), Fukien, Kwangtung, and Kiangsi combined with their compatriots to build concrete testimonials to regional pride and solidarity.[19] The city had a very vigorous commercial life.

The continuing expansion of market influence in Ch'ang-sha can be traced in the increase of rural markets through the eighteenth century. As shown in Table 15, most of the areas in the prefecture participated in this expansion. By definition, periodic markets are temporary and meet at fixed intervals for a brief period. One of the indications of increasing commercialization in Ch'ang-sha is the sudden emergence of permanent shops (*tien*) in the countryside. The most dramatic example of this development appears in Hsiang-t'an hsien. In 1747 there were only 12 markets (*shih*) in the county. By 1781, there were 13 *shih* and 83 *tien;* in 1818, 16 *shih* and 86 *tien*. When the figures for *shih* and *tien* are combined, as in Figure 1, we obtain a visual im-

MAP 7. HSIANG-T'AN, 1818, FROM THE 1818 PREFECTURAL GAZETTEER

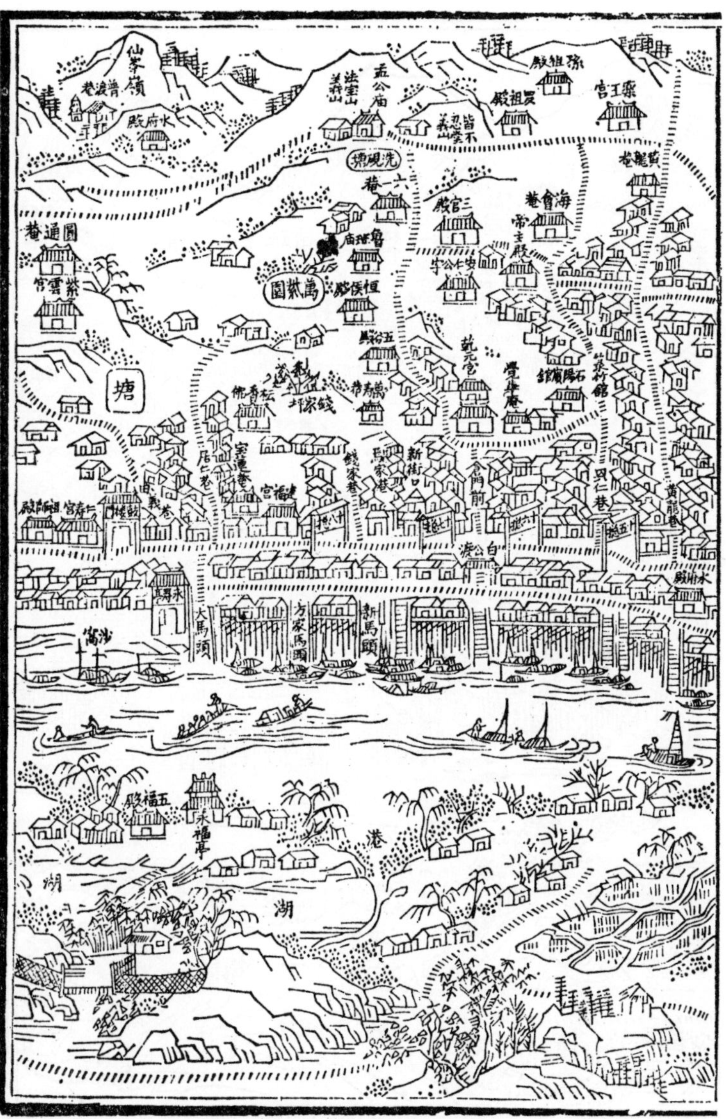

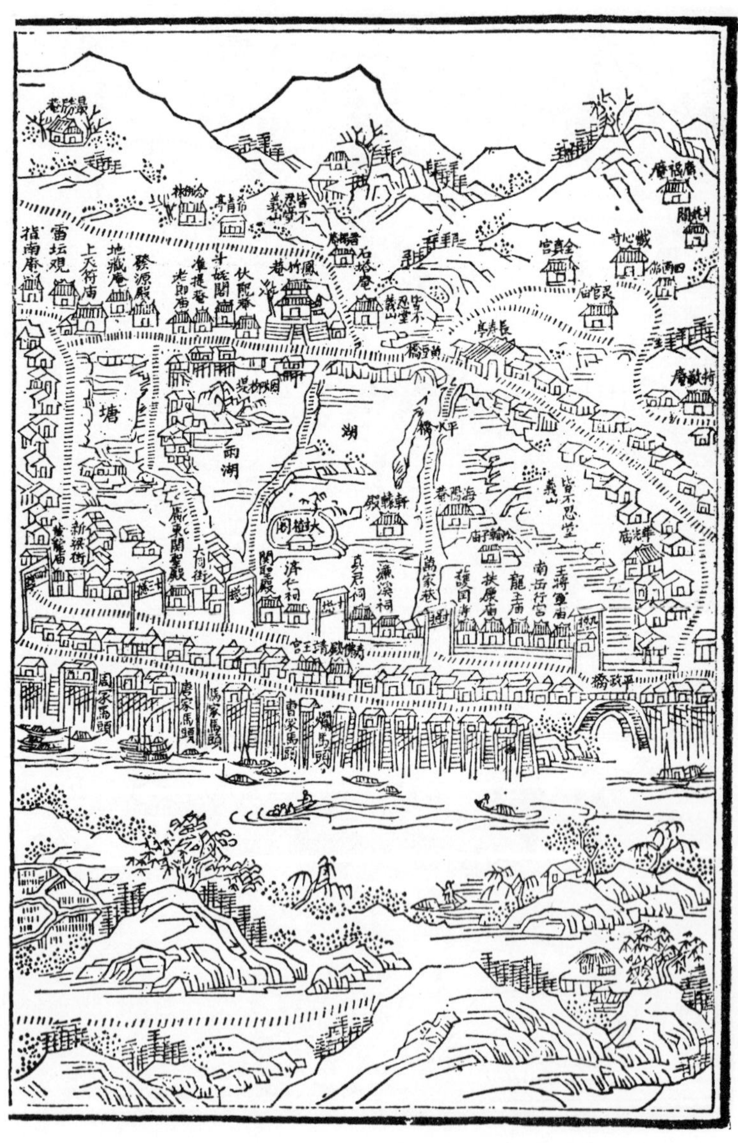
指南庵
雷坛观
上天符庙
地藏庵
石塔庵
塘
雨湖
湖
濂溪祠
真君祠
萬家巷
南岳行宮
龍王庙
周家馬頭
曹家馬頭
馬家馬頭
平政橋
全真宮

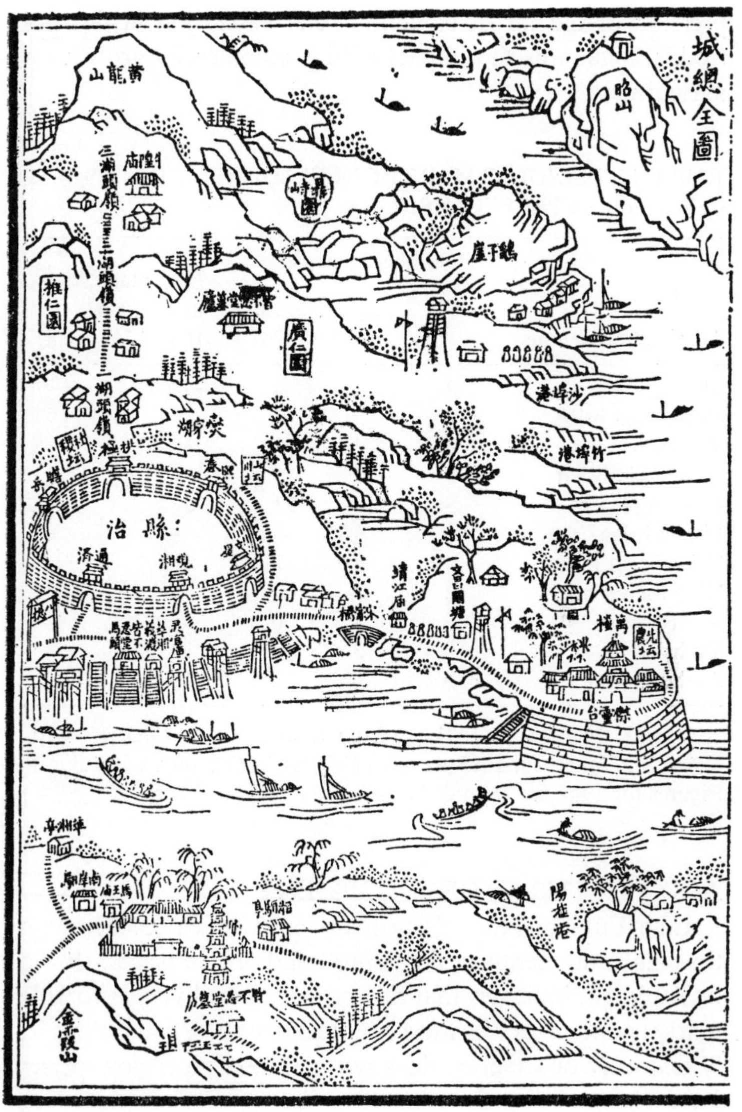
黃龍山
廣仁園
推仁園
縣治
沙埠港
竹埠港

pression of the thrust of commercial expansion in this period.[20] What was the impact of this commercial growth on agriculture?

TABLE 15. PERIODIC MARKET DEVELOPMENT IN CH'ANG-SHA PREFECTURE

Administrative units	Number of markets (*shih*) 1591	1685	1747	Percentage change in markets, 1685–1747
Ch'a-ling (chou)	0	5	4	−20
Ch'ang-sha hsien	0	5	5	0
Shan-hua hsien	0	4	10	150
Hsiang-yin hsien	0	11	16	45
Liu-yang hsien	5	9	33	267
Li-ling hsien	0	5	–	–
Hsiang-t'an hsien	0	3	12	300
Ning-hsiang hsien	2	8	9	12
I-yang hsien	9	1	6	500
Yu hsien	0	3	10	233
An-hua hsien	0	4	12	200

Sources: Figures for 1591 are from *Hukwang tsung-chih*, 1591 ed., chüan 15. Figures for 1685 are from *Ch'ang-sha FC*, 1685 ed., 1.56b ff. Figures for 1747 are from *Ch'ang-sha FC*, 1747 ed., chüan 9.

AGRICULTURAL DEVELOPMENT

Like Fukien, Hunan's primary crop was rice. Through the eighteenth century, the rising trend of rice prices, shown in Table 16, indicates that rice growers faced very favorable market conditions. As the 1746 gazetteer of Yo-chou put it: "Previously one tael could buy six shih of rice; now prices have risen and it is difficult to buy two shih with this

FIGURE 1. RURAL MARKETS IN HSIANG-T'AN HSIEN, 1685–1889

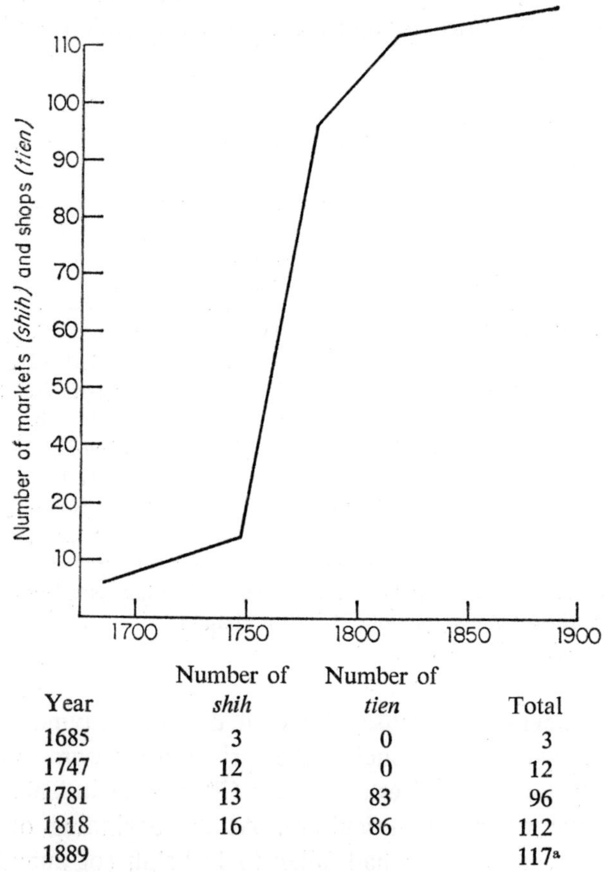

Year	Number of *shih*	Number of *tien*	Total
1685	3	0	3
1747	12	0	12
1781	13	83	96
1818	16	86	112
1889			117[a]

Sources: *Ch'ang-sha FC*, 1685 ed., 1.56b ff.
Ch'ang-sha FC, 1747 ed., chüan 9.
Hsiang-t'an HC, 1781 ed., chüan 5.
Hsiang-t'an HC, 1818 ed., 6.21b-30a.
Hsiang-t'an HC, 1889 ed., chüan 2, map 9.

[a] No separate figures for markets and shops were given in this source.

money." [21] The response of rice cultivators to market stimuli is evident in steadily rising productivity through the period, supported by efforts in land reclamation, irrigation, and increasing seed varieties.

TABLE 16. RICE PRICES IN EIGHTEENTH CENTURY HUNAN[a]

Date	Place	Price (silver liang per shih[b])	Source
ca. 1697–1704	Liu-yang hsien	0.083	*Liu-yang HC*, 1733 ed., 4.19a-21b.
1730's	Hsiang-yin hsien	0.3–0.5	*Hsiang-yin HC*, 1823 ed., 14.29b.
1746	Yo-chou fu	0.5	*Yo-chou FC*, 1746 ed., 12.1b.
1797	Hsiang-yin hsien	1.4–1.5	*Hsiang-yin HC*, 1823 ed., 14.29b.

[a] None of the prices cited referred to years of bad harvests. For evaluation of these figures, see note 21 in this chapter.

[b] Unhusked rice.

The devastation caused by civil disorder around Lake Tung-t'ing destroyed much of the agricultural progress made in Ming times. Yield estimates for Ch'ang-sha in Table 17 show the effect on agriculture. At the beginning of the Ch'ing dynasty, yields had fallen to 1–2 shih (of unhusked rice) per mou, equal to Sung productivity levels in this area. As order was restored, yields rose. By the late eighteenth century, farmers in some areas had tripled their yields.[22]

The steady rise in productivity through the eighteenth century was not achieved through intensification of crop-

TABLE 17. RICE YIELDS IN CH'ANG-SHA PREFECTURE[a]

Date	Area	Yield (unhusked rice, shih/mou)	Source
1685	Li-ling hsien Hsiang-t'an hsien I-yang hsien	1.82 1.6 1.2	*Ch'ang-sha FC*, 1685 ed., 4.74b-80b
1736	Liu-yang hsien	1.7–1.8[b]	*Liu-yang HC*, 1873 ed., reported in Li Wen-chih, "Ch'ing tai," p. 611
1738	Hsiang-t'an hsien	1.68	*Hsiang-t'an HC*, 1781 ed., 10.26a
1743	I-yang hsien	1.46	*I-yang HC*, 1874 ed., 6.18b
1744	Hsiang-t'an hsien	2.0	*Hsiang-t'an HC*, 1781 ed., 10.26a-27a
1745	Ch'ang-sha hsien	1.98	*Ch'ang-sha HC*, 1810 ed., 10.65a. Average of 6 plots, 100+ mou
1746	Ch'ang-sha hsien Shan-hua hsien Liu-yang hsien	1.97	*Ch'ang-sha FC*, 1747 ed., 23.78b-85b
1761	Hsiang-t'an hsien	2.0	*Hsiang-t'an HC*, 1781 ed., 10.26a-27a
1773–75	Hsiang-t'an hsien	2.1	*Hsiang-t'an HC*, 1781 ed., 10.30a-33b. Average of 28 plots, 548 mou
1797	Hsiang-yin hsien	5–6[b]	*Hsiang-yin HC*, 1823 ed., 14.29b
1863	I-yang hsien	3.28	*I-yang HC*, 1874 ed., 6.18b
1869	Hsiang-t'an hsien	5[b]	Wang Yeh-chien, "Agricultural Development," p. 9, table 3
1889	Hsiang-t'an hsien	4[b]	*Ibid.* Yield on medium-grade land

[a] Most of the figures presented in this table were derived from rents on public lands, recorded in gazetteers. The rents were phrased in terms of unhusked rice. They were divided by the acreage to obtain per mou rents, then doubled to obtain a yield estimate. On the use of a 50–50 split of the harvest as the basis for these calculations, see Wang Yeh-chien, "Agricultural Development," p. 31. Note 22, Chapter 5, and note 67, Chapter 4 discuss the comparability of mou and shih units from different parts of Hunan.

[b] These yields are directly obtained and are not derived from rents.

ping. The first mention of double-cropping rice does not occur until 1823.[23] Instead, the cropping cycle consisted of a rice harvest followed by cultivation of a supplementary staple. In Hsiang-t'an hsien, potatoes were planted after the rice harvest;[24] in Ch'ang-sha hsien, bracken roots, Irish and sweet potatoes.[25] Other areas grew beans, buckwheat, and other grains as a winter crop.[26] In the eighteenth century, improved yields stemmed from efforts in land reclamation, irrigation and farming practice, not from major changes in cropping patterns.

The "rice boom" in Hunan was preceded and accompanied by land reclamation and irrigation efforts. In the rich rice lands surrounding Lake Tung-t'ing, the two projects went hand in hand, since land reclamation consisted of diking off part of the lake shore, thus allowing cultivation of the silt of the lake bottom. The embankment projects affected increasingly larger areas of land, from 52,576 mou in the early eighteenth century (1689–1716) to over 166,000 mou by 1723–1746 in Hsiang-yin hsien alone.[27] Even when government policy subsequently shifted from encouragement to prohibition of embankment, the process continued. The most impressive evidence for the perseverance of this trend is provided by a glance at the modern map of Hunan, which shows a largely filled-in area where Lake Tung-t'ing formerly stood (see Map 6).[28] The significance of reclamation to rice cultivation in Hunan is shown by a twentieth century estimate that one fourth of the total rice production in Hunan is grown by the districts bordering the lake.[29]

In the rice districts around Lake Tung-t'ing, the potential danger facing peasant farmers was flood, not drought,[30] and waterworks projects concentrated on drainage and dike systems. For most of the lands in Hunan, however, water scarcity rather than surplus remained the common fear, and the building of irrigation systems with reservoirs and ponds to guard against drought was a major agricultural activity. Descriptions of public landholdings from the late eighteenth century on generally included a list of the ponds (*t'ang*) and reservoirs (*p'i*) attached to the property. The regularity with which these irrigation facilities appear in the records of Ch'ang-sha prefecture indicates that they were a fairly standard part of the agricultural system.[31] Very often the plots themselves were identified by their geographical relationship to an irrigation work, as in the following example from Hsiang-t'an hsien: "Civilian [nonofficial] land, 20 mou, located in the ninth *tu,* seventh *chia,* the plot named *Heng t'ang* (along the side of the pond), with three ponds, one at the head of the field, one alongside, and one towards the road, and a dam with a water wheel to free the water." [32]

Irrigation implements appear in local gazetteers from the late eighteenth century.[33] The 1818 edition of *Hsiang-t'an hsien-chih*[34] contains a detailed description of these. The hsien included several rivers: the Chüan, Lien, and Chin, with a combined length of 330 li, and these banks were lined with water wheels. In areas where the river banks were relatively high, the water wheels were grouped in over ten stages to transport water from the rivers to the fields. In other spots, dams with viaducts led the water to wheels which were propelled by the strength of the current. These were called *t'ung-ch'e* (duct water wheels) and were reportedly able to irrigate over 100 mou in 24 hours.[35] Elsewhere, manpowered water wheels (*shui-ch'e*) drew from the supplies provided by springs, wells, and ponds.[36]

The development of water storage and irrigation systems must have exercised a beneficent influence on rice cultivation in central Hunan. Improvements in farming practice also helped raise productivity. In the early eighteenth century, even a noted rice producing area such as Liu-yang hsien reported that "the land was barren"; no fertilizer was added after the rice seeds were sown, and the result was a maximal yield of about 1.5 shih per mou.[37] By the early nineteenth century, even relatively backward rice growers in areas such as Yung-chou (southern Hunan) used a variety of human and vegetable fertilizers.[38]

The rice boom was also reflected in the successful adaptation of more and more rice seeds to diverse local conditions. In Ch'ang-sha, seed varieties increased through the Ch'ing

TABLE 18. RICE SEED VARIETIES IN CH'ANG-SHA PREFECTURE

		Number of seeds		
Area	Date	Glutinous	Nonglutinous	Sources
Ch'ang-sha prefecture	1534	1	3	*Ch'ang-sha FC*, 1534 ed., 3.25ab
	1747	4	16	*Ch'ang-sha FC*, 1747 ed., 36.1b
Ch'ang-sha hsien	1747	4	10	*Ch'ang-sha HC*, 1747 ed., 2.1ab
	1810	9	18	*Ch'ang-sha HC*, 1810 ed., 14.11b
Hsiang-t'an hsien	1756	3	16	*Hsiang-t'an HC*, 1756 ed., 12.1b
	1781	3	16	*Hsiang-t'an HC*, 1781 ed., 15.1b
	1818	5	24	*Hsiang-t'an HC*, 1818 ed., 39.9b-10a

period, as seen in Table 18. This increase was not necessarily linked to an innovative surge in Hunan. Many, perhaps most, of the seeds were introduced to the province by immigrating peasants. As Ho Ping-ti has noted, a large number of seeds used here in the eighteenth century bear place names which testify to their origins, but the "Kiangsi," "Yunnan," and "Kwangtung" varieties which fall into this category provide only a minimum estimate of the extent of importation.[39]

Seeds were taken from one spot to another not only by peasants, but by public-minded citizens. Take the case of Liu Han-tien, recorded in the annals of Heng-yang hsien. Liu was a boatman in the late eighteenth century. On one of his trips outside the county, he noticed rice growing "amidst frost" and gathered seeds from this region to distribute in Heng-yang. Since Heng-yang farmers suffered from lack of a late ripening rice seed, Liu's action brought a substantial improvement to the agriculture of this area.[40] The issue of seed transmission and development is complex.[41] Happily, evaluation of the significance of seed adaptations does not depend on its solution.

Seed developments in Hunan proceeded along several lines. As in Fukien, the matching of local soils and seed involved a general distinction between seeds suited to marshy soils and those appropriate to hilly plots. In the first instance, seed varieties with long roots, such as the Iron-foot (*T'ieh-chiao tsao*) or Kwangtung[42] were used. Hilly land called for short and shallow-rooted varieties, such as the Hairy (*Mao chan*) and the Yellow Early (*Huang tsao*).[43]

A second line of development focused on an extension of the growing season. In Hunan, seed adaptations moved the growing period of rice forward, modifying the traditional dichotomy of early-late (*tsao-wan*). By the early nineteenth century, the gazetteer of Hsiang-yin talks about three time distinctions in the category of early seeds: early, middle, and delayed. By advancing the growing period, hilly lands with otherwise insufficient rainfall could be planted in rice, taking advantage of the rainy season from April to June. The richer, lowland plots with water reservoirs remained on a later planting schedule, since "the later the planting, the more abundant the harvest." [44]

The normal planting schedule in Hunan called for the rice seeds to be sown about April 5 on the solar calendar. A month later, the sprouts were transplanted.[45] Seed adaptations permitted both processes to be moved forward. By the early nineteenth century, fields in highland areas of Hsiang-t'an were planted by March 20.[46] Slightly over a half century later, further developments allowed fields in some parts of Ch'ang-sha prefecture to be transplanted by April 5, a month ahead of the traditional schedule.[47]

Adoption of double cropping of rice in the nineteenth century also brought new seed varieties to central Hunan. In Li-ling hsien, for example, two varieties of late rice were used in a double-cropping cycle. When the rice was interplanted, the *Ya-ho* (Weighed-down grain) was used; when the two rice crops were planted in succession, a variety called *Fan-tzu* (Turnover) was substituted.[48]

CHANGES IN LANDHOLDING

The success of Ch'ing efforts to resettle abandoned lands in the Hsiang River valley had its effect on landholding patterns in eighteenth century Hunan. In the late seventeenth century, there was probably no tenancy in this region,[49] since land was freely available: as discussed earlier, officials in Ch'ang-sha gave land away to peasants who were willing to cultivate it. By the eighteenth century, the resettlement campaign had succeeded so well that land was again scarce rather than distressingly abundant. A gazetteer of Ch'angsha tells us that by 1734–1735, good land was being sold for 14 to 20 *chin* a mou. A cheaper alternative to land purchase for peasants was to buy the tenant right to cultivate the soil. This cost between one and two silver liang per mou.[50]

Tenancy was therefore an established phenomenon in Ch'ang-sha by the early eighteenth century. Scattered references indicate a trend toward increasing tenancy in this area over the next two centuries. In the mid-eighteenth century, the governor of Hunan, Yang Hsi-fu, reported that 50 to 60 per cent of the cultivated land was owned by wealthy families, while peasants who had formerly owned their own plots had become tenants.[51] A 1781 gazetteer of Hsiang-t'an hsien noted the prevalence of tenancy;[52] in the twentieth century, 70 to 80 per cent of the farmers were reported to be full or part-tenants.[53] Historical evidence of resettlement in the seventeenth century, coupled with findings of widespread tenancy in twentieth century surveys, supports the finding of rising tenancy during the Ch'ing period in Ch'ang-sha. This seems to have been accompanied by increasing land prices, although the limited data does not permit a thorough exploration of the subject.[54]

The effect of tenancy on the welfare of the Hunanese peasant is a complex question,[55] which can be attacked on several levels. By the early part of the eighteenth century, the two major components of tenant obligations to the landlord had already been defined: rent and rent deposit. The available evidence suggests that despite increases in these obligations, the tenant in Hunan enjoyed material improvement in his situation during the century.

RENT

Although the most common tenancy payment in Hunan was fixed rent, paid in kind, sharecropping arrangements also existed. In still other instances, the fixed rent was commuted to a cash payment.

The extent of the landlord's participation in farming is an important factor in determining the form of rent arrangements. In the period of land reclamation and rehabilitation, farming was a cooperative venture, and the harvest was commonly split between the landlord and tenant.[56] In a fixed rent system, the landlord did not provide tools, seed, or oxen and often did not invest funds in land improvement. Even in the Republican period, distinctions in rent arrangements were made according to this criterion. When land was reclaimed, it usually had to be diked, drained, and prepared for paddy culture. If the landlord did this work himself, he and the tenant shared the harvest, the landlord receiving 40 per cent of the crop. When the land was given over to a tenant who improved it without the landlord's aid, a fixed rent was paid.[57] As noted earlier, a fixed rent was the most common form of payment in eighteenth century Hunan.

RENT DEPOSIT

Unlike the Fukienese "guarantee money," paid to the landlord upon first taking up a tenancy contract, the Hunan payment, called *chin chuang* (entering the estate) was customarily returned to a tenant at the end of his contract period. The rent deposit appears in early eighteenth century records of Ch'ang-sha prefecture as a payment of one to two taels of silver a mou. This sum represented from four to six times the annual rent payment, so it was a sizable amount for the tenant to pay.

By the latter part of the eighteenth century, two different kinds of rent deposits are described. Large payments of silver, ranging from one to six taels per mou, called *ta-hsieh* (big deposit) were returned to tenants; small payments of several bits of silver (*hsiao-hsieh*) were kept by the landlord.[58] Yet another set of alternatives is found in an early nineteenth century gazetteer of Hsiang-t'an: those who paid the rent deposit of several taels were given low rents, and those entering a tenancy without rent deposit paid twice as much rent.[59] Variations on these alternatives continued into the twentieth century.[60]

As Wang Yeh-chien has noted, the effect of the rent deposit was to raise the annual obligation of the tenant. Lent out at high interest, the silver brought in additional income for the landlord. It is interesting that landlords sought to increase their income from land not from the produce of the land itself, but from the commercial sector, which promised twice the profit of similar investments in land. Yang Lien-sheng's citation of a Hunanese case in 1825 showed deposits with pawnshops or silversmiths brought an income of 15 to 18 per cent a year, as opposed to less than 7 per cent from land.[61]

Information from Hsiang-yin hsien allows us to examine the effects of rent and rent deposit increases on peasants of that region. Hsiang-yin is a county under Ch'ang-sha fu which was and continues to be one of the most productive rice growing districts in Hunan.[62] In the course of the eighteenth century, rents in this county were sometimes 50 per cent higher than in the neighboring district of Hsiang-t'an.[63] But productivity gains outran increases in rents. In the course of the eighteenth century, yields in Hsiang-yin increased two-fold, from 2 shih to 5 and 6 shih per mou (for unhusked rice).[64] During the same period, rents increased from 1 to 2 shih per mou.[65] Because of the rise in rice prices during the century, both landlords and peasants reaped larger gains than the above figures indicate. In the late 1730's, one shih of rice sold for 0.3 to 0.5 taels of silver. By 1797, the same quantity brought from 1.4 to 1.5 taels on the market.[66] If productivity and rent information are translated into estimates of the money value of the landlord and tenant shares, we can see how all concerned benefited from market conditions. With a rent of 2 shih per mou, the landlord's money income increased five-fold from 1730 to 1797. The tenant, profiting both from rising yields and price increases, increased his potential money income by 800 to 1,100 per cent.[67] Although both sides prospered during the course of the century, the figures show that the tenant's economic position improved more than the landlord's. The rent increases of the eighteenth century were more than offset by the great price increases enjoyed by rice, and their effect on the tenant nullified by productivity increases in the period.

In the same way, rising rent deposits had little significance when compared with the improvements in agricultural yields noted above. Indeed, the rent deposits collected by landlords in the first part of the eighteenth century probably constituted a heavier burden for the cultivator than the higher sums charged about 1781. Earlier, we noted that a rent deposit of 1 to 2 taels per mou represented a sum four to six times the annual rent. If this sum is expressed in terms of rice, it would be equal to 4–6 shih or more. By 1781, rent deposits were sometimes as high as 6 taels per mou, but this sum was equal to only slightly more than 4 shih of rice at current market prices. If anything, the tenant's obligations arising from the rent deposit were eased rather than tightened.

In the preceding sections, we have examined the effects of a rice boom in Ch'ang-sha and the rich rice producing lands adjoining Lake Tung-t'ing. In many ways the dynamic changes which accompanied this boom resembled changes already noted in Fukien. Unlike Fukien, the primary source of Hunan's development was and remained rice. Although other cash crops appeared, none seriously threatened its primacy.[68] The course of development in Hunan was directly linked to its participation in the long distance rice trade.

The areas not favored with easy access to water transportation experienced a different course of development. At one extreme in this group were the areas on the southwest border, such as Ch'en-chou, where battles with the Miao aborigines punctuated an uneasy peace.[69] In many ways, these areas represent the antithesis of the economy and agriculture of the lake area. Where the agricultural basis of the latter was paddy culture, dry land farming often predominated in the frontier economy. Ch'en-chou, for example, was originally not a rice growing area.[70] The minor role of rice cultivation in regions where the primary crop was panicled millet, buckwheat or corn[71] may explain the primitive tools sometimes used. According to a 1760 gazetteer, the *tang pa,* a weeding rake first developed in Yüan times, was still unknown in the southwest hsien of Chih-chiang.[72] In the southern prefecture of Yung-chou, wooden hoes were still in use in the early nineteenth century.[73] Waterworks were notably scarce. In many areas, productivity remained at levels found in Ch'ang-sha only in the early days of the Ch'ing dynasty. In Ching-chou, on the southwest borders, yields of two to three shih per mou continued to prevail in the late nineteenth century.[74]

The rest of Hunan lay somewhere in between these two developmental extremes. Despite natural barriers, most hsien were regularly visited by traveling merchants and were linked to larger marketing systems. These merchants brought rice to exchange for local products such as ramie, t'ung oil, timber, products of the wax tree, and tea.[75]

SHAO-YANG HSIEN

Of the rice growing areas in this group, Shao-yang hsien, site of the prefectural government of Pao-ch'ing, was especially favored by nature. Shao-yang is located on the Tzu River, in the center of a plain, with a correspondingly high percentage of arable land suited to rice culture.[76] The specialization of Shao-yang in rice growing was reflected in a tremendous variety of rice seeds during Ming and Ch'ing times.[77] Today, Shao-yang remains one of Hunan's important rice producing regions.[78]

Although it lies less than 50 miles away from the major market town of Heng-yang, Shao-yang had no direct water links with the Hsiang River system. Nor could it easily ship goods through the rapids on the Tzu River. As the gazetteer put it, "The waters are swift and the rapids dangerous, boats have a difficult time getting through, and for this reason the wealthy and great merchants of the empire do not come." [79] Rice boats which could maneuver the rapids had to be very small and could only carry 40 to 50 shih of rice; and there was always the danger of losing the cargo. The only other route lay over mountain roads, with the expenses of portage.[80] Shao-yang was thus barred from much of the market enjoyed by Ch'ang-sha and the lake hsien. According to an early Ch'ing gazetteer, the area produced barely enough rice for its own population.[81] As we have seen, it also occasionally bought rice from outside the hsien.

The history of rice productivity in Shao-yang during the eighteenth century provides an interesting contrast with Ch'ang-sha's. Shao-yang was also affected adversely by the battles of the mid-seventeenth century; its city walls were burnt down during this period. According to the hsien records, the year 1647–1648, when Ch'ing forces were consolidating their power in this part of China, was marked by a tremendous scarcity. The price of a shih of rice rose to 4 taels of silver, and there was want in the period between the planting of the new grain and its harvest.[82]

Yet Shao-yang passed into the Ch'ing period with relatively little real disruption of agriculture. Where the records of the lake hsien, Ch'ang-sha, and Heng-chou show a sharp break with the Ming and a marked decline in rice yields during the early Ch'ing, Shao-yang's productivity continued at the high levels attained during the early seventeenth century. At a time when yields had dropped to 1–2 shih per mou in the Ch'ang-sha area, Shao-yang rents indicate productivity levels of over 3 shih per mou.[83]

Table 19 makes it possible to trace the course of Shao-yang's productivity and to compare it in Figure 2 with developments in the Ch'ang-sha area. The first conclusion to be drawn from this comparison is the relative slowness of the rehabilitation effort in the devastated Ch'ang-sha area. Although Hunan had already regained a prominent place in Yangtze rice markets by the early eighteenth century, the level of productivity found in the newly resettled paddy districts of east Hunan was still low. In fact, it took over a century after the beginning of the Ch'ing dynasty for agri-

TABLE 19. RICE YIELDS IN SHAO-YANG HSIEN

Year	Derived yield/mou unhusked rice (*shih*)[a]	Sources and comments
1606	2–4	*Shao-yang HC*, 1684 ed., 5.36a-40b. The average yield on plots totaling 253.54 mou was 2.8 shih/mou.
1693	3.36	*Shao-yang HC*, 1877 ed., 4.6b. Derived from average rent on a total of 238 mou.
1820	3.12	*Ibid.*, 4.4b. Derived from average rent on a total of 313 mou.
1854	3.2	*Ibid.*, 4.8b-10a. Derived from average rent on a total of 594.14 mou.
1877	3.2–4.8	Wang Yeh-chien, "Agricultural Development," p. 57, table 16.

[a] See note a to Table 17 for discussion of the method used to obtain these figures.

culture in this region to recover its Ming levels. Much of the "rice boom" of the eighteenth century was thus a recapturing of lost ground, the reconstruction of complex interrelationships between land, water supply, and labor needed for efficient rice culture; it did not represent a breakthrough to historically new levels of productivity.

One of the reasons for this slow recovery may well have been an over-diffusion of labor. In the period of economic rehabilitation, peasants who migrated to Ch'ang-sha could claim large plots for themselves. In the late seventeenth century, peasants in Liu-yang hsien (Ch'ang-sha) were said to farm areas as large as 50 and 100 mou.[84] The land–labor ratios of this period were diametrically opposed to conditions favoring a highly productive rice culture. In order to

FIGURE 2. RICE YIELDS IN VARIOUS AREAS OF HUNAN, 1534–1889.[a]

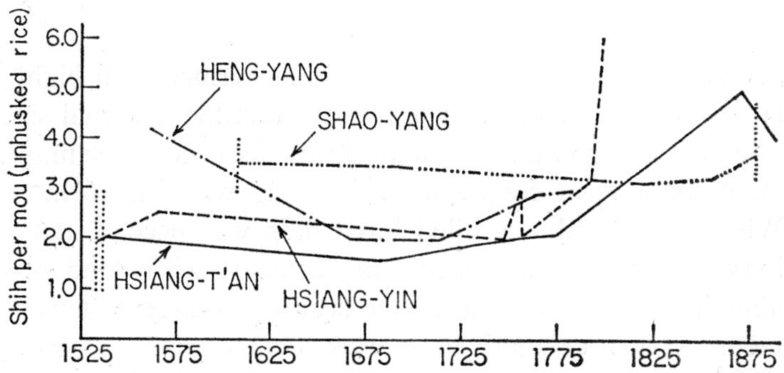

Yield citations: shih of unhusked rice per mou, by hsien and date:

a. Hsiang-t'an		b. Hsiang-yin		c. Heng-yang		d. Shao-yang	
1. 1534	1–3	1. 1534	1–3	1. 1560	4.2	1. 1606	3–4
2. 1685	1.6	2. 1563–4	2.5	2. 1669	2.0	2. 1693	3.36
3. 1744	2.0	3. 1747	2.0	3. 1712	2.0	3. 1820	3.12
4. 1761	2.0	4. 1755	3.0	4. 1763	2.92	4. 1854	3.2
5. 1773–5	2.10	5. 1756	2.0	5. 1789	2.98	5. 1877	3.2–4.8
6. 1869	5.0	6. 1792	3.2				
7. 1889	4.0	7. 1797	5–6				

Sources:

a. 1. *Ch'ang-sha FC*, 1534 ed., 3.25ab.
   2. *Ch'ang-sha FC*, 1685 ed., 4.74b-80b.
   3. *Hsiang-t'an HC*, 1781 ed., 10.26a-27a.
   4. *Ibid.*
   5. *Ibid.*, 10.30a-32b.
   6. and 7. Wang Yeh-chien, "Agricultural Development," p. 9, Table 3. (Data obtained directly, not derived from rents.)

b. 1. *Ch'ang-sha FC*, 1534 ed., 3.25ab.
   2. *Hsiang-yin HC*, 1823 ed., 25.23a.
   3. *Ibid.*, 27.25ab.
   4. and 5. Wang Yeh-chien, "Agricultural Development," p. 54, table 16.
   6. *Hsiang-yin HC*, 1823 ed., 11.8a.
   7. *Ibid.*, 14.29b. (Data obtained directly, not derived from rents.)

c. 1. *Heng-chou FC*, 1593 ed., 7.56a.
   2.–5. *Heng-yang HC*, 1820 ed., 17.68b-84b.

d. 1. *Shao-yang HC*, 1684 ed., 5.36a-40b.
   2.–5. *Shao-yang HC*, 1877 ed., 4.6b-10a. 5. Cited by Wang Yeh-chien, "Agricultural Development," p. 57, table 16.

[a] For a discussion of the comparability of mou and shih units originating in different parts of Hunan, see notes 5.22, 4.67.

achieve maximum yields, rice must be farmed with highly labor-intensive methods. The result is that the maximal size of plots per farm family is small. In modern times, the maximum for a farm couple in Kwangtung was only 6 mou. When more land was tilled hired help was needed at the harvest.[85] In the late seventeenth century, when land was abundant, hired labor must have been very scarce. Extensive methods of rice cultivation were characteristic of early Ch'ing agriculture in Hunan. Peasant families tilled more land and were satisfied with lower yields per mou.

As migration into Hunan continued, the land–labor ratios shifted. By the late eighteenth century, farm holdings in Li-ling hsien (Ch'ang-sha) were reduced in size to somewhat over 10 mou per family.[86] Rising yields during the eighteenth century in this region may be directly linked to a shift toward the more labor-intensive cultivation methods which became possible as family landholdings shrank.

Eastern Hunan recovered from the devastations of the mid-seventeenth century, but Shao-yang hsien's agriculture remained on its former levels. One of the most remarkable aspects of the figures in Table 19 is the near stagnation of yields in this county. In the late nineteenth century, the yields indicated by rents of newly acquired lands in this area remained very close to yields found here almost three hundred years earlier. Shao-yang's pattern of relatively unchanging yields contrasts sharply with the rapid rise of yields in eastern Hunan during the nineteenth century. As Figure 2 illustrates, at least one hsien — Hsiang-yin — had achieved yields of 5 to 6 shih per mou as early as 1797. There is no indication in the records of Shao-yang that yields in this range were reached even a century later.[87] Nor was double cropping adopted in the hsien during the Ch'ing period.[88]

In the nineteenth century, some of the lake counties and others in Ch'ang-sha prefecture began to grow two crops of rice a year, achieving yields of 6 to 7 shih per mou.[89]

As in the Fukien case study in the previous chapter, we propose to rely on interregional differences in market demand to explain Shao-yang's relative stagnation. Our analysis emphasizes the lack of marketing potential in one area and its presence in another. This disparity in commercial possibilities only widened in the course of the nineteenth and early twentieth centuries, as eastern Hunan participated in foreign trade. Hsiang-t'an tea, as tea grown in the Ch'ang-sha districts was called, was exported from Canton and Shanghai.[90] The opening of the Yangtze River to foreign navigation after 1861 and the introduction of steamships stimulated Hunan's rice exports, which rose to a peak of about three million shih a year.[91] Ch'ang-sha and its environs continued to dominate Hunan's commerce in this period. Ch'ang-sha, opened as a treaty port in 1903, and Hsiang-t'an are still the largest rice milling centers in Hunan, and the districts of northeast Hunan produce almost half the rice grown in the province.[92] Demarcations of agricultural areas in eighteenth century Hunan continue to be surprisingly relevant in the twentieth century.

The negative example of Shao-yang throws light on the interrelationships between market expansion and agricultural development in eastern Hunan. In fact, market considerations constituted a positive influence on all of the major factors involved in rice culture: labor, water supply, and improved farming methods.

Eastern Hunan was favored with land appropriate for rice growing, the fertile Tung-t'ing plain and alluvial plains along the middle and lower reaches of the Hsiang River. The very ease of water transportation which enabled these areas to develop commercially also encouraged migrants to move in and settle. The result was the most densely populated region in Hunan and a labor supply which undoubtedly aided some areas in adopting a double-cropping cycle for rice in the nineteenth century.[93]

The provision of adequate water is crucial in ensuring successful rice cultivation. In Hunan, most peasants grew middle season rice to take advantage of the heavy rainfall from April to June, but there was always the fear of drought. In the course of the eighteenth century, irrigation networks with reservoirs for water became a common aspect of the agriculture of eastern Hunan. Most of this represented the investment of private individuals, landlords and tenants. It is not difficult to imagine that rising rice prices during this period supplied the funds which were put into building deep dammed pools and water wheels to guard against drought, and constructing dams to prevent the floods which frequently threatened fields along mountain streams.[94] Water became even more important when rice was double cropped. The rainfall in Hunan declines after June, and without water reservoirs and irrigation, the second rice crop could not be grown.[95] The increased water needs of areas of eastern Hunan were met by this region's heavy investments in waterworks. The rice market provided profits which enabled individuals to undertake the improvements needed to increase productivity.

Market prices of rice provided a concrete incentive for improvements in seeds, fertilizer use, and tillage. The potential importance of psychological factors in rice cultivation is illustrated by a recent example from the lake district of Hunan. Farmers on flood-prone plots responded to the uncertainty of a second harvest by applying smaller amounts of fertilizer and labor to the land. As a result, yields for the second crop were noticeably lower than yields in more secure districts.[96] Conversely, the certainty of a good market price and the prospect of improving market conditions in the future must have provided many peasants in the eighteenth century with motivation to increase productivity through improved farming methods and additional fertilizer. In these ways, the conditions of the rice market may have been responsible for the relatively rapid growth of agriculture in eastern Hunan and may have resulted in its accelerated pace of development.

ACADEMIC SUCCESS

Chang-chou's academic and economic achievements in the sixteenth century signaled the emergence of a formerly obscure area, reflecting a new shift in the power structure of Fukien. In Hunan, the eighteenth century was marked by rehabilitation rather than a totally new regional development. The areas which grew most rapidly were the prefectures of Ch'ang-sha and Heng-chou, devastated during the civil wars of the mid-seventeenth century, which regained their position of dominance in the province.

The list of successful *chin-shih* candidates from Hunan, presented in Table 20, shows a close correspondence between academic and economic developments in the seventeenth and eighteenth centuries. The most extreme example of the disorder of the early Ch'ing can be seen in the record of Ch'ang-sha hsien. Ch'ang-sha and Hsiang-t'an, the largest rice marketing centers in the province, were also the counties with the highest number of *chin-shih* winners in the 1653–1799 period; yet Ch'ang-sha had no winning candi-

TABLE 20. DISTRIBUTION OF *CHIN-SHIH* BY COUNTY, HUNAN, 1653–1799

Area	1653–1679	1685–1706	1709–1724	1727–1745	1748–1763	1766–1781	1784–1799	Total
Ch'ang-sha fu								
Ch'ang-sha	0	0	0	16	7	4	6	33
Shan-hua	1	1	1	7	0	0	2	12
Hsiang-t'an	1	2	6	11	9	10	4	43
Hsiang-yin	0	0	1	5	2	1	2	11
Hsiang-hsiang	0	0	0	0	0	1	2	3
Ning-hsiang	0	0	3	3	2	2	0	10
I-yang	0	1	0	2	2	1	0	6
Liu-yang	0	0	1	0	2	0	0	3
An-hua	0	0	0	1	0	0	0	1
Li-ling	0	0	0	0	0	0	0	0
Yu	1	1	2	2	2	0	0	8
Ch'a-ling chou	1	1	0	1	0	0	0	3
Heng-chou fu								
Heng-yang	1	2	2	5	3	0	4	17
Heng-shan	0	1	1	7	2	2	1	14
Lei-yang	0	0	0	1	0	0	0	1
Ch'ang-ning	0	1	0	4	0	0	0	5
An-jen	0	0	0	0	0	0	1	1
Ling	0	0	0	2	0	0	0	2
Yung-chou								
Ling-ling	0	0	0	1	0	0	2	3
Ch'i-yang	0	0	0	5	1	0	0	6
Tung-an	0	0	0	0	0	0	0	0
Tao-chou	0	0	0	0	0	0	0	0
Ning-yüan	0	0	0	0	0	0	0	0
Yung-ming	0	0	0	0	0	0	1	1
Chiang-hua	0	0	0	0	0	0	0	0
Hsin-t'ien	0	0	0	0	0	0	0	0
Pao-ch'ing fu								
Shao-yang	2	1	2	0	2	0	0	7
Hsin-hua	0	1	1	3	0	3	0	8
Ch'eng-pu	0	0	0	0	0	0	0	0
Wu-kang chou	0	0	0	0	0	1	0	1
Hsin-ning	0	0	0	0	0	0	0	0
Yo-chou fu								
Pa-ling	2	1	1	3	5	0	2	14
Lin-hsiang	1	0	0	0	0	0	0	1
P'ing-chiang	0	0	0	1	0	0	1	2
Hua-jung	0	3	2	1	1	1	0	8
Ch'ang-te fu								
Wu-ling	8	1	5	2	2	2	1	21
T'ao-yüan	1	1	0	0	0	0	0	2
Lung-yang	1	0	0	0	0	0	1	2
Yüan-chiang	0	0	0	0	0	1	0	1

TABLE 20 (Continued)

Area	1653–1679	1685–1706	1709–1724	1727–1745	1748–1763	1766–1781	1784–1799	Total
Ch'en-chou fu								
Yüan-ling	1	0	0	2	0	0	0	3
Lu-ch'i	0	0	0	0	0	0	0	0
Ch'en-ch'i	1	0	0	1	0	0	0	2
Hsü-p'u	0	0	0	1	0	0	0	1
Yüan-chou	0	1	0	0	0	0	0	1
Ch'ien-yang	0	0	0	0	0	0	0	0
Ma-yang	0	0	0	0	0	0	0	0
Kan-chou	0	0	0	0	0	0	0	0
Yung-shun fu								
Yung-shun	0	0	0	0	0	0	0	0
Lung-shan	0	0	0	0	0	0	0	0
Pao-ching	0	0	0	0	0	0	0	0
Sang-chih	0	0	0	0	0	0	0	0
Li-chou[a]	4	0	0	–	–	–	–	–
An-hsiang	1	1	0	1	0	1	1	5
Shih-men	0	0	0	0	0	0	0	0
Tz'u-li	0	0	0	0	0	0	0	0
An-fu	0	0	0	1	0	0	0	1
Ch'en-chou								
Yung-hsing	1	1	0	0	0	0	0	2
I-chang	0	0	0	0	1	0	0	1
Hsing-ning	0	0	0	0	0	0	0	0
Kuei-yang	0	0	0	1	0	1	0	2
Kuei-tung	0	0	0	1	0	0	1	2
Ching-chou								
Sui-ning	0	0	0	0	0	0	0	0
T'ung-tao	0	0	0	0	0	0	0	0
Hui-t'ung	0	0	0	1	1	0	0	2
Kuei-yang chou	0	0	0	1	2	0	0	3
Lin-wu	0	0	0	0	0	0	0	0
Chien-shan	0	0	0	0	0	0	0	0
Chia-ho	0	0	0	1	0	0	0	1

Source: Examination winners section, chüan 134, pp. 2721–2727, in *Hunan t'ung-chih*, 1934 Commercial Press reprint of 1899 work.

[a] Li-chou was a hsien under Yo-chou fu until 1729, when it was made an independent chou. *Hunan t'ung-chih*, pp. 413–425.

dates through the late seventeenth and early eighteenth centuries, and the county with the largest number of winning candidates was not Hsiang-t'an, but Wu-ling hsien.

Table 21, which groups *chin-shih* winners by prefecture,

TABLE 21. *CHIN-SHIH* WINNERS BY PREFECTURE, HUNAN, 1653–1799

	1653–1724		1727–1799	
Prefecture	Number of degree winners	Percentage of total number	Number of degree winners	Percentage of total number
Ch'ang-sha	24	31.4	109	53.0
Heng-chou	8	10.5	32	15.5
Yung-chou	0	–	10	4.9
Pao-ch'ing	7	9.2	9	4.4
Yo-chou	10	13.2	15	7.7
Ch'ang-te	17	22.4	9	4.4
Ch'en-chou fu	2	2.6	5	2.4
Yung-shun	0	–	0	–
Li-chou	6	7.9	4	1.9
Ch'en-chou	2	2.6	5	2.4
Ching-chou	0	–	2	1.0
Kuei-yang	0	–	4	1.9
Total	76		204	

Source: Table 20.

illustrates the shifts in academic success more clearly. In the period of economic rehabilitation, residents of Yo-chou and Ch'ang-te were able to win over one third of the *chin-shih* degrees awarded in Hunan. By the latter part of the eighteenth century, as the proportion of *chin-shih* from Ch'ang-sha and Heng-chou increased by two thirds, the share of Yo-chou and Ch'ang-te *chin-shih* winners declined by almost the same proportion. The eighteenth century saw a shift in the relative balance of power in Hunan, but serious competition for academic success remained confined to the major commercial centers in the province.[97] Ch'ang-te prefecture, located at the western end of Lake Tung-t'ing, dominated the trade of western Hunan, and Yo-chou, in eastern Hunan, benefited from its location between the lake and the Yangtze River. Together with Ch'ang-sha and Heng-chou, these prefectures produced over three fourths of the *chin-shih* in Hunan throughout the period.[98]

The dominance of commercial centers in academic success also emerges from an examination of *chin-shih* from hsien with central rice markets, listed in Table 20. The nine counties with specialized rice markets before 1720 together produced 60 per cent of all *chin-shih* between 1653 and 1799; the sixteen counties with such markets at mid-century produced almost 70 per cent of the *chin-shih* in this period.

This finding is not surprising. Although they represented less than one fourth of the administrative units in Hunan, these counties surely held a much higher proportion of the region's wealth and population. Wealth, which enabled the expensive investment in education necessary for academic success, gave these counties an advantage over their neighbors. For regions, if not individuals, wealth and degree winning marched hand in hand in a predictable fashion.[99] The competition for degrees in Hunan was dominated by the wealthy trading counties; in the course of the eighteenth century the exact shares of each changed as a result of the growing prosperity of the Hsiang River valley.

In this and the previous chapter, we have presented two historical case studies of market expansion and its influence on a primarily agrarian economy. Both Fukien and Hunan illustrate the reality of development in Ming and Ch'ing times, but at the same time they point sharply to the limitations imposed by geography and transportation. The specific ways in which market movements influenced and changed not only the urban but the rural peasant economy as well amount to a general interpretation which emphasizes market movements as a major stimulus for change in agriculture. In essence, the process of commercialization of agriculture which took place in Sung times can be explained in the same way. The applicability of this approach to Chinese economic history extends beyond the boundaries of the regions we have examined.

Chapter Six / AGRICULTURAL CHANGE AND THE PEASANT ECONOMY

Fukien and Hunan represent case studies of change within the context of a largely agrarian economy. In Fukien and Hunan, expanding long distance markets stimulated the agriculture of the surrounding countryside in similar ways. On the one hand, high profits encouraged farmers to intensify cultivation by increasing the water, labor, and fertilizer applied to the soil. Intensification resulted in higher acreage yields for rice. On the other hand, marketing opportunities could divert efforts away from grains into production for trade. The development of specialization in cash crops and rural handicrafts were two aspects of this trend.

The changes that occurred in sixteenth century Fukien and eighteenth century Hunan were only a small part of a long historical process, involving intensification and diversification of farming. With the aid of twentieth century materials, it is possible to examine different points in this process more fully and to investigate the effects of agricultural change on peasant life.

AGRICULTURAL CHANGE IN HISTORICAL PERSPECTIVE

Twentieth century studies of village life covering areas in north as well as south China show a tremendous diversity in the agriculture of different regions. These differences are rooted in the history and geography of various localities, but at the same time, they represent different stages in the process of agricultural change in China. The path along which the agriculture of Fukien and Hunan must have moved and the direction in which they were headed can be seen from the information provided by recent materials describing a cross-section of Chinese agricultural systems.

Intensification of agriculture was accompanied by increasing population density. The relationship of population to arable land can be concretely expressed in terms of farm size. There are very broad regional differences in population density in the twentieth century: in the Shensi villages, a family of five might till lands of over ten acres, and holdings of over 20 acres were considered to be "not much" in Yenan.[1] In Yunnan, a family of the same size tilled less than two acres;[2] in Kwangtung, from 0.8 to 1.6 acres.[3] Farm size clearly influenced the manner in which the soil could be cultivated. The number of man-days per acre devoted to the primary crop, shown in Table 22, is a partial expression of the continuum from extensive to intensive cultivation.

Different crops require differing amounts of care. Millet, the primary crop in Ting hsien, Hopei, demands much less tillage than does rice, the major crop in Yunnan.[4] Contrasting labor requirements for Ting hsien and the Yunnan villages thus reflect a more general relationship between the extensive cultivation of grains grown in north China and the labor-intensive cultivation of rice. The labor requirements inherent in the cultivation of a specific crop, however, allowed for considerable variation. For example, rice was grown under all sorts of conditions. In Shantung, where it was rarely planted, the seeds were sown directly, and the plots were not irrigated.[5] Even in south China, where farm-

TABLE 22. FARM SIZE, FAMILY SIZE, AND LABOR EXPENDED ON THE PRINCIPAL CROP

Area	Average farm size (acres)	Average family size	Number of man-days/acre devoted to the principal crop
1. Ting hsien, Hopei	3.53	5.8	36
2. Lu ts'un, Yunnan	1.46	5.0	244.8
3. Yi ts'un, Yunnan	1.25	4.4	212–260
4. Yu ts'un, Yunnan	0.85	5.0	122.4[a]

Sources:

1. Ting hsien: Sidney Gamble, *Ting Hsien: A North China Rural Community* (New York: Institute of Pacific Relations, 1954), p. 240.

2–4. Fei Hsiao-t'ung and Chang Chih-i, *Earthbound China: A Study of Rural Economy in Yunnan* (London: Routledge & Kegan Paul, Ltd., 1949), information on size of farm and household size, pp. 298–299, table 49. Information on labor expended, pp. 213, 146, and 214 respectively.

[a] Fei explains the comparatively low number of man-days devoted to rice in terms of a transition from rice to vegetable growing in this area. Fei and Chang, p. 214.

ers practiced more conventional tilling methods, there was great variation. The labor requirements for Yunnan villages in Table 22 represent estimates of the labor expended in growing one crop of rice, yet the villagers of Lu ts'un used twice as much labor on their plots as the farmers of Yu ts'un. Thus, "weeding and watering take all the farmer's time" [6] in some regions, but in other areas the same period was punctuated by long intervals of idleness.[7]

Available information suggests that over the long run all the important inputs in rice growing were increased: water, fertilizer, and labor.[8] The trend from single to double cropping of rice, which began in Sung (960–1280) times, was simply the most obvious manifestation of an intensification of agriculture resulting in increased productivity. Intensification of agriculture was linked to population growth.

DIVERSIFICATION OF AGRICULTURE

Diversification of agriculture in a more wholistic sense developed in rural areas with access to urban markets. Here expanded marketing opportunities affected the peasant economy, as in sixteenth century Chang-chou. The Soochow area provides a model of the ways in which urban markets could stimulate cash cropping, rural handicrafts, and supplementary farm activities. The resulting diversification of income yielding activities meant that farmers often paid less attention to rice cultivation as its importance to farm income diminished. This may be one reason for the stagnation in rice productivity through the Ch'ing period in a region like Soochow.

The Soochow plain has been at the forefront of Chinese agriculture from the Sung period. Here the most advanced tools, irrigation instruments, fertilizers, and general farming practice found in China were applied to rice cultivation and brought significant increases in yields. Nor were advances in productivity confined to the Sung. By the mid-seventeenth century, rice yields in Soochow had quadrupled from the thirteenth century record of 200–300 catties to highs of 1,123 catties per mou.[9] In the light of these impressive precedents, the virtual stagnation of yields over the next two centuries — the highest rice yields achieved in 1955 were only 1,250 catties per mou — is puzzling if examined by itself.[10] In the context of the entire peasant economy, however, this standstill in yields can be seen as a reflection of agricultural diversification. Labor diverted to handicrafts and other sources of income left the farmer with neither the interest nor the inclination to plunge more deeply into rice culture: indeed, there was a "manpower shortage" hindering expansion of rice cultivation, but abundant labor for other activities, such as growing vegetables for sale to urban markets.[11] The transition from staple grains to truck farming, found in some parts of China as early as the Sung period,[12] entailed heavy increments of labor, fertilizer, and in some cases additional equipment, but the returns were superior to those for rice.[13] Not only did it have the advantage of producing income throughout the year, but it allowed the farmers to follow a more flexible tilling schedule.[14] Vegetable farming represents yet another stage in agricultural intensification, both in terms of reduced farm size and the extra fertilizer and labor expended on the plot.[15]

Intensification of cultivation and diversification of rural economic activity changed the tempo of peasant life. The previous farming cycle of peak seasons and periods of idleness, dictated by the growing season of a cereal crop, was supplanted by more constant demands for labor. In areas with a commercialized agriculture, there are no idle seasons. The Yunnan rice farmer enjoyed 40 to 45 days of rest before and after transplanting and after weeding,[16] but the Kwangtung peasant spent spare moments during the rice growing period tending his vegetable plots, which "demanded continuous attention."[17] In south China, vegetables could be grown throughout the year, eliminating the slack season entirely.

Rural handicrafts also represented a move away from the seasonality commonly associated with the agricultural cycle. The peasant economy of Soochow, with its emphasis on sericulture and weaving, thus represented a further stage along the process of agricultural change seen in the systems of sixteenth century Fukien and eighteenth century Hunan. It is interesting that the modernization of villages in present day Taiwan and the New Territories has followed along the same lines described above.[18]

AGRICULTURAL CHANGE AND TENANCY

The effect of agricultural developments on peasant life has been studied by many scholars, but the discussion has been dominated by a Marxist perspective which looked at the process in terms of class struggle and focused on the landlord-tenant relationship because areas with intensive agriculture also had high rates of tenancy.[19] In fact, the historical data contradict many commonly held assumptions on the causation and effect of agricultural intensification and diversification. A recent study has challenged the notion that reduction in farm size was accompanied by increasing tenancy and has denied that tenancy is necessarily detrimental to productivity.[20] The view that the peasant was forced by rising rents into supplementary non-farm activities is not substantiated by evidence from Fukien and Hunan. In the previous chapters, we cited instances when the real rent burden grew progressively lighter as productivity rose[21] and other cases where rent increases were a response to inflation and did not constitute real rent increases at all. Historians who have cited rent figures to argue that tenants were oppressed must remember that frequently the rents were not paid. Eighteenth and nineteenth century Hunan gazetteers give numerous instances in which tenants postponed or defaulted on rent payments with impunity.[22]

The strongest evidence of the frequency of rent arrears

comes from the Kiangsu bursary records studied by Muramatsu Yūji. In one bursary, it was common to find about 20 to 30 per cent of the accounts unpaid in a year; at times rent arrears affected from 40 to 50 per cent of all of the tenant accounts.[23] Nor were such unsatisfactory tenants subject to retaliatory action. In Kiangsu, customary security of tenure seems to have been stronger than landlord will. Out of 175 cases of rent default between 1906 and 1909, 19 of these being cases of continuous delinquency in payments, only seven tenants were actually arrested.[24] Rent collectors, responsible for dunning tenants, were sometimes themselves involved. One of the seven tenants arrested for rent arrears was himself a rent collector! [25]

One of the most startling findings resulting from study of the Fei bursary accounts concerns the practice of reducing rents for peasants who did not meet the deadlines for payments. Theoretically, peasants agreed to pay their rents by a stipulated deadline when they signed tenancy contracts. They were notified each year of this deadline and informed of the collection spot as well as the amount to be paid. In actuality, Kiangsu landlords represented by bursaries had no confidence that rents would be paid at the designated time. The 1906 account books of the Fei bursary show that substantial discounts of 30 and 40 per cent were offered as an inducement for prompt payment.[26]

Rents which remained unpaid after the deadline had passed were regarded as delinquent. Muramatsu was able to examine records of rents paid long after the deadline and to compare the rates charged these tenants with the discounted rates offered with prompt payment. He found that in every instance, the delinquent tenants received larger rent reductions than early payers. These extra discounts were 16 to 30 per cent larger than those given for prompt payment.[27] Indeed, the later the date of payment, the larger the discount given.[28] Late payment brought benefits rather than penalties for the erring tenant.

It is difficult to reconcile these findings with generalizations about landlord exploitation. Although this information bears on only one area, the details presented in Muramatsu's rent bursary sources are uniquely rich and are supported by observations of tenancy in Soochow during the 1930's, when discounts for prompt payment continued to be common practice.[29] At the very least, the rent bursary studies suggest that no uniform generalizations can be made concerning the effect of a commercialized agriculture on peasant welfare. A survey of tenancy in twentieth century Fukien demonstrates, for example, that tenancy was not necessarily correlated with commercialization, as is commonly assumed. On the contrary, tenancy was lowest in the areas along the urbanized coast and highest in the rural interior.

TENANCY IN FUKIEN

Despite the advent of railroads, Fukien continued to be not one but at least two disparate economic regions into the 1950's. The interior, particularly northwest Fukien, was a sparsely populated region practicing a primitive and low yielding agriculture. The coastal strip, particularly in the southern part of the province, differed from it in almost every aspect. It was urbanized, with population densities of 300 to 500 persons per square mile. Here lived 40 per cent of the Fukienese population. Agriculture was marked by low land–population ratios, with three to four times more people on the soil than in northwest Fukien. In Hsing-hua, Ch'üan-chou, and Chang-chou none of the shortages in fertilizer, labor, and inadequate water control that plagued the northwest existed.[30] The result was a markedly different agricultural system. In place of the one crop cycle common in the northwest, southern Fukien generally grew two and in some areas even three crops each year. This was the heart of the rice double cropping region in the province.[31]

Urbanization, with concomitant marketing opportunities, and a high yielding agriculture were thus found along the coast of south Fukien, in sharp contrast to conditions in the interior. If commercial activity worked to increase tenancy, the coast should have experienced a markedly higher incidence of tenancy than the interior, but the situation in Fukien was precisely the reverse. A survey of tenancy conditions in 1937 discovered that tenancy was most widespread in the areas of west, north, and east Fukien, where 74 to 84 per cent of the agricultural households rented at least part of their land, and lowest in the Hsing-hua, Ch'üan-chou, and Chang-chou region, where only 57 to 60 per cent of the agricultural households were full or part tenants.[32] The precise figures are presented in Table 23.

The evidence from Fukien suggests that there was no simple cause and effect relationship between commerce and tenancy. Nor did commercialization lead to a decline in the economic position of the tenant in Fukien; indeed, it was along the commercialized coast that tenants enjoyed greatest security of tenure and most favorable rent conditions.

There were three different kinds of arrangements governing length of tenure in Fukien. The most common was an unspecified tenure, with the term depending on mutual agreement: this was prevalent in coastal areas such as Ch'üan-chou and Chang-chou as well as in northern Fukien, but there is no information on how it worked in practice. About

TABLE 23. REGIONAL VARIANCE IN TENANCY, FUKIEN, 1937

Area	a. Percentage of farmers who are part tenants	b. Percentage of farmers who are full tenants	c. Percentage of full or part tenants (a + b)
Fu-chou and Fu-ning	28.7	37.8	66.5
Hsing-hua	37.5	20.0	57.5
Ch'üan-chou	33.2	24.6	57.8
Chang-chou	32.8	26.8	59.6
West Fukien	35.6	48.7	84.3
North Fukien	35.5	38.9	74.4
East Fukien	36.9	37.4	74.3

Source: Hsü T'ien-t'ai, "Fu-chien tsu-tien chih-tu yen-chiu," *Fu-chien wen-hua chi k'an*, 1.1: 60 (1941).

a quarter of the tenancy contracts specified a definite time period, which could be as long as 100 years or as short as one year. Three years was the most common term found in the province, but in the coastal prefectures of Hsing-hua and Chang-chou, tenancy contracts of five and ten years duration were normal. It is generally agreed that the longer the period of tenure, the better off is the tenant. The most favorable form of tenancy is permanent tenure, which was found in one fifth of the cases in Fukien. Permanent tenancy was most common along the coast, where it was enjoyed by 38 per cent of the tenants in Hsing-hua, and least practiced in north Fukien, where it affected less than 5 per cent of the tenants. Tenants in coastal Fukien thus tended to receive longer terms of tenure when these were specified or to be favored with permanent tenure.

Rents in Fukien continued to be paid primarily in kind.

In 1937, only 12 per cent of the tenants in the province were paying cash; this practice was generally confined to the coast, where it was the dominant form of rent in some hsien.[33] There were two ways of paying rent in kind. In north Fukien, over a third of rent payments were of the share cropping type. This form of rent was virtually non-existent in highly commercial areas such as Hsing-hua or P'u-t'ien hsien.[34] Where share cropping did exist, the landlord's share varied greatly. In the coastal areas of Hai-ch'eng and Chin-chiang it was as low as 35 per cent of the yield. In the interior, it was more commonly 60, 70, and as much as 80 per cent of the crop.[35]

Fixed rents in kind were the most common form of payment in Fukien. Here again payments varied greatly from region to region. The average rent for the province for the best paddy land was 288 catties per mou, but rents for such plots in some coastal areas of Chang-chou were over twice this figure.[36] On the other end of the scale, rents for the best land were as low as 150 catties per mou in the northwestern hsien of Ch'ung-an.

Under share cropping, the tenant in the interior usually received a smaller share of a smaller total crop than did his coastal counterpart. Under a system of fixed rents in kind, roughly the same proportion, slightly less than 60 per cent, of the crop was being paid to the landlord.[37] The variance in rice rents noted above was a reflection of divergent regional yields.

In 1932, the provincial average rice yield for Fukien was slightly over 361 catties per mou.[38] This figure masked large regional differences. In many areas of the northwest, average yields were 200 to 250 catties per mou,[39] while some regions on the coast had average yields of three times this figure.[40]

The effect of rent in kind on peasant income was quite different even though the landlord's share in percentage terms may have been the same. After rent payments, the tenant in northwestern Fukien was probably left with only one fourth the product of the coastal peasant.[41] The coastal tenant was better off because he had a larger harvest to begin with.

Peasants who paid cash rents enjoyed still more favorable conditions when cash rents were converted to equivalent rice payments at market prices.[42] The tenant on the best plots paid a cash rent which was equal to only 300 catties of rice. When converted to real terms in this manner, cash rents were only three quarters of the fixed rent in kind paid on the same grade of land.[43]

Of the three kinds of rent systems, we have seen that cash rents were most, and share cropping least, advantageous to the tenant, with fixed rent falling in between. Tenants in the coastal areas enjoyed a two-fold advantage over their counterparts in the interior: not only was the most favored form of rent concentrated on the coast, but within each rent system, coastal tenants received more favorable contract terms than their inland cousins.[44] In addition, the coastal tenant enjoyed greater security of tenure.

Regional differences in farm size are crucial in comparisons of peasant income on the coast with the interior, since higher yields on the coast were partially offset by larger farms inland.[45] Tenants in the interior, with more acreage under cultivation, might obtain lower yields per mou and still emerge with a higher income. Several factors support the belief that this was not the case in Fukien. The northwest was essentially a single crop area in the 1930's, but the coast grew two, and sometimes three crops.[46] Because the coastal areas generally enjoyed much higher yields, one mou of land in coastal Fukien was literally the equivalent of two and perhaps more mou in a single cropping region. When alternative sources of income are also considered, the peasant on the coast probably received a larger income than his inland counterpart despite tilling a smaller farm.[47]

The importance of evaluating rents within the context of the whole economy is highlighted by information derived from Ch'ang-sha and Soochow, demonstrating that a given rent can mean entirely different things in different areas.

CH'ANG-SHA AND SOOCHOW RENTS

Ch'ang-sha and Soochow are densely populated regions with a commercialized agriculture. Ch'ang-sha prefecture has already been extensively described in Chapter Five. In the twentieth century, it was the most populous and urbanized part of Hunan: the provincial capital, Ch'ang-sha was a city of 395,000 persons by 1935.[48] The countryside surrounding Ch'ang-sha and Hsiang-t'an was also densely populated. The city of Ch'ang-sha accounted for only one third the total population of the hsien.[49] Of the ten counties in the prefecture, six had population densities above 150 persons per square kilometer.[50]

Soochow was located in the most urbanized part of China, close to large markets which directly affected the livelihood of the rural population. Although the statistics of the 1930's counted over 78 per cent of the Kiangsu population as "agricultural," indicating village residence, the character of village economy masked by these statistics was quite different from the meaning commonly ascribed to this term. Indeed, in some parts of Kiangsu, over half the villagers were no longer engaged in agriculture.[51]

Ch'ang-sha and Soochow were essentially rice growing districts, with high rates of tenancy: about 70 to 80 per cent of the farmers rented at least part of the land they tilled.[52] A comparison of rents from Soochow rent bursaries with Ch'ang-sha rents, presented in Table 24, coupled with information on average yields, presented in Table 25, gives the impression that tenants in the two areas experienced roughly equivalent conditions.[53] In the twentieth century, average yields in the Ch'ang-sha area were similar to those found in Soochow and the rents were not very different. However, institutional differences in the manner of collecting rent resulted in great differences in the effect of rent on tenant income. In Ch'ang-sha,[54] rents were paid in kind, while in Soochow, cash rents were collected from the 1890's.

Unlike the cash rents found in earlier periods on government or corporately owned lands,[55] the Soochow cash rents were collected by rent bursaries for private landlords. The fact that Muramatsu found cash rents being collected by several bursaries suggests that this was not unusual in Soochow.[56] In the late 1930's, Amano noted that this was the form in which rents in this region were customarily collected.[57]

Although rents in Soochow were paid in cash, they were still computed in kind. In the tenancy contracts, a set rent, generally a picul of husked rice per mou, was stipulated.[58] Every year this rent was translated into a sum of silver at rates determined by the landlord.[59] The amount of the actual payment was affected first by the widespread practice of discounting, and secondly by the commutation rate.

In an earlier section the discounts given by bursaries were discussed in some detail. Amano's information for the 1930's suggests that discounts were frequently given for prompt

TABLE 24. RENTS IN SOOCHOW AND CH'ANG-SHA

Soochow			Ch'ang-sha		
Date	Rent[a] shih/mou	Hsien	Date	Rent[a] shih/mou	Hsien
			1863	0.82	I-yang
1866–1870	1.07[b]	Wu	1867	0.6–1.4	Ch'ang-sha
			1867	1.1[b]	Ning-hsiang
1866–1878	0.5[b]	Wu, Ch'ang-chou, Yüan-ho	1871	0.25–1.5	Yu
			1872	0.75[b]	Hsiang-hsiang
			1873	0.65[b]	Liu-yang
			1873	0.9–1.45	Liu-yang
1885	1.02[b]	Ch'ang-chou			
			1889	1.0	Hsiang-t'an
1893	0.70[b]	Ch'ang-chou, Yüan-ho			
1906	0.78[b]	Wu-chiang, Chen-tse[c]			
1899–1928	0.72[b] 0.76[b]	Yüan-ho			
1899–1928	0.84[b]	Wu			
1920	1.07[b]	Ch'ang-chou			
1922	0.86[b]	Ch'ang-chou[c]			
			1926	1.5	Li-ling

Sources: Soochow 1866–1870 data from Feng bursary cited in Muramatsu Yūji, "Shin-matsu Soshū fukin no ichi sosan ni okeru jinushi shoyūchi no chōzei kosaku kankei — Kōso-shō Go-ken Ma Rin issan chichō sōryō kankei bosatsu ni tsuite," (*Hitotsubashi*) *Keizaigaku kenkyū*, 6:308–309, table 14. 1866–1878 data from Muramatsu's "Shin-matsu no Kōnan ni okeru kosaku jōken to kosaku ryō ni tsuite — Kōso-shō Go-ken Han shi gisō, onajiku Go-shi Yo-kei-san no 'shōyu,' 'shōran,' 'soyu,' 'jijō,' 'sekkyaku,' oyobi 'shussetsu bisa' satsu no kenkyū," (*Hitotsubashi daigaku*) *Shakaigaku kenkyū*, no. 5 (1963), Fan charitable estate, p. 145, table 1; 1885 data from Feng bursary, cited in Muramatsu, "Shin-matsu Soshū no ichi sosan," pp. 314–315, table 18; 1893 data from Wu clan bursary, cited in Muramatsu, "Shin-matsu Min-sho no Kōnan ni okeru hōran kankei no jittai to sono kessan hōkoku — Soshū Go-shi yo-keisan 'Hōshō kaku-gō bi-sa' satsu no kenkyū," *Kindai Chūgoku kenkyū* 6:17, 23 (1964). 1906 data from Kung-shou t'ang, cited in Muramatsu's "Nijū seiki shotō ni okeru Soshū kinbō no ichi sosan to sono kosaku seido — Kōso-shō Go-ken Hi-shi kyōju-san kankei 'soseki bensa' satsu no kenkyū," *Kindai Chūgoku kenkyū*, 5:118, table 13. 1899–1928 data from Yüan-ho hsien cited in Muramatsu's "Shin-matsu Min-sho no Kōnan," pp. 39–40, tables 9 and 10. For Wu hsien, from Muramatsu's "Shin-matsu Min-sho no Kōnan," p. 41, table 11. 1920 data derived from rent bills held at the Harvard-Yenching Library, presented in Muramatsu, "Saikin gūmoku shita jakkan no Chūgoku jinushi-sei kankei bunsho ni tsuite — Harvard-Yenching kenkyū-jo shūzō no soyo sono ta," *Tōyōgakuhō* 46.4:3–9 (1964). 1922 data from the Chün hao (under the Kung-shou t'ang), presented in Muramatsu's "Nijū seiki Soshū no ichi sosan," p. 119, table 14.

Ch'ang-sha: 1863 data from *I-yang HC*, 1874 ed., 6.18b. 1867 and subsequent data from Wang Yeh-chien, "Agricultural Development," pp. 55–57, table 16, selecting high rents and converting to husked rice at the ratio of 2 unhusked to 1 husked.

[a] Rent is in husked rice. For a discussion of the comparability of mou and shih from the two areas, see note 53 in this chapter.

[b] Averages; the unmarked items are single citations.

[c] These represent the real or discounted rent rates.

TABLE 25. RICE YIELDS IN SOOCHOW AND CH'ANG-SHA

	Husked rice (catties/mou)[a]			
	Soochow		*Ch'ang-sha*	
Date	Average	High	Average	High
1658	481.5	1,123.5		
1868			241	401
1908	273–401			
1930's			428	495
1955	433	1,250		
1957			341–426	760

Sources: Soochow 1658 and 1955 figures from Ch'en Heng-li, *Pu nung shu yen-chiu* (Shanghai: Chung-hua shu-chü, 1958), p. 32. 1908 information from Amano Motonosuke, *Chūgoku nōgyō-shi*, p. 389. Ch'ang-sha 1868 data from gazetteers cited by Wang Yeh-chien, "Agricultural Development," p. 9, table 3. 1930's information is for double cropped rice land of best quality (high column): Kanda Masao, *Konan-shō sōran* (Tokyo: Kai-gai sha, 1937), p. 521. The average yield is a 1933 statistic cited in Kanda, p. 517. 1957 information is from *Economic Geography of Central China*, p. 322.

[a] Shih catties per shih mou. For a discussion of the comparability of mou and shih from the two areas, see note 53 in this chapter.

payment; Muramatsu's data reveal that in all of the instances when such information was available, the actual rent charged was less than the rent stipulated in the tenancy contract.[60] The discounts given were substantial, averaging 20 to 30 per cent of the titular rent. While Muramatsu's landlords received cash, their tenants were left with rice, which they sold to wholesale rice stores in Soochow. What was the result of this change in the form of rent payments? A perusal of the records shows that the tenant gained by paying his rent in cash and retaining his rice crop.

In order for the landlord to have retained the full "value"

of his rents, he would have had to receive in cash whatever increases accrued in the market price of rice. Landlords tried to do this by changing the commutation rates applied to the rents in kind. Muramatsu discovered in studying the Wu bursary records from 1899 to 1928 that though the rent in kind remained virtually unchanged during these three decades, the commutation rates moved in response to market fluctuations in the price of rice.[61] While this method of computing rents did serve as a hedge against inflation,[62] it was consistently ineffective in capturing the full value of the rice rents originally stipulated.

When Muramatsu studied commutation rates recorded in bursary accounts, he found they were almost always substantially below the Shanghai market price. In the forty instances for which there is information, presented in Table 26, the commutation rate was exactly equal to the Shanghai market price only once. As is shown in Table 27, the Soochow landlord most commonly levied rates which were only 60 per cent of the market price in Shanghai.

The Soochow tenant was in a very favorable position for selling his rice. He could transport it himself to the hsien city, Soochow, for sale. Or, for less than 2 per cent of the eventual price, he could ship it by traditional or modern means to Shanghai.[63] In fact, most peasants probably chose the first alternative and sold their rice in Soochow at a price lower than the Shanghai price. By selling his own grain and paying the landlord in cash, the peasant retained about a quarter of the value of the rice rent stipulated in the contract.[64] The shift from payment in kind to payment in cash enabled the Soochow peasant to retain part of the landlord's contractual share in addition to his own part of the harvest.

Landlord incomes were further reduced by taxes, bursary

TABLE 26. THE COMMUTATION RATE AS A PERCENTAGE OF THE SHANGHAI MARKET PRICE

Date	Commutation rate[a] (yüan)	Shanghai market price (yüan)	Commutation rate as a percentage of the market price
1899	2.900	4.80	60
1900	2.523	4.45	57
1901	3.051	4.75	64
1902	3.302	6.66	50
1903	3.424	6.31	54
1904	3.075	5.48	56
1905	2.869	4.31	67
1906	3.792	5.86	65
	4.0[b]	5.86	68
	3.9, 4.16[c]	5.86	71, 67
1907	4.351	7.51	58
	4.3, 4.4, 4.8[b]	7.51	57, 59, 64
	4.36, 4.40[c]	7.51	58, 59
1908	6.015	7.06	85
	3.9, 4.0[b]	7.06	55, 57
	3.9, 4.0[c]	7.06	55, 57
1909	5.922	5.93	100
	4.1[a]	5.93	69
	4.2[b]	5.93	71
1910	5.562	7.13	78
1912	4.473	7.94	56
1913	4.248	7.21	59
1914	4.454	6.42	69
1915	4.656	7.40	63
1916	4.445	7.12	62
1917	4.434	6.52	68
1918	4.468	6.62	67
1922	6.624	11.26	59
	5.39[d]	11.26	48
1923	7.024	11.20	63
1927	9.654	14.77	65
	6.32[d]	14.77	43
1928	8.421	11.17	75
1929	7.29[d]	12.51	58

TABLE 26 (Continued)

[a] Unless otherwise indicated, figures in the table are taken from Muramatsu Yūji, "Shin-matsu no Kōnan," p. 48, table 15. There are several problems concerning the money units in this table. The first is that the commutation rates before 1912 are in thousands of copper cash (*wen*) and not in yüan. Money rents in the Soochow records were phrased in both yüan and copper cash; examples are presented in Muramatsu's "Shin-matsu no Kōnan," p. 11, and "Nijū seiki Soshū no ichi sosan," pp. 96–97. In several instances, Muramatsu converts copper cash into sums comparable with the yüan by taking 1 yüan = 1,100 *wen*. He derives this from 1907–1908 records in "Nijū seiki Soshū no ichi sosan," pp. 96–98, and applies it to money units in records dated 1893–1919 in "Shin-matsu no Kōnan," p. 43, table 12. Hence the commutation rates before 1912 in the table, expressed in thousands of copper cash, are slightly upwardly biased. Were these rates to be converted into yüan at the rate 1 yüan = 1,100 wen, the resulting figures would be smaller than they now stand. Our conclusions would be strengthened rather than weakened by this correction.

A second problem concerns the yüan unit which appears after 1912 in the Soochow commutation rates. In "Nijū seiki Soshū no ichi sosan," p. 96, Muramatsu identifies this yüan as the *ta-yang yüan*, or foreign-style silver dollar (see L. S. Yang, *Money and Credit in China*, item 5.36, p. 50). In the late nineteenth and early twentieth centuries, this was probably the Mexican silver dollar; see P'eng Hsin-wei, 1965 edition, p. 782 for a description of the circulation of the Mexican dollar in the lower Yangtze region. But by 1929, the date of the last item in the table, the Mexican dollar had been supplanted by the Republican dollar; the 1929–1930 *China Yearbook*, p. 289, notes that the Mexican dollar was still circulating in the Shanghai district but the total was "by no means large." It is therefore possible that the commuted rates in the 1920's were in terms of Republican yüan and not the Mexican dollar.

This leads to the final issue, that of the comparability between the money units in which the Soochow rates and the Shanghai rice prices are phrased. The Shanghai rice prices were taken by Muramatsu from vol. 1 of *Shang-p'in tiao-ch'a ts'ung-k'an*, compiled by the Shanghai shang-yeh ch'u-hsü yin-hang (Shanghai, 1931), pp. 90–94; the compilers converted the original rice prices into Republican dollars. How comparable were the Mexican dollar and the Republican dollar? Since $1.50

TABLE 26 (Continued)

Mexican was = 1 Haikwan tael, 1 Haikwan tael = 1.114 Shanghai taels, and 1 Republican dollar = 0.728 Shanghai taels, it follows that 1 Republican dollar = 0.981 Mexican dollar, and the two units are close enough to be comparable. On the value of the Mexican dollar, see Inspector General of Customs, China Imperial Maritime Customs, *Returns of Trade and Trade Reports*, which published the exchange rates annually through 1919. The rates from 1910–1920 are also in *The China Yearbook, 1921–1922*, p. 286. *The China Yearbook, 1925–1926*, p. 952, published the exchange rates for the Mexican dollar 1921–1924. The rate of conversion between Haikwan taels and Shanghai taels is provided by H. B. Morse, *The Trade and Administration of China*, p. 170. Eduard Kann presents the legal exchange rate of Republican dollars to Shanghai taels in *The China Yearbook, 1929–1930*, p. 290, and describes the daily fluctuations in the rate of exchange in his book, *The Currencies of China* (Shanghai: Kelly and Walsh, 1927), p. 171.

[b] Data taken from Muramatsu Yūji, "Nijū seiki Soshū no ichi sosan," p. 111, table 11. (In yüan.)

[c] Data taken from Muramatsu Yūji, "Nijū seiki Soshū no ichi sosan," p. 114, table 12. (In yüan.)

[d] Data taken from Muramatsu Yūji, "Nijū seiki Soshū no ichi sosan," p. 130, table 19. (In yüan.)

TABLE 27. DISTRIBUTION OF COMMUTATION RATES AS A PERCENTAGE OF THE SHANGHAI RICE PRICE

Rate as percentage of Shanghai rice price	Number of observations	Percentage of observations
80–100	2	5
70–79	4	10
60–69	15	38
50–59	17	42
Under 50	2	5
Total	40	100

Source: Table 26.

charges, and the expense of dunning delinquent tenants. The average income from land was in fact very small. When expressed in terms of rice, as in Table 28, it is clear that landlords received only a fraction of the rice rent written into the contract. As shown graphically in Figure 3, landlords would have fared much better had they collected rents in kind rather than in cash.[65]

Another way in which location benefited the Soochow peasant was in the higher prices he could command for his crops. Even with the same crop in hand, the lower prices of rice on the Ch'ang-sha market resulted in different incomes for the farmers of the two regions.[66] In addition, as described earlier, the Soochow peasant had many sources outside rice cultivation for earning an income, and there can be little doubt that the Ch'ang-sha peasant fared more poorly in this respect.[67]

If the contrast between Ch'ang-sha and Soochow underlines the importance of institutional arrangements for rent payment in determining the effect of a particular rent on tenant households, it also points to the need for inspecting tenure within the context of the whole economy in which tenurial relations functioned. Cash rents were advantageous to the Soochow tenant because the period was one of rising prices; in another market situation, the tenant paying rents in kind may have been better off. In this regard, market conditions affected peasants who may not have participated directly in production for trade.

CONCLUSION

The changes which occurred in sixteenth century Fukien and eighteenth century Hunan were part of a long historical process continuing in China to the present day. In Fukien

TABLE 28. THE REAL INCOME OF A BURSARY

Date	Net income per mou[a]		Shanghai rice price yüan/shih	Real income per mou (shih of rice)	
	Chi hao	Kung hao		Chi hao	Kung hao
1899	1.26	1.16	4.80	.26	.24
1900	1.11	1.16	4.45	.25	.26
1901	1.15	1.22	4.75	.24	.26
1902	1.40	1.53	6.66	.17	.23
1903	1.23	1.38	6.31	.20	.22
1904	1.20	1.30	5.48	.22	.24
1905	1.14	1.38	4.31	.26	.32
1906	1.38	1.58	5.86	.23	.27
1907	1.90	2.10	7.51	.25	.28
1908	2.63	2.66	7.06	.32	.38
1909	2.10	2.20	5.93	.35	.37
1910	2.60	2.75	7.13	.36	.39
1912	1.93	1.95	7.94	.24	.25
1913	2.32	2.45	7.21	.32	.34
1914	1.97	2.12	6.42	.31	.33
1915	2.52	2.45	7.40	.35	.33
1916	2.68	2.51	7.12	.38	.35
1917	2.03	2.08	6.52	.31	.32
1918	2.32	2.39	6.62	.36	.36
1922	4.18	4.24	11.26	.31	.38
1923	4.88	4.72	11.20	.44	.43
1927	3.98	4.00	14.77	.27	.27
1928	3.68	3.58	11.17	.33	.32

Sources: Information on net income is from tables 9 and 10 in Muramatsu Yūji, "Shin-matsu Min-sho no Kōnan," pp. 39–40. Rice prices from p. 48, table 15. These were applied to the money income of the two subunits of the Wu bursary to obtain rice equivalents.

[a] 1899–1910 money income in 1,000 *wen* copper cash units; 1912–1928 figures are in yüan. 1 yüan = 1,100 *wen* so the 1899–1910 figures are upwardly biased, and the real income per mou was lower than the figures noted above.

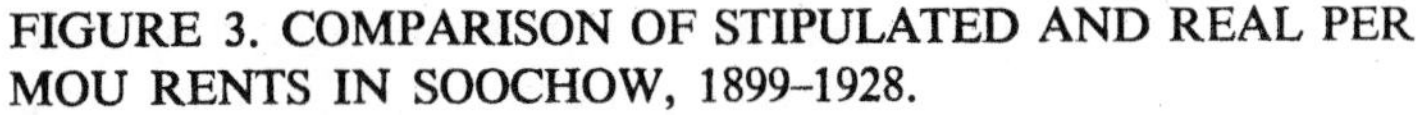

FIGURE 3. COMPARISON OF STIPULATED AND REAL PER MOU RENTS IN SOOCHOW, 1899–1928.

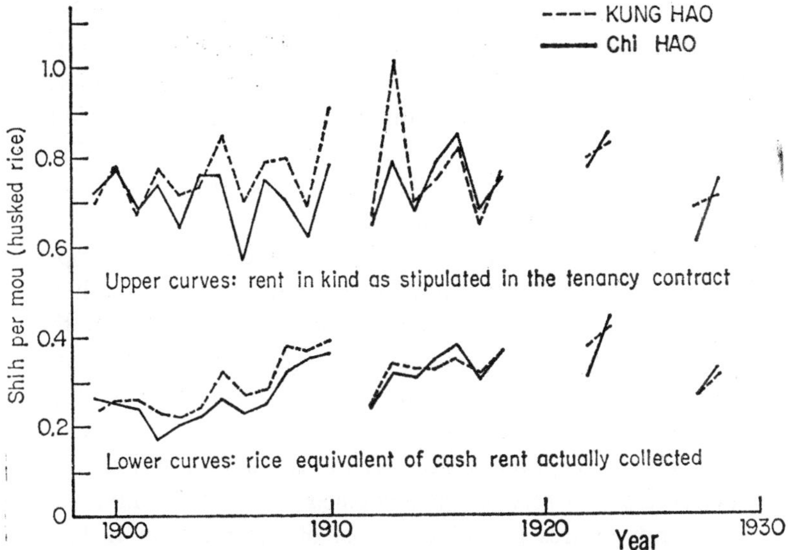

Sources: Information on stipulated rents in kind from tables 9 and 10, Muramatsu Yūji, "Shin-matsu Min-sho no Kōnan," pp. 39–40. Figures on real rents, reconverted to rice, obtained from last two columns, Table 28.

and Hunan, these changes brought identifiable benefits to peasant households. The twentieth century materials on tenancy indicate that these were not unique or isolated incidents, and suggest that the effect of agricultural change on peasant life cannot be evaluated without considering the specific institutional and economic framework within which these changes occurred.

There were great disparities in the extent to which regions within Fukien and Hunan could participate in economic expansion, stemming from the severe limitations on marketing imposed by transport costs in areas not on water routes. In an earlier chapter, the implications of transportation as a barrier to change for much of China's large land mass were discussed briefly. The extent of regional variance has important implications for interpretations of Chinese history. Most broadly, it casts doubt on generalizations about China which imply a standardization which did not exist. The academic debate among Japanese scholars on the nature of Sung landholding provides a concrete example of the perils of assuming uniformity in China: two diametrically opposed interpretations proved to be equally valid, since they were based on evidence from different regions.[68] Yet both schools claimed that their conclusions on Sung society, derived from such limited sources, were applicable to the whole empire.

With the exception of Chapter Four, which describes the repercussions of foreign trade expansion on local commerce and manufactures in Fukien, most of the material in this book deals with agriculture and not commerce, yet the importance of commerce as an underlying theme should not be underestimated. Indeed, agricultural change in China was at least partly a reflection of the qualitative changes wrought by trade in the village economy which has always dominated the Chinese scene. This aspect of the subject attains added significance in the absence of information on the quantitative aspects of commerce in the Ming and early Ch'ing periods. To the extent that commercial influence penetrated agriculture and produced changes in rural as well as urban economy, we can say that the Chinese economy in pre-modern times was capable of a dynamic response to changing economic conditions. That this response was largely independent of government action is also significant.

The central government appears in local markets as a licensing authority. Even in areas in which it had an urgent interest, as in the basic price of food grains or the value of money, it was powerless to do more than forestall market fluctuations. Its role was a passive one: it reacted to, rather than determined, market trends. The source for change should be sought instead in the actions of individual merchants and peasants, acting as private economic agents. It is at this level that we have sought to analyze the interaction of commerce and the rural economy, one of the important elements in Chinese economic history.

Appendix

Notes

Bibliography

Glossary

Index

Appendix / FUKIEN'S POPULATION IN THE MING PERIOD

This search for hsien break-downs of Fukien's population in Ming times began with a survey of local gazetteers of the province. The most important sources of information were Ming gazetteers, extant in Japanese libraries, which often contained materials edited out of subsequent editions; in addition, gazetteers of later date were used to fill in gaps in coverage. In this way, every hsien in the province was covered at least three times, by two provincial gazetteers and at least one prefectural gazetteer. It is doubtful whether the comprehensiveness of this survey could be improved without access to works held in mainland Chinese libraries. The sources provided a collection of population figures, including some sex ratios and age distributions. One of the provincial gazetteers included a list of population by hsien for the year 1482.[1]

THE IMPOSSIBILITY OF RECONSTRUCTING POPULATION TOTALS

It was clear from the beginning that the 1482 figures could not be used without adjustment. The general unreliability of Ming population totals was heightened in Fukien, where even the 1391 census, the only Ming population record which was the product of a concerted effort to count heads, was falsified and downwardly biased.[2] The conclusion that population records had to be either corrected or discarded was easily reached, but the question of what method, if any, could correct these totals is very complicated. Not only were several different traditions of under-reporting simultaneously at work, but their combinations were difficult to sort out. The pages which follow should clarify our decision to discard these population records. The conclusion that our original goal — reconstruction of population movements over time on the hsien level — is impossible because of inadequate data, follows from rejection of these totals. The hsien populations for 1393 presented in Table A.3 were then reconstructed on the basis of reported acreage.

UNDER-REPORTING

Under-reporting produced an almost continual decline in the recorded provincial population. From 1393 to 1482, Fukien's household totals declined by 40 per cent; from 1482 to 1578, they declined by 17 per cent.[3] The testimony of many gazetteers supports the conclusion that these declines were not historically valid.[4] In analyzing the sources of these declines, we can first eliminate omission of women and children as an important factor.

The complete omission or under-reporting of women and children is probably the most common cause of downward biases in Chinese population reports of all periods. In Fukien, however, women were generally included in the recorded population. Information for 1391 suggests that in what is considered the most reliable population count for the dynasty, a serious effort was made to count all the women. The sex ratios of 107 and 130 found for that date in two hsien both fall within the range of potentially valid demographic figures.[5] Information on sex ratios throughout the rest of the Ming period gives no basis for concluding that the percentage of women reported fell; in the majority of the 15 hsien for which this information exists, the opposite trend occurred.[6] The proportion of women reported increased; the sex ratio fell.

The Fukien materials suggest that a more serious factor in under-reporting throughout the dynasty was the complete omission in most cases of the aged and of those below taxable age. Information found for a hsien in 1391 permits us to look at the combined downward bias introduced by not counting those over taxable age (60 and over) and minors; roughly 40 per cent of the population was omitted.[7] This isolated example suggests that under the best of circumstances, when the government made an integrated effort to actually carry out a census, it may still have omitted 40 per cent of the total population. The 1393 population of 3.9 million for Fukien should actually have been at least 6.5 million. Since almost all Ming records for Fukien continued this neglect, however, omission of the young and aged represents a constant downward bias in the population totals and plays no part in the increased under-reporting represented by declines in the recorded population. These declines were caused by the following tax evasion measures: (1) flight of households from the tax registers; (2) under-reporting of household members; (3) flight of individuals and households from the registers, as represented by the practice of amalgamating nonkin households.

EVASIVE PRACTICES

The most obvious trend was the flight of peasant households from the population registers. Had population grown at an estimated rate of 0.5 per cent a year,[8] household totals should have increased by 251 per cent from 1393 to 1578, instead of declining by 56 per cent, as was reported.

Yet another trend was the flight of individuals from the registered households, reflected in declines in average household size. Even in 1391, the Fukien average household size of 4.0 was far below the national average of 5.3 for the same year.[9] While twentieth century studies of Chinese population have shown that household size varies impressively with degree of wealth, they have also indicated that average household size remains fairly close to 5. This was true even for small samples of several hundred households;[10] for hsien units, the likelihood of its holding true is even stronger. For that reason, the low average household size of 4.0 for 1391 suggests that individuals were not being fully reported and not that Fukien's households were significantly smaller than the national average.

All available information on household size from records dated 1393 and earlier is presented in Table A.1. The extremely low household size figures for the coastal prefectures of Fu-chou and Fu-ning chou suggest that hsien in these areas were especially active in concealing household members from the records. On the other hand, the average household size of 6.2 reported in Lung-yen and Shang-yang hsien indicates that even in this part of China, some hsien were resorting to a practice more common in the southwest, the amalgamation of nonkin households. According to the prefectural gazetteer of Ch'üan-chou, amalgamation of households was the reason the registered populations of four of its hsien declined while the actual populations flourished.[11] Although the number of taxable males (*ting*) was generally under-reported, amalgamation on a sufficiently large scale

TABLE A.1. AVERAGE HOUSEHOLD SIZE, BY HSIEN, IN THE FOURTEENTH CENTURY RECORDS[a]

County	Average household size	County	Average household size
A. Fu-chou fu		D. T'ing-chou fu	
Min	2.8	Ch'ang-t'ing	4.5
Hou-kuan	2.3	Ning-hua	3.6
Huai-an	2.3	Shang-hang	6.2
Ch'ang-lo	3.3	Wu-p'ing	4.2
Lien-chiang	2.8	Ch'ing-liu	4.1
Fu-ch'ing	3.6	Lien-ch'eng	5.5
Ku-t'ien	2.9	E. Yen-p'ing fu	
Yung-fu	2.7	Yu-ch'i	3.3
Min-ch'ing	3.4	Sha	5.2
Lo-yüan	3.2	F. Shao-wu fu	
B. Chien-ning fu		Shao-wu	4.1
Chien-an	3.1	T'ai-ning	3.9
O-ning	4.8	Chien-ning	4.3
P'u-ch'eng	3.4	Kuang-tse	4.2
Chien-yang	4.0	G. Fu-ning chou	
Sung-ch'i	4.7	Ning-te	2.2
Ch'ung-an	3.8	Fu-an	3.5
Cheng-ho	3.5		
C. Chang-chou fu			
Lung-yen	6.2		

Sources: A. *Fu-chou FC*, 1596 ed., 7.1b-3b (1381 figures). B. *Chien-ning FC*, 1541 ed., 12.1b-9a (1381 figures). C. *Lung-yen HC*, 1558 ed., 1.44b-45b (1391 figures). D. *T'ing-chou FC*, 1637 ed., 9.1a-6b (1391 figures). E. 1. *Yu-ch'i HC*, 1636 ed., 3.6b (1391 figures). 2. *Sha HC*, 1545 ed., 4.1b (1391 figures). F. *Shao-wu FC*, 1601 ed., 5.2a-7b (1391 figures). G. *Fu-ning CC*, 1593 ed., 4.1b-3a (1391 figures).

[a] Only hsien for which there was information are listed.

often resulted in an unusually high average household size.

Both under-reporting of household members and amalgamation of households increased through the fifteenth and sixteenth centuries. The continued decline in provincial average household size shows that the first was the stronger trend. By 1578, this stood at 3.4 for Fukien, while the national average household size was 5.7.[12] In the same period, however, some hsien reported average household sizes of up to 10.5;[13] amalgamation was a secondary but continuing trend.

A final complication to be considered is that the evasive processes described above occurred in various degrees in different hsien, with no predictable pattern. If successful tax evasion were linked to gentry representation,[14] one would expect the geographical division between the academically successful coastal prefectures and the unsuccessful interior areas to appear in the pattern of population distortion. When population totals over time are studied, there is evidence that hsien differed markedly in their ability to satisfy tax evasion desires, but a coastal-interior distinction does not appear.

Table A.2 presents information on household totals by prefecture and hsien from 1393 to 1578. Although the provincial population declined during this period, the picture on the prefectural and hsien levels was different. Four prefectures showed increases in household numbers. These increases may have been genuine, but the totals were almost certainly still downwardly biased; in no case was the increase as great as anticipated by external estimates of growth (Column D). The areas with increasing population totals may simply be those which were least successful in under-reporting their numbers and may not necessarily be the ones

TABLE A.2. HOUSEHOLD TOTALS OVER TIME, FUKIEN

Unit	A Popu- lation 1	B Popu- lation 2	C Per cent change in reported popu- lation	D Per cent change in pop. under assumed growth rate, 0.5 per cent/year
A. Fu-chou fu	94,541	98,984	5	167
Min	20,075	23,784	18	167
Hou-kuan	10,854	10,696	−2	167
Huai-an	8,136	9,813	121	167
Ku-t'ien	7,085	8,336	18	167
Min-ch'ing	903	1,421	57	167
Ch'ang-lo	16,350	19,620	20	167
Lien-chiang	5,908	6,378	8	167
Lo-yüan	1,937	1,998	3	167
Yung-fu	1,218	1,453	19	167
Fu-ch'ing	21,848	15,485	−29	167
B. Chien-ning fu	112,142	120,914	8	28
Chien-an	11,492	21,536	87	28
O-ning	25,213	25,397	1	28
P'u-ch'eng	21,156	21,166	0	28
Chien-yang	24,755	24,731	0	28
Sung-ch'i	8,968	8,844	−1	28
Ch'ung-an	10,506	10,973	4	28
Cheng-ho	6,800	5,572	−18	28
Shou-ning	3,252	2,696	−17	28
C. Ch'üan-chou fu	41,152	48,704	18	87
Chin-chiang	18,079	21,368	18	87
Nan-an	6,395	9,364	46	87
T'ung-an	6,711	7,565	13	87
Te-hua	1,173	1,110	−5	87
Yung-ch'un	1,908	1,549	−19	87
An-ch'i	2,380	3,474	46	87
Hui-an	4,506	4,274	−5	87
D. Chang-chou fu	49,354	45,917	−7	91
Lung-ch'i	21,476	13,865	−36	91
Chang-p'u	11,593	7,260	−37	91
Lung-yen	4,985	4,124	−17	91

TABLE A.2 (Continued)

Unit	A Population 1	B Population 2	C Per cent change in reported population	D Per cent change in pop. under assumed growth rate, 0.5 per cent/year
Ch'ang-t'ai	1,550	1,428	−8	91
Nan-ching	4,568	2,802	−39	91
Chang-p'ing	5,182	3,399	−34	91
E. T'ing-chou fu	60,033	36,174	−40	218
Ch'ang-t'ing	13,693	10,270	−25	218
Ning-hua	12,588	5,393	−57	218
Shang-hang	11,158	4,777	−57	218
Wu-p'ing	4,157	1,903	−54	218
Ch'ing-liu	12,613	4,584	−64	218
Lien-ch'eng	5,824	2,480	−58	218
Kuei-hua	5,903	3,585	−39	102
Yung-ting	2,298	2,184	−5	102
F. Yen-p'ing fu	63,584	64,205	1	57
Nan-p'ing	12,027	12,870	7	57
Chiang-lo	8,030	8,349	4	57
Yu-ch'i	15,861	8,878	−44	57
Sha	12,767	14,693	15	57
Shun-ch'ang	6,948	7,449	7	57
Yung-an	7,951	7,722	−3	57
G. Shao-wu fu	56,682	39,793	−30	202
Shao-wu h.	26,604	20,114	−24	202
T'ai-ning	9,480	7,680	−19	202
Chien-ning	10,506	5,694	−46	202
Kuang-tse	10,092	7,260	−28	202
H. Hsing-hua fu	64,241	34,237	−47	147
P'u-t'ien	51,151	25,855	−50	147
Ch'ien-yu	9,530	8,382	−12	147
I. Fu-ning chou	43,157	16,937	−61	202
Fu-ning	20,177	6,550	−68	202
Ning-te	15,570	3,812	−76	202
Fu-an	7,410	6,575	−11	202

TABLE A.2 (Continued)

Sources:

A. 1382 figures from 1596 ed., *Fu-chou FC*, 7.1b-3b. 1578 totals from 1613 ed., *Fu-chou FC*, 26.1b-5a.

B. 1482 and 1532 figures: 1482 figures, *Pa Min t'ung-chih*, 20.2a-6a; 1532 figures, 1541 ed., *Chien-ning FC*, 12.1b-9a.

C. 1482 and 1608 figures: 1482 figures, *Pa Min t'ung-chih*, 20.2a-6a; 1608 figures, 1612 ed., *Ch'üan-chou FC*, 6.3a-4b.

D. 1482 and 1612 figures: 1482 figures from *Pa Min t'ung-chih*, 20.2a-6a; 1612 figures from 1628 ed., *Chang-chou FC*, 8.15b-17a.

E. 1391 and 1623 figures: both from 1637 ed., *T'ing-chou FC*, 9.1a-6b.

F. 1482 and 1572 figures: 1482 figures from *Pa Min t'ung-chih*, 20.2a-6a; 1572 figures from 1660 ed., *Yen-p'ing FC*, 4.1a.

G. 1391 and 1613 figures: both from *Shao-wu FC*, 1623 ed., 5.2a-7b.

H. 1391 and 1572 figures: both from 1575 ed., *Hsing-hua FC*, 4.1a-6b.

I. 1391 and 1613 figures: both from 1616 ed., *Fu-ning CC*, 7.1b-4b.

with the highest actual growth rates or largest increases in population. On the other hand, the four prefectures showing increases in recorded totals include the academically successful coastal areas of Fu-chou and Ch'üan-chou, but they also include the academically mediocre prefectures of Yen-p'ing and Chien-ning.[15] A similarly inconclusive picture appears on the hsien level, where one third of the hsien recorded increases over previous totals, contrary to the provincial trend. Again, some were in coastal areas, others in the interior. A similar finding appears when the geographical distribution of evasive practices is studied. A survey of changes in average household size on the hsien level found no discernible pattern: in both the coast and the interior there were some counties with rising household size, others with declining household size, and occasionally some whose household size remained constant.

Despite our certainty that populations in Fukien were

being under-reported, we could not find a method to predict where and to what extent these evasive practices introduced a downward bias into the recorded totals. In the next section, we shall see that the information at our disposal does not permit us to reconstruct corrected totals which would be useful for studying regional variance.

CORRECTION OF BIASES

To correct for the omission of children and the aged from the population registers, we can simply increase the recorded totals by 40 per cent to compensate for their absence. The effect of this correction is to increase all totals, since the omission of these age groups was always a problem. It does not explain the increased under-reporting indicated by declines in the recorded population.

The second distortion cited was the general decline in household totals. There seems to be no alternative to applying an external correction factor, that of a 0.5 per cent annual growth rate. Information on sex ratios cannot be used to correct the totals because under-reporting of women was not a major contributor to the declines. Having corrected for the artificial diminution of the household totals by applying a 0.5 per cent annual growth rate, we are left with the problem of determining the appropriate relationship between household numbers and individuals. Two methods come to mind: first, to correct the totals for each form of evasive practice described above; second, to discard the figures for individuals which are recorded and substitute instead a reconstructed total based on the assumption that the "true" average household size for Fukien was 5. Only the second method is feasible.[16]

We can construct a table showing hsien populations from

the fourteenth to the sixteenth century by applying an estimate of provincial growth to the household totals for a given year. When these totals are multiplied by five (the average household size), we obtain figures representing hsien populations over time. The estimates produced by this method ignore population shifts from region to region. From what we know of peasant movements in Fukien during this period, we can assume that people often migrated in search of better opportunity. The economic success of some regions and the relative decline of others was reflected in these migrations. As a result, some areas grew much more rapidly than others. Because the Ming totals are so unreliable, these different growth patterns cannot be ascertained. But use of a uniform growth rate fails to capture the relative shifts in population which are an important factor in regional differentiation. We must conclude that with the materials at hand, it is not possible to produce population totals which would be useful for regional study.

The next section takes up a method of examining under-reporting, a serious problem in Fukien. If the assumption that this was primarily a gentry-linked phenomenon is true, hsien in the province should have had varying success in evading the tax rolls. In order to examine the extent of under-reporting, the hsien populations of 1393 were reconstructed. These were compared with actually recorded totals for 1482, and the discrepancy was used as an indicator of the extent of under-reporting.

RECONSTRUCTION OF 1393 POPULATION

There are obvious advantages to obtaining a list of hsien populations for 1393 rather than 1482. First is the belief that a real attempt to register people was made in 1393.

Despite the flaws in the Fukien totals for that year, the 1393 figures are apt to be more accurate than subsequent totals, especially since under-reporting increased in the course of the fifteenth century.

The problem in using 1393 hsien breakdowns is that although the provincial total is available, there is no list of all hsien populations for that year. These subtotals had to be reconstructed. Our method, based on hsien acreage totals, follows from the observation that cultivated acreage totals were more stable than population figures. Though the latter declined by 40 per cent from 1393 to 1482, acreage remained almost constant; the total provincial acreage of 14,492,323 mou recorded in the 1491 gazetteer was 99 per cent of the 1393 total.[17] Since 1393 acreage totals by hsien are not available, the 1491 totals were used. The provincial average per capita acreage for 1393 was applied to these figures, and the result (Column A, Table A.3) are estimates of hsien population in 1393.[18]

In order to measure the degree of under-reporting in 1482, the 1393 hsien reconstructed populations were compared with their 1482 counterparts. Had population stagnated in the 99 years, these totals should have been identical. If population grew at an estimated rate of 0.5 per cent a year, the 1482 populations should have been over one and one half times the 1393 figures. Comparison of these populations reveals that under-reporting occurred almost universally; in only 5 out of 54 cases was the recorded 1482 population greater than its 1393 predecessor, and in only one instance did the 1482 population approach the expected growth rate.

The divergence of the 1482 totals from the 1393 figures was recorded in percentage terms (Column C). This repre-

TABLE A.3. ESTIMATED HSIEN POPULATIONS, 1393, AND MEASUREMENT OF UNDER-REPORTING, 1482

Hsien	A 1393 hypothetical population	B 1482 population totals	C Degree of under-reporting (A–B as percentage of A)
Fu-chou fu			
Min	88,400	58,448	34
Hou-kuan	108,000	22,716	79
Huai-an	57,600	19,153	67
Ch'ang-lo	61,400	54,262	12
Lien-chiang	42,800	16,917	60
Fu-ch'ing	148,000	78,523	47
Ku-t'ien	66,000	20,112	70
Yung-fu	20,000	3,273	84
Min-ch'ing	36,400	3,082	92
Lo-yüan	35,200	6,187	82
Chien-ning fu			
Chien-an	130,000	50,506	61
O-ning	97,500	84,974	13
P'u-ch'eng	140,000	61,934	56
Chien-yang	164,500	83,947	49
Sung-ch'i	41,700	31,922	23
Ch'ung-an	98,000	83,947	14
Cheng-ho	31,000	24,704	20
Shou-ning	10,000	11,651	[a]
Ch'üan-chou fu			
Chin-chiang	116,900	67,407	42
Nan-an	96,500	22,343	77
T'ung-an	69,400	38,926	44
Te-hua	28,400	4,971	82
Yung-ch'un	43,200	5,866	86
An-ch'i	37,200	8,675	77
Hui-an	65,500	32,625	50
Chang-chou fu			
Lung-ch'i	103,000	127,151	[a]
Chang-p'u	69,400	62,282	10
Lung-yen	44,400	39,609	11

TABLE A.3 (Continued)

Hsien	A 1393 hypothetical population	B 1482 population totals	C Degree of under-reporting (A–B as percentage of A)
Ch'ang-t'ai	38,000	16,360	57
Nan-ching	50,600	34,315	32
Chang-p'ing	25,200	37,934	[a]
T'ing-chou fu			
Ch'ang-t'ing	105,000	42,817	59
Ning-hua	61,400	36,133	41
Shang-hang	48,800	26,801	45
Wu-p'ing	33,900	14,597	57
Ch'ing-liu	23,400	56,272	[a]
Lien-ch'eng	35,000	30,569	13
Kuei-hua	42,400	33,917	20
Yung-ting	26,200	13,767	47
Yen-p'ing fu			
Nan-p'ing	59,600	52,458	12
Chiang-lo	47,800	34,682	27
Yu-ch'i	66,000	48,189	27
Sha	61,500	38,408	38
Shun-ch'ang	45,000	33,334	26
Yung-an	25,600	29,244	[a]
Shao-wu fu			
Shao-wu h.	136,000	56,903	58
T'ai-ning	35,000	26,212	25
Chien-ning	51,500	21,121	59
Kuang-tse	54,000	27,046	50
Hsing-hua fu			
P'u-t'ien	242,000	165,470	32
Ch'ien-yu	126,000	14,356	89
Fu-ning chou			
Fu-ning	57,600	18,335	68
Ning-te	46,800	21,329	54
Fu-an	32,600	28,259	13

Source: 1482 totals from *Pa Min t'ung-chih*, 20.2a-6a.
[a] 1482 total exceeds 1393 hypothetical population.

sents the degree to which a hsien succeeded in evading the population registers, not in absolute but in relative terms. In other words, a hsien which lost 33 per cent of its population between 1393 and 1482 was assumed to have been significantly less successful in suppressing its population records than a hsien which had lost 85 per cent of its 1393 population.[19]

It is possible that some of the "under-reporting" measured in Table A.3 was instead a genuine loss of population. During the fifteenth century it is possible that the interior prefectures lost more people in migrations than they gained, but highly improbable that these areas experienced a halving of their population, as the figures for Shao-wu prefecture indicate. The divergences which emerge in Column C are so marked that it is difficult to see how they could have been produced by anything other than deliberate evasion. Not only did hsien differ significantly in the degree to which they under-reported their populations, but this difference was not predictable by location, despite the fact that academic success, usually cited as the source of successful evasion, was clearly a coastal phenomenon.

CONCLUSION

That an examination of Ming population figures is really an exercise in fiscal practice is not a surprising finding, nor is the conclusion of this survey an unqualified rejection of all Ming data on the subject. Local gazetteers are unpredictable sources, and much depends on the number and quality of available editions. For another province, enough information may exist for direct corrections of population totals, but in the case of Fukien it was not possible to construct a method which could explain and predict differential success in under-reporting.

Notes

Chapter One / INTRODUCTION

1. The essays in *Chung-kuo tzu-pen-chu-i meng-ya wen-t'i t'ao-lun chi,* published in 1957, and its sequel, *Chung-kuo tzu-pen-chu-i meng-ya wen-t'i t'ao-lun chi hsü-pien,* issued in 1960, constitute the main body of articles studying "sprouts of capitalism" in Ming and Ch'ing China. See also the earlier collection of four studies, reissued in 1957 under the title *Ming Ch'ing she-hui ching-chi hsing-t'ai ti yen-chiu.* See Albert Feuerwerker, "China's Modern Economic History in Communist Chinese Historiography," *The China Quarterly,* 22:44–45 (1965).

2. With the possible exception of the Ching-te-chen kilns in the Ch'ing period: see Margaret Medley, "Ching-te-chen and the Problem of the 'Imperial Kilns,'" *Bulletin of the School of Oriental and African Studies,* 39.2:326–338 (1966).

3. The pioneering works of Ho Ping-ti on population and economic development in this period have established a framework for studying Ming and Ch'ing economy. See also Dwight Perkins, *Agricultural Development in China, 1368–1968* (Chicago: Aldine, 1969), p. 13.

4. Carlo Cipolla, *Money, Prices, and Civilization in the Mediterranean World: Fifth to Seventeenth Century* (Princeton, 1956), p. 57. For a discussion of the relevance of transport costs to nineteenth century history, see pp. 482–485 in Dwight Perkins, "Government as an Obstacle to Industrialization: The Case of Nineteenth Century China," *The Journal of Economic History,* 27.4:478–492 (1967).

5. See Perkins, *Agricultural Development,* pp. 140–143.

6. The Chiang-nan plain has the greatest river density in China. *Economic Geography of East China,* ed. Sun Ching-chih (Joint Publications Research Service translation: Washington, 1961), p. 10.

7. Sun Ching-chih, ed., *Hua-nan ti-ch'ü ching-chi ti-li* (Peking, 1959), pp. 140–146. *Economic Geography of Central China,* ed. Sun Ching-chih (Joint Publications Research Service translation: Washington, 1960), pp. 203–207.

8. Perkins, *Agricultural Development,* pp. 115–116.

9. John Meskill, tr., *Ch'oe Pu's Diary: A Record of Drifting across the Sea* (Tucson: Association for Asian Studies, 1965), p. 154.

10. *Ibid.,* pp. 68, 91–92.

11. Louis J. Gallagher, *China in the Sixteenth Century: The Journals of Matthew Ricci, 1585–1610* (New York: Random House, 1953), p. 261.

12. There are many studies dealing with this topic: nearly all the articles collected in *Chung-kuo tzu-pen-chu-i meng-ya wen-t'i t'ao-lun chi* which treat the Ming period describe the efflorescence of commerce, as does the study by Han Ta-ch'eng, "Ming tai shang-p'in ching-chi ti fa-chan yü tzu-pen-chu-i ti meng-ya," pp. 18–37 in *Ming Ch'ing she-hui ching-chi hsing-t'ai ti yen-chiu.* The largest such study is by Fu I-ling, *Ming Ch'ing shih-tai shang-jen chi shang-yeh tzu-pen* (Peking: Jen-min ch'u-pan she, 1956). See also Fujii Hiroshi, "Shin-an shōnin no kenkyū," *Tōyōgakuhō,* 36.1, 2, 3, 4: 1–44, 32–60, 65–118, 115–145 (1953–1954). The monetization of silver which accompanied economic development in the fifteenth century is studied in detail by Liang Fang-chung in his studies of the Ming tax system and the "Single Whip" tax reform: see *The Single-Whip Method of Taxation in China,* tr. Wang Yü-ch'üan (Cambridge: Harvard University Press, 1956). This should be read together with his articles studying domestic and foreign sources of silver: "Ming tai yin-k'uang k'ao," *Chung-kuo she-hui ching-chi shih chi-k'an,* 6.1:65–112 (1939); and "Ming tai kuo-chi mao-i yü yin ti shu ch'u-ju," *Chung-kuo she-hui ching-chi shih chi-k'an,* 6.2:267–324 (1939).

13. Although various sources of information are available, none provides a satisfactory method of measuring Ming trade. One potential source is the data on the commercial tax, or *shang-shui.* The commercial tax of Ming times was directly descended from imposts first recorded in late T'ang documents and regularly collected by Chinese governments since Sung times. It is an unreliable

measure of Ming commerce, for the following reasons: (1) the tax never encompassed coastal trade, an important part of domestic commerce along the southeastern coast; (2) after 1409 it was frozen into quota payments which bore no relationship to the actual volume of commerce. Like most Ming taxes, the *shang-shui* declined until the late sixteenth century, when eunuchs under the Wan-li emperor (1573–1620) increased imperial revenues through levies on commercial traffic outside the *shang-shui* system. These new taxes were not uniformly imposed, however, and do not reflect the overall commerce of that period. The subject is treated in detail in Evelyn Sakakida, "Fukien in the Mid-Sixteenth Century," Ph.D. diss. Harvard University, 1967, pp. 55–70.

Sixteenth century guidebooks are another potentially useful source. Often written by merchants and intended for their use, the guidebooks provide detailed information on routes throughout China, including notations of distance and travel conditions, with occasional citations of local products. Unfortunately, they provide no means for distinguishing and comparing trade volumes on the routes described. These guidebooks, found in Japanese libraries, have been discussed by Niida Noboru, "Gen Min jidai no mura kiyaku to kosaku shōsho nado — Nichiyō hyakka-zensho no rui nijū shu no naka kara," *Tōyō bunka kenkyū-jo kiyō,* 8:123–166 (1956), and by Sakai Tadao, "Mindai no nichiyō ruisho to shomin kyōiku," in Hayashi Tomoharu, ed., *Kinsei Chūgoku kyōiku-shi kenkyū* (Tokyo, 1958), pp. 25–155.

14. Wu Chi-hua, *Ming-tai hai-yün chi yün-ho ti yen-chiu* (Taipei: Institute of History and Philology, Academia Sinica, 1961), Table 4, p. 102, and Tables 13, 14, pp. 198, 200. At its peak, the Grand Canal actually delivered 6.7 million piculs to Peking (1432). One reason for increased commutations and decreased shipments of tribute grain to the capital in the sixteenth century is suggested in a memorial recorded by Wu: this is the 1568 memorial of Meng Chao, who noted that the grain transport boats carried 472 shih of official grain, whereas their capacity was 700 to 800 shih. Private trade in grain was thus sizable. Wu Chi-hua, p. 203.

15. Abe Takeo, "Beikoku jukyū no kenkyū: Yōseishi no isshō to shite mita," *Tōyōshi kenkyū,* 15.4:120–214 (1957).

16. Dwight Perkins, *Agricultural Development,* p. 119.

17. Terada Takanobu, "Mindai So-shū heiya no nōka keizai ni tsuite," *Tōyōshi kenkyū,* 16.1:1–26 (1957). This topic is treated in numerous essays in the collection *Chung-kuo tzu-pen-chu-i meng-ya wen-t'i t'ao-lun chi,* for example: Wang Chung-lo, "Ming tai Su-Sung-Chia-Hu ssu-fu ti tsu-o ho Chiang-nan fang-chih yeh," I,12; Fu I-ling, "Ming tai Su-chou chih-kung, Chiang-hsi t'ao-kung fan feng-chien tou-cheng shih-liao lei-chi," I,22–24; Li Kuang-pi, "Ming tai shou-kung-yeh ti fa-chan," I,36, 38.

18. G. William Skinner, "Marketing and Social Structure in Rural China," *Journal of Asian Studies,* 24.1:1–43 (1964), 24.2:195–228 and 24.3:363–399 (1965).

19. The rigid hexagonal structures of Christaller-Löschian central place theory are not applicable in an extremely mountainous terrain such as Fukien's.

20. Shiba Yoshinobu, "Sōdai Kō-nan no mura-ichi to byō-ichi," *Tōyōgakuhō,* 44.1:41–76 and 2:89–97 (1961). In his study of Sung markets, Shiba, p. 59, found that periodicity did not of itself connote the scale of the market, i.e., more frequently held markets were not necessarily on a higher level in the market hierarchy. The Ming gazetteers for Fukien did not generally record meeting dates, so changes in periodicity over time could not be studied. For a discussion of this and other aspects of the market information found for Ming Fukien, see Sakakida, *Fukien in the Mid-Sixteenth Century,* pp. 90–93.

21. For an example, see discussion of the role of population in stimulating the Industrial Revolution: "Conference Report: The Origins of the Industrial Revolution," *Past and Present,* 17:71–81 (1960). On the treatment of population as a factor see the comprehensive work of Phyllis Deane and W. A. Cole, *British Economic Growth, 1688–1959: Trends and Structure* (Cambridge, England: Department of Applied Economic Monographs No. 8, 1962).

Chapter Two / CONDITIONS OF RICE CULTURE

1. Shiba Yoshinobu, "Nan Sō kome shijō no bunseki," *Tōyōgakuhō,* 39.3:36 (1956). Yields in Fukien were on a par with those of the most advanced rice growing regions, Kiangsu and Chekiang.

2. Liu Ta-chung and Yeh Kung-chia, *The Economy of the Chinese Mainland: National Income and Economic Development, 1933–1959* (Princeton: Princeton University Press, 1965), Table A-2, p. 285. This is a downward revision of Buck's estimate of 128.3 per cent (because of double cropping); nevertheless, Liu and Yeh classify Fukien as a major rice producer.

3. J. J. Ochse, M. J. Soule Jr., M. J. Dijkman, C. Wehlburg, *Tropical and Subtropical Agriculture* (New York: Macmillan, 1961), p. 1256.

4. Clifford Geertz, *Agricultural Involution: The Process of Ecological Change in Indonesia* (Berkeley: University of California Press, 1966), pp. 30–35. D. H. Grist, *Rice* (London: Longmans, Green & Co., 1959), pp. 28, 31.

5. For example, the records on Hai-ch'eng hsien (*Chang-chou FC,* 1573 ed., 30.55b–58a) include four inscriptions on waterworks, all of which mention land reclamation.

6. *Chang-chou FC,* 1628 ed., 8.5ab.

7. *Ibid.,* 25.4a–5a.

8. *Chang-chou FC,* 1573 ed., 1.15b.

9. *Ibid.,* 30.55b–56b. Two records: the record of Wang dike by Lin Chün and "The new repairs to the Ch'en dike" by Chao Hun. Chao was mistaken in assigning the first building of the dike by Wang to the early years of the Hung-chih reign period; see the dates mentioned by Lin Chün for the completion of the project, 30.56a.

10. *Chang-chou FC,* 1573 ed., 30.55b–56a. The Wang dike was repaired by a group of citizens led by Ch'en, for whom the dike was renamed. Ch'ü T'ung-tsu treats the subject of gentry participation in public works in Chapter 11, *Local Government in China under the Ch'ing* (Cambridge: Harvard University Press, 1962). In *Chinese Lineage and Society: Fukien and Kwangtung* (New York: Humanities Press, 1966), pp. 159–162, Maurice Freedman suggests that this need for large-scale water control projects promoted the large localized lineage found in the rice growing southeast. His interesting point parallels the argument of Japanese historians that the water needs underlying rice cultivation were important in explaining the social cohesion and close economic cooperation in Japanese rural communities. See Richard Beardsley, Robert Ward, and John Hall, *Village Japan* (Chicago: University of Chicago Press, 1959), p. 115;

Tadashi Fukutake, *Japanese Rural Society,* tr. R. P. Dore (London: Oxford University Press, 1967), pp. 82–83; Chie Nakane, *Kinship and Economic Organization in Rural Japan* (New York: Humanities Press, 1967), pp. 76–79. The Chinese lineage may have provided the institutional framework for labor cooperation and coordination which was supplied by the Japanese village.

11. "Ch'üan nung shu," *Chang-chou FC,* 1573 ed., 11.43b–44b.

12. *Ibid.*

13. According to a study conducted in Japan, the optimal period for transplanting, which depends on the flow of water and on climate, may be as short as a week. Chie Nakane reports this finding of Oishi Shinzaburō, pp. 76–77.

14. Ch'en Fu-liang, *Chih-chai hsien-sheng wen-chi,* 44.6b–8a, "Kwei-yang chün ch'üan nung wen."

15. Geertz, pp. 32–35. "The capacity of most terraces to respond to loving care is amazing," p. 35.

16. "Ch'üan nung shu," *Chang-chou FC,* 1573 ed., 11.44b.

17. As C. K. Yang notes in his study of a Kwangtung village, "A frequent change of tenants was undesirable for proper maintenance of the land." *A Chinese Village in Early Communist Transition* (Cambridge: Technology Press, 1959), p. 48.

18. *Ning-yang HC,* 1692 ed., 4.3b–4a.

19. *Chin-chiang HC,* 1765 ed., 3.5a–8b.

20. The Yung-an contracts are found on pp. 28–32, the Min-ch'ing contracts on pp. 60–63 of Fu I-ling, *Ming Ch'ing nung-ts'un she-hui ching-chi* (Peking: San-lien shu-tien, 1961). Tenancy contracts dating from the eighteenth century are also presented by Imabori Seiji, "Shindai ni okeru kosaku seido ni tsuite," *Tōyō bunka,* 42:57–86 (1967), but in these contracts the acreage is not recorded in mou.

21. The Min-ch'ing sales contract is dated 1577 and published as note 1, p. 158 in Fu I-ling, *Ming Ch'ing nung-ts'un.* The 1558 Yung-an sales contract was published by Fu in "Ming Ch'ing shih-tai Fu-chien tien-nung feng-ch'ao k'ao lüeh," *Fu-chien wen-hua chi-k'an,* 1.1:16 (1941). There is also a sales contract from Yung-an hsien dated 1585 described on pp. 22 and 24 in Fu I-ling, *Ming Ch'ing nung-ts'un.*

22. Fu I-ling, *Ming Ch'ing nung-ts'un,* p. 60.

23. Niida Noboru, *Chūgoku hōsei-shi kenkyū: Tochi-hō torihiki-hō* (Tokyo: University of Tokyo Press, 1960), pp. 551–552. The contract represents a synthesis of the nearly identical contract forms found by Niida in the Ming editions of *Wan-shu tsu-pao, Wan-shu yüan-hai, Wan-yung cheng-tsung* and *Po-lan ch'üan-shu.* On these encyclopedia of daily use, which were somewhat like Western almanacs, see Niida Noboru, "Gen Min no mura kiyaku." Also see his *Chūgoku hōsei-shi kenkyū: dorei nōdo-hō, kazoku sonraku-hō* (Tokyo: University of Tokyo Press, 1962), pp. 742–746, 790–823.

24. In some coastal areas, the land was defined in hillocks or *ch'iu.* See *Ku-t'ien HC,* 1606 ed., 4.20b–32a, and *Fu-ning CC,* 1616 ed., 7.31a.

25. Amano Motonosuke, *Chūgoku nōgyō-shi kenkyū* (Tokyo: Ochanomizu shobō, 1962), p. 303.

26. Amounts of 0.5 tou per mou are recorded for Chiang-lo hsien in 1556; *Yen-p'ing FC,* 1660 ed., 5.16a. *Chang-p'u HC,* 1700 ed., 9.11b–12a; *Hai-ch'eng HC,* 1693 ed., 2.11b.

27. *Ibid.*

28. When there are two different measures, and the second is specifically described as a local measure, it is likely that the first is the abstract "official" unit of measure. For a discussion of official vs. local measures, see Perkins, *Agricultural Development,* pp. 308–311. In this instance, the catty was the local measure, and the *tan* refers to the official measuring unit.

29. According to J. L. Buck, *Land Utilization in China* (Nanking: University of Nanking, 1937), I,198, only 10 per cent of the farms in the rice-tea area had a share-rent system. C. K. Yang also states that in rice-growing Kwangtung, share-rents were not common: C. K. Yang, p. 49.

30. D. K. Lieu, "Land Tenure Systems in China," *Chinese Economic Journal,* 2.6:467 (1928).

31. For Tawney, tenancy and debt seemed to be correlated: *Land and Labour in China* (London: Allen & Unwin, 1932), chap. 3. Most of the Japanese historians listed in the next footnote assume an exploitative situation between landlord and tenant. See Chapter 5, note 5 for further discussion.

32. The system of two levels of land ownership was studied by Niida Noboru, "Shina kinsei no ichi-den ryō-shu kankō to sono

seiritsu," *Hōgaku kyōkai zasshi,* 64.3:129–154, 64.4:241–261 (1946). Niida used Ch'ing gazetteers and twentieth century data. In an interpretive essay, "Chūgoku kinsei no nōmin bōdō — toku ni To Mo-shichi no ran ni tsuite," *Tōyōshi kenkyū,* 30.1:1–13 (1947; reprinted in his *Ajia shi kenkyū,* III, 213–226), Miyazaki Ichisada suggested that the *i-t'ien liang-chu* system was a result of improved conditions resulting from the Teng Mao-ch'i rebellion of 1448–1449. This view was criticized by Shimizu Taiji, "Mindai Fukken no nōka keizai — toku ni ichi-den san-shu no shukō ni tsuite," *Shigaku zasshi,* 63.7:1–21 (1954). Shimizu stressed the tax evasive orientation of the system. Meanwhile, Niida's attempt to trace the origin of the system to Sung times was criticized and rejected by Sudō Yoshiyuki, "Nan Sō no den-kotsu, ya-kotsu, en-kotsu ni tsuite — toku ni 'kai-ten shū-bai' to no kankei," *Tōhōgaku,* 21:73–86 (1961). A Yüan document stipulating the deed rights of the cultivator was subsequently found by Kataoka Shibako, "Fukken no ichi-den ryō-shu sei ni tsuite," *Rekishigaku kenkyū,* no. 294:42–49 (1964). Kataoka differed from earlier writers in linking the development of the system to commercialization of agriculture. The subject has also been treated by Fu I-ling, *Ming Ch'ing nung-ts'un,* who agrees with Miyazaki's hypothesis, p. 49. There may also have been improvements in tenancy conditions independent of the *i-t'ien liang-chu* system: this is suggested by Fu I-ling, "Ming tai Chiang-nan fu-hu ti fen-hsi," *Chung-kuo tzu-pen-chu-i meng-ya wen-t'i t'ao-lun chi,* I,542, who cites contracts from this period which give tenants compensation for work done for their landlords.

33. Niida Noboru, "Shina no ichi-den ryō-shu kankō," pp. 129–130, cites the provinces of Kiangsu, Kiangsi, Fukien, Anhwei, and Chekiang. D. K. Lieu, pp. 457–474, found the system in Kiangsu, Kiangsi, Chekiang, Anhwei, Hunan, and Hupei. The occurrence of this practice in Fukien is described by Hsü T'ien-t'ai, "Fu-chien tsu tien chih-tu yen-chiu," *Fu-chien wen-hua chi-k'an,* 1.1:59–80 (1941). The suggestion that the origins of the system are linked to the labor investment required to prepare land for rice cultivation contradicts Buck's explanation: "The landlords have devised this system of ownership for the purpose of preventing struggle amongst the tenants for obtaining the privilege of renting land and to facilitate the collec-

tion of rents on time and of good quality." Buck, *Farm Ownership and Tenancy in China* (Shanghai, n.d.), pp. 22–23. Fu I-ling offers another explanation (*Ming Ch'ing nung-ts'un,* pp. 49–50): he cites records in Min-ch'ing hsien of peasants who originally pretended to give away land to avoid paying taxes. After a time, the powerful local "protectors" to whom the land had been entrusted became the real landlords, and the original owners could only protect their cultivation rights. Niida's examples are much more directly linked to the *i-t'ien liang-chu* system, and Fu's explanation does not answer why the practice was confined to rice growing regions. I therefore prefer Niida's explanation.

34. Niida Noboru, "Shina no ichi-den ryō-shu kankō," pp. 132–133.

35. *Lung-yen HC,* 1558 ed., 1.46ab; *Hai-ch'eng HC,* 1633 ed., 4.2b–3a; *Chang-chou FC,* 1628 ed., 8.6b–12b.

36. See Niida Noboru, "Shina no ichi-den ryō-shu kankō," for the terms used in each locality.

37. *Ibid.,* pp. 136–138. Pierre Hoang, *Notions techniques sur la propriété en Chine avec un choix d'actes et de documents officiels* (Shanghai, 1897), p. 30, describes the transferral procedure. Besides the sales contract, the bottom soil holder signed a second form, a *hui tsu chü,* which was given to the cultivator to save him the trouble of hunting out the new owner to sign a new act of location. The same procedure was followed when the topsoil right was sold.

38. According to D. K. Lieu, pp. 464–465, the landlord might void the contract under continued failure to pay rent, but Niida Noboru, "Shina no ichi-den ryō-shu kankō," p. 131 shows how strong the tenant's position was, and Muramatsu's study of Kiangsu rentals bears him out. See Chapter Six for detailed discussion.

39. Most explicitly stated in *Ch'ung-an HC,* 1670 ed., 1.19b–20a.

40. Niida Noboru, "Gen Min no mura kiyaku," pp. 140, 143, 147.

41. *Chia-li chien-i,* 1607 ed.; see Niida Noboru, "Gen Min no mura kiyaku," p. 165.

42. The *i-t'ien san-chu* system is described in Niida Noboru, "Shina no ichi-den ryō-shu kankō," Shimizu Taiji, and is amply documented in Ming gazetteers. Into the two-level system described

previously a third party was introduced. The subsoil holder (*hsiao-tsu*) transferred the tax payment obligation to a third person (*ta-tsu*) who received in exchange part of the rent. The tax motivation behind the system is clearly stated: "The wealthy households have much land and so their taxes are heavy. They transfer the land to other people; calculating the tax, they supply these culprits with just enough of the rent to cover the tax payments." *Lung-yen HC,* 1558 ed., 1.46ab. A further elaboration was the farming out of the tax payment to yet another, fourth party, the *pai-tui. Lan-na hu,* powerful households who specialized in tax payments and tax evasion, were often *pai-tui.* The details of these practices appear in most Chang-chou gazetteers from the late sixteenth century on. See *Chang-chou FC,* 1573 ed., 5.6b–7a; 1628 ed., 8.6a–12b. Also described in *Hai-ch'eng HC,* 1633 ed., 4.2b–3a; *Chang-p'u HC,* 1700 ed., 7.47b–50b; *Lung-ch'i HC,* 1762 ed., 5.5b–6a. Most of these citations concern government efforts to abolish the practice, but even in Chang-chou there is a recorded instance of the government as a participant in the system. See the 1609 purchase of the *ta-tsu* (third party) share which went into the school fund, *Chang-p'u HC,* 1700 ed., 9.11b, and *Chang-chou FC,* 1628 ed., 5.26a.

43. Niida Noboru, "Shina no ichi-den ryō-shu kankō," pp. 245, 248. *Yen-p'ing FC,* 1660 ed., 5.13a; *Yu-ch'i HC,* 1636 ed., 3.17a–18a; *Ch'ung-an HC,* 1670 ed., 1.19b–20a.

44. Fu I-ling, *Ming Ch'ing nung-ts'un,* pp. 44–59.

45. Niida Noboru, "Shina no ichi-den ryō-shu kankō," pp. 129–130; *Agrarian China* (Chicago, 1938), p. 25; D. K. Lieu.

46. C. K. Yang, pp. 48–50; *Chiang-su sheng nung-yeh tiao-ch'a lu* (Agricultural Department, Tung-nan University, 1925).

47. Quoted by C. K. Yang, p. 50, who found the same phenomenon in the village he studied, and says T. H. Shen also made the same observation.

48. Fu I-ling, *Ming Ch'ing nung-ts'un,* contract no. 6, pp. 30, 35.

49. For example, Miyazaki Ichisada identifies the *tung-hsi* as a primary cause for the Teng Mao-ch'i rebellion: Miyazaki, "Chūgoku kinsei nōmin bōdō." Fu I-ling lists these fees as some of the "feudal" traits found in Ming and Ch'ing agriculture in "Ming Ch'ing Fu-chien tien-nung" and "Fu-chien tien-nung ching-chi shih ts'ung

k'ao," *Fu-chien hsieh-ho ta-hsüeh wen shih ts'ung k'ao,* no. 2:3–34 (1944). Also Ipponsugi Reiko, "To-sei — Min-moku Shin-sho no Fukken ni okeru," *Shiron,* 1:36–49 (1953). Perhaps it should be stated that neither here, nor in the subsequent discussions of peasant welfare is there any denial of the existence of a group of subsistence level, marginal peasantry, who were heavily in debt and unable to make ends meet; such a group must surely have existed in any period. Instead, the attention of this book is focused on the potential and possible conditions confronting an able, ambitious peasant. That this group also existed in the period is difficult to doubt. The condition of the majority of the peasantry is of course the crucial question. Because Chinese peasants were for the most part free to migrate and did so (see Ho Ping-ti, *Studies on the Population of China, 1368–1953* [Cambridge: Harvard University Press, 1959] Chap. 7), it is possible to argue that the majority must have enjoyed a stable if not slightly rising standard of living in the regions around coastal Fukien and eastern Hunan in the time periods which form the focus for our study. There are, of course, no data to quantify these speculations.

50. Fu I-ling, "Fu-chien tien-nung," pp. 10–14. Shimizu Taiji, pp. 15–16. *Chang-chou FC,* 1628 ed., 8.6b–7a; *Lung-yen HC,* 1558 ed., 1.46ab; *Hai-ch'eng HC,* 1633 ed., 4.2b–3a.

51. Ipponsugi Reiko, p. 38. These fees were also found in other provinces: p. 36. Fu I-ling, "Fu-chien tien-nung," p. 9; *Ming Ch'ing nung-ts'un,* p. 164.

52. Ipponsugi Reiko, p. 37.

53. Tenancy contracts no. 1, p. 24, and no. 3, p. 28 in Fu I-ling, *Ming Ch'ing nung-ts'un.*

54. Fu I-ling, *Ming Ch'ing nung-ts'un,* pp. 60–63, p. 158. By the nineteenth century, the *t'un-hsi* was paid in copper cash.

55. Fu I-ling, *Ming Ch'ing nung-ts'un,* pp. 25, 158.

56. 1714 contract, 1.5 per cent; 1817 contract, 2 per cent of the primary rent payment. Contracts in Fu I-ling, *Ming Ch'ing nung-ts'un,* pp. 60–63.

57. In the 1770 Yu-ch'i rent list (Table 1) they were 3.8 per cent of the rent.

58. Fu I-ling, *Ming Ch'ing nung-ts'un,* p. 64.

59. Fu I-ling, *Ming Ch'ing nung-ts'un,* pp. 36–37. The fact that these were institutionally owned lands may lead to the conclusion that they were special cases: it can be argued that corporately owned lands were never managed as rapaciously as privately owned plots. The difficulty in investigating this issue lies in the absence of comparative material from private holdings. There are several factors which suggest that conclusions based on the data presented in the text may be generally applicable: (1) the practice of permanent tenure made it difficult for landlords to change tenants; the rent was fixed by contract as noted in the text. See Perkins, *Agricultural Development,* p. 104, for an evaluation of the effect of this rent arrangement on productivity. (2) Absentee landownership tended to weaken the landlord's position. This is discussed in Chapter Two. Chapter Six presents modern information on Soochow pertinent to this point. (3) Even in areas in Fukien without permanent tenure, the period of tenure seems to have been long: it was never less than 10 years for rice paddies in the Ming and Ch'ing contracts discovered by Fu I-ling. Again, for the duration of the contract, one can argue that rents were not changed. On the difficulty of introducing new tenants, see Perkins, *Agricultural Development,* pp. 102–103 and Chapter Six.

60. From scattered evidence over the seventeeth and early eighteenth centuries, a Marxist historian also concludes that there was no change in rent levels during this period, and ascribes the lack of movement to stagnant productivity conditions: Ch'en Chen-han, "Ming-mo Ch'ing-ch'u (1620–1720) Chung-kuo ti nung-yeh laotung sheng-ch'an lü, ti-tsu ho t'u-ti chi-chung," *Chung-kuo tzu-pen-chu-i meng-ya wen-t'i t'ao-lun chi* (Peking: San-lien shu-tien, 1957), I,279.

61. Fu I-ling, *Ming Ch'ing nung-ts'un,* p. 63.

62. From the *Min-ch'ing HC,* chüan 7: "In Ming times many rich families in the province collected rents here, and they built houses and temporarily dwelt here. After a long time their descendants set up households here." Cited by Fu I-ling, *Ming Ch'ing nung-ts'un,* p. 65.

63. Fu I-ling, *Ming Ch'ing nung-ts'un,* p. 64.

64. *Ch'ung-an HC,* 1670 ed., 1.19b–20a.

Chapter Three / FACTORS IN RICE CULTIVATION

1. See Ramon Myers, *The Chinese Peasant Economy: Agricultural Development in Hopei and Shantung, 1880–1949* (Cambridge: Harvard University Press, 1970), particularly pp. 192–194. The assertion in this chapter, which underlies the whole study, namely that commerce and the peasant economy were closely linked, has been extensively explored by students of Tokugawa economic history. Recent work, reviewed by Susan B. Hanley and Kozo Yamamura, "A Quiet Transformation in Tokugawa Economic History," *Journal of Asian Studies,* 30.2:373–384 (1971), includes investigations of increasing commercialization and rising output in Japanese agriculture. The conclusion of Chapter 2, that Chinese peasants, both owner-tillers and tenants, shared in the economic gains from increased agricultural productivity is echoed in the Tokugawa studies. As Hanley and Yamamura conclude (p. 374), "The most significant and obvious consensus emerging is that the Tokugawa economy grew steadily throughout the entire period (1600–1868) and that the peasant class was not excluded from the benefits derived from this growth."

2. R. H. Tawney, Chapter Three.

3. *Lung-yen HC,* 1558 ed., 2.60a.

4. Dwight Perkins, *Agricultural Development,* p. 41.

5. *Economic Geography of South China,* p. 382.

6. There are exceptions to this generalization and to Buck's regional categories: Lin Yüeh-hwa, in a novelistic treatment of his own village, located in Ku-t'ien hsien, Fu-chou prefecture, describes how the villagers grew two crops of rice a year, using the interplanting method. *The Golden Wing: A Sociological Study of Chinese Familism* (London: Kegan Paul, Trench, Trubner & Co., 1948), pp. 74–75.

7. Buck, *Land Utilization,* I,74–75.

8. *Ibid.,* p. 75, p. 84.

9. Hung Fu, "Land Utilization Maps of Fukien Province with Notes on the Physical Environment in Its Bearing upon Land-use and the Distribution of Population," *Tsing-hua University Science Reports. Series C: Geological and geographical series,* 1.1:21 (1936).

10. C. K. Yang, p. 30.

11. Buck, *Land Utilization,* I,216.

12. *San shan chih,* 41.1b. Sudō Yoshiyuki comments extensively on Fukien rice growing practices in "Nan Sō inesaku no chiiki sei," *Sōdai keizai-shi kenkyū* (Tokyo: Tokyo University Press, 1962), pp. 154–155, 169–173, p. 196. On the introduction of Champa rice to Fukien, see Ho Ping-ti, "Early Ripening Rice in Chinese History," *Economic History Review,* second series, 9.2:200–218 (1956). Its role in stimulating the terracing of hills in Fukien is described by Ho in *Huang-t'u yü Chung-kuo nung-yeh ti ch'i-yüan* (Hong Kong: Chinese University of Hong Kong, 1969), pp. 99–101.

13. *P'u-ch'eng HC,* 1650 ed., 4.8a.

14. *Economic Geography of South China,* p. 382.

15. Dwight Perkins, *Agricultural Development,* p. 45.

16. Ho Ping-ti, *Studies on the Population of China,* pp. 163–164, 167–168.

17. Fu I-ling, "Fu-chien tien-nung," p. 5. Contract forms are presented by Niida Noboru, "Gen Min no mura kiyaku," p. 165.

18. Katō Shigeshi, "Keizai-shi jō yori mitaru Kita Shina to Minami Shina," *Shakai keizai shigaku,* 12.11–12:4 (1943). Amano Motonosuke, "Mindai nōgyō no tenkai," *Shakai keizai shigaku,* 23.5–6:26 (1958).

19. Fu I-ling, *Ming Ch'ing nung-ts'un,* pp. 60–62.

20. Fu I-ling, *Ming Ch'ing nung-ts'un,* p. 24.

21. Fu I-ling, *Ming Ch'ing nung-ts'un,* pp. 24, 25, 28–32, 158.

22. See Amano Motonosuke, "Mindai nōgyō," pp. 21–22 on Ming developments in tools. For a brief discussion and illustrations of Sung tools, see Amano Motonosuke, "Chin Fu no nōsho to suitōsaku gijutsu no tenkai," *Tōhōgakuhō,* no. 19:23–64 (1950), and no. 21:37–133 (1952). On Sung rice cultivation see Sudō Yoshiyuki, *Sōdai keizai-shi kenkyū,* pp. 73–138 and pp. 139–206. The subject is also treated in Amano Motonosuke, *Chūgoku nōgyō-shi,* pp. 211–256. Ming developments are treated in pp. 278–332.

23. The mou measure remained constant (Wu Ch'eng-lo, *Chung-kuo tu-liang-heng shih,* Shanghai, Commercial Press, 1937, pp. 75–76), but the Sung picul measure was smaller than the Ming picul, so that 1 Sung picul = 0.64 Ming piculs (Wu, Table 5). As a re-

sult, the Sung yield of 3 shih (Amano Motonosuke, *Chūgoku nōgyō-shi,* pp. 255–256) was equivalent to a Ming yield of 2.02 piculs per mou (of husked rice). When converted to husked rice, the highest Ming yield for Fukien is 4 piculs per mou (Hai-ch'eng hsien, recorded in *Chang-chou FC,* 1573 ed., 5.53a), which is about twice the Sung figure. The *Chang-chou FC* discusses local and standard measures: this would be the "official" measure.

24. A total of 31 Ming editions and various Ch'ing editions was canvassed for information on seeds. These included two provincial gazetteers, at least one prefectural gazetteer for each prefecture in Fukien, and 24 hsien gazetteers of Ming and early Ch'ing date.

25. *Chin-chou* seed, found in Fu-chou: *Min shu,* 150.1a; *Fu-chou FC,* 1596 ed., 8.1a; 1613 ed., 37.1a. This seed had been used in Sung times. *T'u-lun: Fu-chou FC,* 1596 ed., 37.1a–b; this grew on the plains. *Min shu,* 150.1a also lists this seed. *Huang-mang: Fu-chou FC,* 1596 ed., 8.1a; 1613 ed., 37.1a–b; *Min shu,* 150.1a–*b. Fen-ch'ih tsao: Fu-ning CC,* 1593 ed., 1.43a; *Fu-an HC,* 1597 ed., 1.19a.

26. Out of 77 nonglutinous rice seeds, 38 of them, or 49 per cent, were Champa. For the coastal area, the figure is 17 out of 47, or 36 per cent of the total.

27. Sudō Yoshiyuki, *Sōdai keizai-shi,* pp. 158–159. He quotes a memorial on granaries to show that *keng* rice was stipulated for general military supplies as well as for rents and taxes. Sudō's discovery of late-ripening Champa strains in Sung pushes the date of this development several centuries earlier than seems to be generally known: see Ho Ping-ti, *Studies on the Population of China,* p. 174, which ascribes this to "Ming times at the latest."

28. Some gazetteers divided rice into just two categories: nonglutinous rice, which was eaten, and glutinous rice, used to make wine. See *Min shu,* 150.1a; *Fu-chou FC,* 1596 ed., 8.1a; *Ch'üan-chou FC,* 1612 ed., 3.38b–40b; *T'ing-chou FC,* 1637 ed., 4.8a. On the warehouses, see *Kuo ch'ao tien-hui,* chüan 101. Chüan 97 has information on grain transport.

The Ch'ing government also made no distinction in collection of tribute rice between the *hsien* (early ripening rice) and *keng* (late ripening) varieties: see the grain transport section in *Chechiang t'ung-chih,* 1934 reprint of 1899 ed., p. 1507.

29. *Yin-shih shu,* 1.4a.

30. Both seeds were found in Chien-ning fu: *Chien-yang HC,* 1607 ed., 3.26a–27a.

31. *Ibid.*

32. *Ch'üan-chou FC,* 1612 ed., 3.38b–40b. See Ho Ping-ti, *Studies on the Population of China,* pp. 172–174.

33. Both are cited in *Chien-yang HC,* 1607 ed., 3.26a–27a; the *Lan-ni tsao* (Soft Mud) is also cited in *Min shu,* 150.2a–b, and *Chien-ning FC,* 1541 ed., 13.1a–2a.

34. "The seed comes from the Liao and Man (barbarians) who in the deep mountains and fertile spots fell trees and burn them to profit from the fertility. In two or three years, the fertility wears thin, and they move elsewhere." *Hai-ch'eng HC,* 1633 ed., 11.10a–11a. Also cited in *Ch'üan-chou FC,* 1612 ed., 3.38b–40b; *Min shu,* 150.1a–2a; *Chang-chou FC,* 1628 ed., 27.1a–b; *Hsing-hua FC,* 1503 ed., 13.1a–2a. Although *She* in this context refers to the She people, the term is used in T'ang texts to describe a method of tillage. See Ho Ping-ti, *Huang-t'u yü Chung-kuo nung-yeh,* pp. 98–99.

35. "The soaked seed's seed-cover is slightly broken and the seed is put into the ground. When the seed sprouts it is taken out. It ripens with the Red Late; in the more brackish of alkaline soils, it does well." *Ch'üan-chou FC,* 1612 ed., 3.38b–40b; *Min shu,* 150.1b–2a.

36. *T'ien-hsiang tsao: Chien-ning FC,* 1541 ed., 13.1a–2a; *Chien-yang HC,* 1607 ed., 3.26a–27a; *Min shu,* 150.2a–b; *Yen-p'ing FC,* 1660 ed., 4.1a. *Ta-tung: Fu-chou FC,* 1596 ed., 8.1a; 1613 ed., 37.1a–b; *Pa Min t'ung-chih,* 25.1a–b; *Ch'üan-chou FC,* 1612 ed., 3.38b–40b; *Min shu,* 150.1b–2a. *Erh-shou:* "Planted in the warm spring on the plains, it ripens in autumn; planted again in the autumn, it ripens in the winter." *Yu-ch'i HC,* 1636 ed., 4.7a–8a.

37. *Te-hua HC,* 1687 ed., 2.7b–8a.

38. The dated references to the "Lodger" seed in the 1573 ed. of *Chang-chou FC,* 13.9a–b, and the 1612 ed. of *Ch'üan-chou FC,* 3.38b–40b, predate Amano Motonosuke's earliest citation of the interplanting method, from "Nung-t'ien yü-hua," dated 1615: "Mindai nōgyō," pp. 23–24. Amano discusses the Lodger seed in *Chūgoku nōgyō-shi,* p. 331, using later editions of Fukien gazetteers.

39. Sources noted in note 36. Yield information in *Fu-ch'ing HC,* 2.2a–8b.

40. *Hsing-hua FC,* 1503 ed., 13.2a.

41. Ch'üan Han-sheng, "Nan Sung tao-mi ti sheng-ch'an yü yün-hsiao," *Li-shih yü-yen yen-chiu so chi-k'an,* 10:403–431 (1942).

42. Information on consumption in *Shou-ning HC,* 1637 ed., 1.49a. On the sweet potato, see *Hui-an hsien hsü-chih,* 1612 ed., 1.30b–32b. On rice price trends in Ming, see P'eng Hsin-wei, II, 459. Also Miyazaki Ichisada, "Chūgoku kinsei gin mondai ryaku-setsu," *Ajia shi kenkyū* (Kyoto, 1963), III, 245.

43. E-tu Sun and Shiou-chuan Sun, p. 6.

44. Amano Motonosuke, *Chūgoku nōgyō-shi,* p. 309.

45. *Min shu,* 38.3b.

46. *Chang-chou FC,* 1573 ed., 11.43b–44b.

47. *Ibid.*

48. E-tu Sun and Shiou-chuan Sun, p. 19.

49. The case of Soochow farmers who chose to grow the older *keng* grain rather than the new Champa is described in the section on handicrafts in this chapter. The relationship of labor and fertilizer inputs to the market price is made explicit in a discussion describing the effects of a low rice price: tenants calculating the cultivation costs against the low market price reduced the amount of fertilizer and labor expended on the crop, with a consequent diminution of yield. In this way, concluded the writer, a low rice price was hurtful to agriculture. *Ning-hsiang HC,* 1867 ed., 24.8b.

50. See Terada Takanobu, "Mindai Soshū nōka keizai."

51. *Hsing-hua FC,* 1503 ed., 12.10a. On the textile trade in general, see Maeda Katsutarō, "Min Shin no Fukken ni okeru nōka fukugyō," *Suzuki Shun kyōju kanreki kinen Tōyōshi ronsō* (Tokyo: Sanyo-sha, 1964), pp. 573–574.

52. *Hsing-hua FC,* 1503 ed., 12.10a.

53. *Te-hua HC,* 1687 ed., 2.1b, 2.7b–8a.

54. *Ibid.,* 2.7b. Government officials sometimes tried to prevent local rice from being shipped to markets outside the hsien. A 1595–1596 example from Fu-an hsien, Fu-ning chou, is provided in *Shih-cheng lu,* 1.26a–30b, 1.39a–42a. Others adopted a laissez-faire policy. In Ch'üan-chou prefecture, which depended on rice imports,

1606 was a bad year. The prefectural authorities were troubled by the high rice prices resulting from a poor harvest but decided to let the market price prevail with the view that by thus encouraging merchants to import more rice, the price would eventually fall. *Ch'üan-nan tsa-chih,* 2.13b. Perhaps the most striking example of rice marketing is provided by Fei Hsiao-tung's and Chang Chih-i's study of Yi-ts'un, a village in Yunnan, whose villagers took their rice and sold it, then went to a cheaper market elsewhere to buy rice for their own consumption: Fei Hsiao-t'ung and Chang Chih-i, p. 152.

55. *Shou-ning HC,* 1637 ed., 1.43a.

56. Fu I-ling, *Ming Ch'ing nung-ts'un,* pp. 60–63.

57. For historical background, see Katō Shigeshi, "Shina ni okeru kansho oyobi satō no kigen ni tsuite," *Shina keizai-shi kōshō* (Tokyo: Tōyō bunko, 1953), II, 676–677.

58. *Hsing-hua FC,* 1503 ed., 12.11a–b.

59. *Ibid.,* 13.10b.

60. Maeda Katsutarō, "Min Shin no Fukken," p. 576.

61. *Lung-yen HC,* 1689 ed., 2.26b–27a. *Yung-an HC,* chüan 9, cited by Fu I-ling, *Ming Ch'ing nung-ts'un,* p. 27. In Ch'ing times, P'u-ch'eng tobacco was quite famous. See citation in Li Wen-chih, "Ch'ing-tai ya-p'ien chan-cheng ch'ien ti ti-tsu, shang-yeh tzu-pen, kao-li tai yü nung-min sheng-huo," *Chung-kuo tzu-pen-chu-i meng-ya wen-t'i t'ao-lun chi* (Peking: San-lien shu-tien, 1957), II, 624, 625.

62. *Ibid.* Li Wen-chih, p. 625, presents a citation comparing rice cultivation with tobacco and calculating the increased rice yields which could be obtained were the fertilizer and labor devoted to tobacco cultivation switched to rice.

63. E-tu Sun and Shiou-chuan Sun, pp. 124–125.

64. Lychee is omitted from this discussion although it was an important cash crop, because it seems to have been grown on ridges, along canals and streams, and in spots where it is difficult to discuss alternative land use. See Ochse et al., p. 728. Maeda Katsutarō "Min Shin no Fukken," discusses many of the specialized local cash crops grown in Fukien.

65. Ochse et al., pp. 1141–1142. Two to three crops a year of

ramie are cited in *T'ien-kung k'ai-wu:* E-tu Sun and Shiou-chuan Sun, pp. 63–64; four crops a year are cited in *Chien-yang HC,* 1607 ed., 3.26a–27a. On ramie cloth, see Maeda Katsutarō, "Min Shin no Fukken," pp. 554–555. According to the *Chin-chiang HC,* 1765 ed., 1.51b, ramie cloth was woven in the mountain districts, rarely in towns.

66. L. H. Bailey, *The Standard Cyclopedia of Horticulture* (New York: Macmillan, 1929), pp. 1645–1646. E-tu Sun and Shiou-chuan Sun, pp. 75–76.

67. *Yin-shih shu,* 5.28a–30b has a general discussion of Fukien tea. *Chien-yang HC,* 1607 ed., 3.26a–27a is the source of the inforation in the text. Tea was also grown in the hills in coastal areas: *Ch'üan-chou FC,* 1612 ed., 3.43b–44b.

68. Bailey, p. 245; E-tu Sun and Shiou-chuan Sun, p. 216.

69. *An-ch'i HC,* 1757 ed., 4.6a.

70. In Chang-chou, Ch'üan-chou, and parts of Fu-chou, barley was a third crop in the annual planting cycle, grown after the second rice harvest: *Fu-ch'ing HC,* 2.2a–8b; *Ch'üan-chou FC,* 1612 ed., 3.38b–40b; *Chang-chou FC,* 1573 ed., 13.9ab.

71. *Economic Geography of East China,* ed. by Sun Ching-chih. Joint Publications Research Service translation (Washington, 1961), p. 10.

72. At least in modern times, the farmers in this area owned their own boats, although they entrusted goods for sale to "agent boats." Fei Hsiao-t'ung, *Pleasant Life in China: A Field Study of Country Life in the Yangtze Valley* (London: Routledge & Kegan Paul, Ltd., 1939), pp. 123, 254–256.

73. Sudō Yoshiyuki, *Sōdai keizai-shi,* pp. 139–161, 187.

74. Amano Motonosuke, "Mindai nōgyō," pp. 24, 26.

75. Shen Ch'i, *Shen-shih nung-shu* (1643), and Chang Lü-hsiang, *Pu nung shu* (1658), were combined and published under the title *Pu nung shu* in 1871 as part of Chang's collected writings. Described in Amano Motonosuke, *Chūgoku nōgyō-shi,* pp. 288–289 and in Ch'en Heng-li, p. 1. See Furushima Kazuo, "Min-matsu Chōkō deruta ni okeru jinushi keiei — Shin-shi nōsho no ichi kōsatsu," *Rekishigaku kenkyū,* 148:11–23 (1950), and "Ho nō-sho no seiritsu to sono jiban," *Tōyō bunka kenkyū-jo kiyō,* 3:18–117 (1952). Both

Shen and Chang were natives of Chekiang province, from areas close to Soochow, and market conditions in Soochow could not have been very different from those described in their books. The Soochow economy in mid-Ming times was a major focus for many scholars interested in the "sprouts of capitalism" theory: see the articles by Hsü Ta-ling, Hung Huan-ch'un, Li Kuang-pi, Fu I-ling in *Chung-kuo tzu-pen-chu-i meng-ya wen-t'i t'ao-lun chi.*

76. Ch'en Heng-li, p. 26.

77. All of the Soochow yield figures are in husked rice.

78. Ch'en Heng-li, p. 49.

79. Alternate farm plans drawn up by the two writers are compared in Ch'en Heng-li, p. 91.

80. Calculations are presented in Furushima Kazuo, "Min-matsu Chōkō deruta," p. 20, and in Ch'en Heng-li, p. 93.

81. See Wang Chung-lo, I,12; Fu I-ling "Ming tai Chiang-nan fu-hu," pp. 22–24; and Li Kuang-pi, I,36, 38. On silk and cotton weaving, see Terada Takanobu, "Mindai Soshū nōka keizai": he concludes that by the end of Ming, subsidiary handicrafts were as important as basic farming to the Soochow peasant economy. See Miyazaki Ichisada, "Mindai So-Shō chihō no shi-dai-fu to min-shū — Mindai shisō-byō no kokoromi," *Shirin,* 37.3:1–33 (1954). Although cotton replaced rice as the major crop in eastern Kiangsu, it was little grown in Soochow. But Amano Motonosuke, *Chūgoku nōgyō-shi,* has numerous citations on cotton weaving in Soochow from Ming times into the 1930's: pp. 516, 557, 558, 559, 563.

82. This was true from Sung times: Ch'üan Han-sheng, pp. 404–409.

83. Ch'en Heng-li, pp. 91–92.

84. This excludes the cost of her food, calculated at 5 liang a year: Furushima Kazuo, "Min-matsu Chōkō deruta," p. 20.

85. Ch'üan Han-sheng, pp. 413–415, 422–429; Shiba Yoshinobu, "Sōdai ni okeru Fukken shōnin to sono shakai keizai teki haikei," *Wada hakase kōki kinen Tōyōshi ronsō* (Tokyo: Kodansha, 1960), p. 489. Also Maeda Katsutarō, "Min Shin no Fukken," p. 569, who argues, p. 572, that the high rents forced peasants to turn to supplementary industries.

86. Shiba Yoshinobu, "Sōdai Fukken shōnin."

Chapter Four / MARKET STIMULUS AND ECONOMIC CHANGE

1. Neither this chapter on Fukien nor the subsequent chapter on Hunan is intended to be an economic geography; only selected areas are compared and other areas are ignored or mentioned only to illustrate a point.

2. Ernest B. Price, "Transportation and Public Works," *Fukien, A Study of a Province in China* (Shanghai: Presbyterian Mission Press, 1925), p. 72. For a detailed description of Fukien topography, see Sun Ching-chih, pp. 341–349.

3. Chao Yüan-jen, in "Languages and Dialects in China," *Geographical Journal,* 102.2:964–965 (1943), finds two dialect areas: the Fu-chou dialect area in north Fukien, and the Amoy-Swatow dialect area in the south. Floy Hurlbut adds another, the northwest part of the province, where a form of Mandarin is spoken which is also the dialect of the contiguous Kiangsi region. Hurlbut, *The Fukienese: A Study in Human Geography* (Ph. D. diss., University of Nebraska. Published by the author, May 1930), p. 63. This area in fact enjoys its closest relations with Kiangsi rather than with the rest of Fukien.

4. Sixteenth century guidebooks, some of them written by merchants and all intended for merchants, provided the information on these routes. Five texts were used as primary sources for this topic: the earliest in date (1570) is the *I-t'ung lu-ch'eng t'u-chi* (Maps and records of the itineraries of the empire) compiled by a Hsin-an merchant, Huang P'ei, held by the Naikaku bunko in Tokyo. The *Shang-ch'eng i-lan* (Survey of commercial routes) was printed in Fukien and is perhaps contemporaneous with the first; it is also at the Naikaku bunko. The *Shui-lu lu-ch'eng* (Itinerary of water and overland routes), dated cyclically *ting-i* (1557–58 or 1617–18) is held by the Sonkeikaku bunko in Tokyo. The last two texts are portions of larger works: chüan 19 and 20 of the small geography entitled *Kuang huang yü k'ao* (Geography of the empire), preface dated 1626–1627, and chüan 2 of the "popular" encyclopedia *Wan-yung cheng-tsung* (A multi-purpose "how to do it" guide.) Both are held by the Naikaku bunko.

5. River systems are described in G. Cressey, *Land of the 500 Million* (New York: McGraw-Hill, 1955), pp. 86–87, 210; Hurlbut, p. 6; and Sun Ching-chih, pp. 347–349.

6. *T'ien-kung k'ai-wu,* the Japanese edition, edited by Yabuuchi Kiyoshi (Tokyo, 1953), p. 446 (p. 179 in the Sun translation). Stanley Wright lists the types of junks used in twentieth century Kiangsi, along with their tonnage, normal runs, and cargoes, in *Kiangsi Native Trade and Its Taxation* (Shanghai, 1920), p. 4, and provides ample evidence of the great specialization in craft. He attributes modifications in boat size and type to the depth and nature of particular streams, but G. Worcester, *The Junks and Sampans of the Yangtze* (2 vols.; Shanghai: Inspectorate General of Customs, 1947), II, 249–250, has suggested that minimization of tax payments, which were based on hull measurement, also acted as a powerful incentive influencing boat design.

7. Hurlbut, p. 9.

8. Samuel Ball, *An Account of the Cultivation and Manufacture of Tea in China* (London: Longman, Brown, Green and Longman, 1848), pp. 352–353, 356. Since Ball was inspector of teas for the East India Company in China, his cost estimates should be reliable. Because there were no technological changes in inland travel, the comparative cost differences were probably not so different for the Ming dynasty, but we have no information on the topic. Actually the cost comparison lay between shipping tea to Canton or Fu-chou, since at either port the tea could then be loaded onto ships for passage to England: the ocean distance between Canton and Fu-chou was so negligible a part of the total cost of shipment from the tea country to England that it is not discussed by Ball. In addition to the savings in transport cost, Ball (pp. 352–353, 356) states that the Fu-chou route was much faster: it took only four or five days to ship tea from the Bohea country to Fu-chou, as opposed to the six weeks to two months involved in shipments on the overland route to Canton.

9. Robert Fortune, *The Tea-Districts of China and India* (2 vols.; London: John Murray, 1853), I, 220–221.

10. Galeote Pereira, p. 8, in C. R. Boxer, ed., *South China in the Sixteenth Century* (London: Hakluyt Society, 1953), whose account of the excellence of this coastal highway is corroborated by later

European observers: Martin de Rada and Cornelius Ryerson, pp. 8, 254 in the same book. A nineteenth century Commissioner of Imperial Maritime Customs at Amoy described this road as "the only practicable one for commerce, which exists in all this region." George Hughes, *Amoy and the Surrounding Districts* (Hong Kong: de Souza & Co., 1872), p. 78.

11. See note 3 in this chapter.

12. Henry Yule, *The Book of Ser Marco Polo* (New York: Charles Scribner's Sons, 1903), pp. 218–246. Price, p. 73.

13. Miyazaki Ichisada, *Tōyōteki kinsei* (Osaka, 1950), p. 57; *Min shu,* 39.29b–30a.

14. Wu Kuang-ch'ing, "Ming Printing and Printers," *Harvard Journal of Asiatic Studies,* 7.3:209 (1943). Hsü Ta-ling, "Shih-liu shih-chi, shih-ch'i shih-chi ch'u-ch'i Chung-kuo feng-chien she-hui nei-pu tzu-pen-chu-i ti meng-ya," *Chung-kuo tzu-pen-chu-i meng-ya wen-t'i t'ao-lun chi,* II,903, 904; Li Kuang-pi, "Ming tai shou-kung-yeh ti fa-chan," p. 42 in vol. I of the same work.

15. *Shou-ning HC,* 1637 ed., 1.54b–55a. Silver was mined in this region at various points in the Ming dynasty, and a quota levy was collected by the government. These are recorded in *Chien-ning FC,* 1541 ed., 14.6a–b, 14.15a, 14.19b–20a, 14.28b, 14.35b, 14.40b, 14.45b, 14.50a, and 14.56a.

16. Kuwabara Jitsuzō, "On P'u Shou-keng, a Man of the Western Regions who was the Superintendent of the Trading Ships Office in Ch'üan-chou towards the end of the Sung dynasty, together with a general sketch of (the) trade of the Arabs in China during the T'ang and Sung eras," *Memoirs of the Research Department of the Tōyō Bunko,* no. 2:1–79 (1928) and no. 7:1–102 (1935).

17. J. J. L. Duyvendak, "The True Dates of the Chinese Maritime Expeditions in the Early Fifteenth Century," *T'oung Pao,* 34:341–342 (1939).

18. *Pa Min t'ung-chih,* 25.2a–3a, 26.1a–b, 26.6a, 26.18a–b. For sugar exports see Fu I-ling, *Ming Ch'ing shih-tai shang-jen chi shang-yeh tzu-pen* (Peking: Jen min ch'u-pan she, 1956), p. 148; Emma H. Blair and James A. Robertson, *The Philippine Islands, 1492–1898* (3 vols.; Cleveland: Arthur H. Clark Co., 1903), III, 287. Sugar was taken to Bantam and Batavia and refined there; see M. A. P. Meilink-Roelofsz, *Asian Trade and European Influence in the Indo-*

nesian Archipelago between 1500 and about 1630 (The Hague: Martinus Nijhoff, 1962), p. 258. Some of it is said to have eventually reached the Netherlands. Ts'ao Yung-ho, "Chinese Overseas Trade in the late Ming Period," *Proceedings: Second Biennial Conference of the International Association of Historians of Asia* (Taipei, 1962), p. 451.

Fruit was a commercial specialty of Fukien by Sung times: see Shiba Yoshinobu, "Sōdai Fukken shōnin," p. 490. As a Ming product it is described in *Pa Min t'ung-chih, chüan* 25–26, and *Min shu,* 38.2a, and chüan 150. On lychee, see Maeda Katsutarō, "Min Shin no Fukken," p. 579. According to *Min shu,* 150.12b, Hsing-hua produced the best lychee and Fu-chou the greatest quantities. It was grown in all of the coastal prefectures.

19. As the prefectural gazetteer puts it: "The marketing of cloth is the primary category of man-made products in Chang-chou." *Chang-chou FC,* 1573 ed., 1.15b. On textiles, see 13.19b–20a. Dyes are listed on 13.20a–21a. Silk weaving is described by Saeki Yūichi, "Mindai shōyaku-sei no hōkai to toshi kinu orimono-gyō shijō no tenkai," *Tōyō bunka kenkyū-jo kiyō,* 10:385–386 (1956). Cotton textiles are discussed by Nishijima Sadao, "Mindai ni okeru momen no fukyū ni tsuite," *Shigaku zasshi,* 57.4:203 (1948), and 57.5:41 (1948); by Maeda Katsutarō, "Min Shin no Fukken," pp. 573–574.

20. Fu I-ling, *Ming Ch'ing shih-tai shang-jen,* p. 148. *Chang-chou FC,* 1573 ed., 23a–b in chüan 5, part 2, discusses the government levy on iron.

21. The kilns were in Chang-p'ing and P'ing-ho hsien: *Chang-chou FC,* 1573 ed., 1.16a. In Japan these wares were called "Gosu-aka-e." Hayashida Seizo and Gakuji Hasebe, *Chinese Ceramics,* tr. Charles A. Pomeroy (Tokyo: Tuttle, 1966), p. 86. See Fu I-ling, *Ming Ch'ing shih-tai shang-jen,* pp. 147–148. Ku Ching-yen, "Ming tai tz'u-ch'i ti hai-wai mao-i," *Chung-kuo tzu-pen-chu-i meng-ya wen-t'i t'ao-lun chi,* I,50, describes the importation of ceramic wares into Nagasaki on ships from Fu-chou and Chang-chou.

22. Meilink-Roelofsz, p. 258.

23. Cited by Katayama Seijirō, "Gekkō nijū-shi shō no han-ran," *Shimizu hakase tsuitō kinen Mindai shiron sō* (Tokyo: Dai-an, 1962), p. 391.

24. The Ming dynasty followed customary practice in forbidding

trade outside tributary channels, so the junk trade described in the text was also clandestine.

25. Gaspar da Cruz, tr. in Boxer, *South China,* p. 192. The *Shih-lu* references, dated 1524, 1525, 1533, and 1534 are cited by Fu I-ling, *Ming Ch'ing shih-tai shang-jen,* pp. 108–109. Cheng Jo-ts'eng, *Ch'ou ch'ung-pien,* cited by Liang Fang-chung, "Ming-tai kuo-chi mao-i yü yin ti shu ch'u-ju," *Chung-kuo she-hui ching-chi shih chi-k'an,* 6.2:290 (1939), footnote. Other contemporary sources cited by Fu I-ling, *Ming Ch'ing shih-tai shang-jen,* pp. 109–112.

26. Katayama Seijirō, "Mindai kaijō mitsu-bōeki to enkai chihō gōshinsō — 'Chu Wan' no kai-kin seisaku kyōkō to sono zasetsu no katei o tōshite no ichi kōsatsu," *Rekishigaku kenkyū,* 164:23–32 (1953); Sakuma Shigeo, "Mindai kai-gai shi-bōeki no rekishiteki haikei — Fukken shō o chūshin to shite," *Shigaku zasshi,* 62.1:1–25 (1953); Sakuma, "Min-chō no kai-kin seisaku," *Tōhōgaku,* 6:42–51 (1953); Kobata Atsushi, "Mindai Shō Sen-nin no kai-gai tsūshō hatten, toku ni Kaichō no shozei-sei to Nichi-Min bōeki ni tsuite," *Tōa ronsō,* 4:125–169 (1941), examine the illegal trade. From the Portuguese side, there is Chang T'ien-tse, *Sino-Portuguese Trade from 1514 to 1644* (Leiden: Brill, 1934), and translations of Portuguese accounts in Boxer, *South China.*

27. The voyage of Garcia de Loaisa (1525–1526), p. 35, in Blair and Robertson. A Chinese description of the expansion in trade with Luzon after the Spanish settlement describes the initial returns to investment as "several-fold"; see *Min shu,* 39.34 a–b.

28. Edgar Wickberg, *The Chinese in Philippine Life, 1850–1898* (New Haven: Yale University Press, 1965), pp. 6, 80. C. R. Boxer, "The Manila Galleon, 1565–1815," *History Today,* 8.8:546 (1958).

29. C. R. Boxer, *Fidalgos in the Far East, 1550–1770* (The Hague: Martinus Nijhoff, 1948), pp. 12–13.

30. Liang Fang-chung, "Ming tai kuo-chi mao-i," p. 308.

31. In Chu's collected works, *P'i yü chi,* 2.16b–17a. The opening of Hai-ch'eng as a legalized trading port specifically excluded trade with the Japanese, but Sino-Japanese commerce seems to have flourished: see *Hui-an hsien hsü-chih,* 1612 ed., 1.41a–b. The studies cited in note 26 present details on Ch'üan-chou and Chang-chou trading activities. For information on Chinese traders living abroad, see Iwao Seiichi, "Li Tan, Chief of the Chinese Residents at Hirado:

Japan in the Last Days of the Ming Dynasty," *Memoirs of the Research Department of the Tōyō Bunko,* no. 17:26–83 (1958). In addition to previously cited studies of Chinese trade with the Philippines, there is Wu Ching-hong, "The Rise and Decline of Ch'üan-chou's International Trade and Its Relation to the Philippine Islands," *Proceedings: Second Biennial Conference of International Association of Historians of Asia,* pp. 469–483; see also Chao Ch'üan-ch'eng, "A Ship's Voyage from Luzon to China in the Eighteenth Century," in Sun and de Francis, tr., *Chinese Social History* (Washington: American Council of Learned Societies, 1956), pp. 353–360.

32. These markets are all *shih.*

33. The 0.5 per cent growth rate estimate is taken from Dwight Perkins, *Agricultural Development,* p. 24. Problems attached to using Chinese population records are discussed in the appendix. What is meant by a natural increase of population in this section is the rate of population growth to be expected under conditions of normalcy: peace and ordinary economic activity, but no unusual increase in the economic stimuli. It is of course obvious that "boom" conditions bring with them correspondingly abnormal rates of population growth; the California gold rush is an example of very high rates of population increase resulting from migration into the gold fields. To a less dramatic degree, any flourishing economy attracts migrants from less prosperous environs, and it is very likely that in Chang-chou too in-migration occurred to swell the local population. For analytic purposes, however, it is important to distinguish between the demographic increase which would have occurred without the stimulus of expanding foreign trade and the probable population increase which resulted from the new prosperity. That is what this calculation attempts to do.

34. *Chang-chou FC,* 1573 ed., 12.13a–b. On the continued presence of the Japanese in the 1560's, see *Huang Ming chih-fang t'u,* second chüan, 52a–53a. Hai-ch'eng was established after an abortive rebellion in the area; see Katayama Seijirō, "Gekkō no han-ran," pp. 389–419.

35. These subdistricts are called *tu. Pa Min t'ung-chih,* 14.14b–15b; *Chang-chou FC,* 1573 ed., 2.15b, 12.27b, 19.12b, 21.12a, 23.13b, 25.8b, 27.8a, 29.9a, 30.11a, 31.5b; 1628 ed., 29.9a–10b.

36. *Hai-ch'eng HC,* 1633 ed., 11.14b.

37. E-tu Sun and Shiou-chuan Sun, p. 60.

38. *Chang-chou FC,* 1628 ed., 27.2a–b. Chang-chou silk weavers also adopted techniques from Chekiang which are noted in this source.

39. Charles Singer, E. J. Holmyard, A. R. Hall, and Trevor I. Williams, eds., *A History of Technology* (Oxford: Clarendon Press, 1957), III, 42. On its impact in Europe see John U. Nef, "Mining and Metallurgy in Medieval Civilization," in M. M. Postan and E. E. Rich, eds., *The Cambridge Economic History,* vol. II, *Trade and Industry in the Middle Ages* (Cambridge: Cambridge University Press, 1952), p. 463. Although Japanese silver production began to increase in the 1530's, the great and sustained expansion of output came in the late sixteenth and seventeenth centuries. The Sumitomo family mss., dated 1580, describes the liquation process, which was largely responsible for the increased output. Delmer Brown, *Money Economy in Medieval Japan* (New Haven: Far Eastern Association, 1951), pp. 56–57; Nishio Keijirō, "Kodai ni okeru kōzan gijutsu no kenkyū — nuki gin hō no denrai," *Nihon kōgyō kaishi,* no. 452:682–685 (1922).

40. E-tu Sun and Shiou-chuan Sun, p. 247. Fu I-ling, *Ming Ch'ing shih-tai shang-jen,* p. 151.

41. *Yin-shih shu,* 5.27b.

42. *Chang-chou FC,* 1628 ed., 27.25a.

43. *Ning-yang HC,* 1692 ed., 2.11b–12a.

44. A 1765 gazetteer of Chin-chiang comments that its tobacco did not equal Chang-chou's. *Chin-chiang HC,* 1.52a–b.

45. *Min shu,* 38.10a.

46. Chu Yüan, cited by Nishijima Sadao, "Shina chokki mengyō shijō no kōsatsu," *Tōyōgakuhō,* 31.2:128 (1947), and Ho Ping-ti, "The Introduction of American Food Plants into China," *American Anthropologist,* 57.2 (pt. 1): p. 199 (1965). According to Wu Han, "Ming ch'u she-hui sheng-ch'an li ti fa-chan," *Chung-kuo tzu-pen-chu-i meng-ya wen-t'i t'ao-lun chi,* I,138,139, Fukien was an important cotton growing area in Sung and Yüan times, but the Ming local histories report that cotton was little grown in this region: Nishijima Sadao "Shina shokki mengyō," discusses this on pp. 32–33. See also Wang Chung-lo, pp. 8–9 for a discussion of Fukien cloth.

47. Wickberg, p. 81.

48. *Chang-chou FC,* 1573 ed., 13.20a. The importation of silk thread for weaving is also mentioned in *Hsing-hua FC,* 1503 ed., 12.10a.

49. *Chang-chou FC,* 1573 ed., 13.20b.

50. *Chang-chou FC,* 1573 ed., 13.19b–20a; *Chang-p'u HC,* 1700 ed., 4.1b.

51. *Hai-ch'eng HC,* 1633 ed., 11.11a. See Liang Fang-chung, "Ming tai kuo-chi mao-i," pp. 318–320, for identification of coins. See also Hsü Ta-ling, p. 911.

52. *Hai-ch'eng HC,* 1633 ed., 11.11a.

53. Fu I-ling, *Ming Ch'ing shih-tai shang-jen,* pp. 125–126.

54. Miyazaki Ichisada, "Chūgoku kinsei gin mondai ryakusetsu," *Ajia shi kenkyū,* III,244, cites an undated reference stating that one ounce of silver in Japan brought 250 *wen* (copper cash) in Japan as opposed to 750 *wen* in China.

55. Undated, cited by Fu I-ling, *Ming Ch'ing shih-tai shang-jen,* pp. 125–126.

56. Kobata Atsushi, "Nihon no kin gin gaikoku bōeki ni kansuru kenkyū," *Shigaku zasshi,* 44.11:1417–1418 (1953).

57. The Portuguese themselves had twenty ships in the 1560's. Boxer, *Fidalgos,* pp. 12–13. Liang Fang-chung, "Ming tai kuo-chi mao-i," p. 307, estimates that 370,000 ounces of silver were being imported annually.

58. Although Pinto's accounts, cited by Kobata Atsushi, "Nihon no kin gin," p. 1423, have been rejected by Boxer, *South China,* n.2, p. xxi, Pinto was in Asian waters, and may even have served on one of the Portuguese ships involved in the illegal trade. For a favorable estimate of his writings, see p. xiv, Charles D. Ley, ed., *Portuguese Voyages, 1498–1663* (New York: Dutton, 1947). True or not, the report that the quantity of silver in circulation in Ningpo increased with the Portuguese trade is plausible from other information on silver inflows into this area.

59. Kobata, tr. W. D. Burton, "The Production and Uses of Gold and Silver in 16th and 17th Century Japan," *Economic History Review,* 2nd ser., 18.2:247–248 (1965); Liang Fang-chung, "Ming tai kuo-chi mao-i," pp. 314–318.

60. Liang Fang-chung, "Ming tai kuo-chi mao-i," pp. 308–313, studies the revenues from this trade.

61. *Chang-chou FC,* 1573 ed.: 8 liang/mou price cited 5.7a, 7–10 liang/mou price cited 5.53a. Supported by information for 1578 in *Chang-chou FC,* 1877–1878 ed., 7.39b: school land in P'ing-ho hsien was purchased for 8.1 liang/mou. Prices for Chien-ning from *Chien-ning FC,* 1693 ed., 9.6a.

62. *Chien-ning FC,* 1693 ed., 9.6a.

63. *Ku-t'ien HC,* 1606 ed., 4.20b–32a. In 1594, a plot purchased for 2.4 liang of silver per mou carried a rent of 1 shih (of unhusked rice) per mou. Another plot, purchased in 1600 for 3 liang of silver/mou, brought a rent of 2.2 shih/mou.

64. *Ch'üan-chou FC,* 1612 ed., 6.6b.

65. *Chang-chou FC,* 1628 ed., 8.7b–12b.

66. *Chang-chou FC,* 1573 ed., 5.6b; 1628 ed., 8.5a–b.

67. A 1571 citation for Chien-an hsien, which produced a yield estimate of 7.08 shih/mou, and a 1611 citation for Chien-ning fu, with a yield estimate of 7.2 shih/mou (both in unhusked rice), were rejected on the basis of silver rent information for the same time period. For both 1610 and 1611, the gazetteer records the acreage, price paid for the land, and rent obtained from it. The rent for the 1610 plot is in terms of silver, 19.84 liang for 63.746 mou of land, an average of 0.32 liang/mou. The 1611 plot records rent in kind of 1.8 shih/mou (all calculations here are in terms of husked rice). To obtain the silver rent equivalent of this sum, the rent in kind is multiplied by the average price of rice, 0.638 liang/shih, obtained from P'eng Hsin-wei, *Chung-kuo huo-pi shih,* II, 459. The silver rent equivalent of 1.8 shih is then 1.1484 liang, almost four times the 0.32 liang rent, found on the 1610 plot. But land prices suggest that the latter was more productive land. The two plots were purchased in consecutive years, years unmarked by large-scale disaster in agriculture, according to the 1693 prefectural gazetteer, 46.8ab. Chien-an is the prefectural capital, so the plots are in the same land market, and should enjoy similar price levels. This enables us to infer that the 1610 land was of higher quality than the 1611 plot because of its higher price: 3.187 liang/mou as compared to 2.095 liang per mou. In other words, if the 1610 plot yielded a rent of 0.32 liang, the rent of the 1611 plot should probably have been less than this, and certainly not four times larger. Additional support for rejection of the 1611 figure is provided by the following comparison: if the

1.8 shih rent were equivalent to the 0.32 liang silver rent of 1610, what would have been the market price of rice? In order for the two rents to be equivalent, the price of rice would have had to be 0.177 liang/shih; a price this low was never seen on the rice markets of Ming China. See P'eng, II, 459. The same objections apply to the Chien-an county figure of 1.77 shih/mou.

Silver rents and rent in kind were taken from *Chien-ning FC,* 1693 ed., 9.6a–24b. Scholars have used rent information to estimate yields because so little direct information on productivity is available: see Perkins, *Agricultural Development,* pp. 312–313, for discussion, including the assumption that rents were about half of the harvest. But, as Fu I-ling, "Fu-chien tien-nung," p. 7, shows, rents in Ming Fukien varied greatly. Along the coast, fixed rents represented half of the harvest, but in some interior areas, the landlord received as much as 80 per cent of the crop. Clearly, these local differences greatly affect the validity of our yield estimates, all of which assume the landlord received half of the primary crop. In the absence of direct information on yields, we must rely on these estimates. It should be noted that my procedure understates the difference in yields between Chang-chou and Chien-ning. Since the landlord in Chien-ning probably received more than half of the harvest, estimates based on the assumption of a 50–50 split overestimate the actual yield in this prefecture. If we had information on rent shares in Chien-ning to correct the yield estimates, our conclusion that productivity was greater in Chang-chou would be strengthened. There is also the problem, stated by Ho Ping-ti, *Studies on the Population of China,* Chapter Six, and Perkins, *Agricultural Development,* pp. 218–221, of variance in the size of the land measure, the mou. In Fukien, the practice of using local land measures, with different names, suggests that the mou was an artificial unit, whose use represented an attempt to use the "official" measure. The Chien-ning *lo* and Chang-chou *tou* which measure land by the seed sown, seem to have been more commonly used than was the mou. As noted in Chapter Two, the tenancy, land sale and mortgage contracts discovered by Fu I-ling in Min-ch'ing (Fu-chou fu) and Yung-an (Yen-p'ing fu) hsien also phrased land units in terms of the seed sown, so Chien-ning and Chang-chou were not unique in this respect. See also

Ku-t'ien HC, 1590 ed., 4.24a; 1627 ed., 4.24a; *Shao-wu FC,* 1623 ed., 14.3a; *Yen-p'ing FC,* 1660 ed., 5.16a. The final question, of whether the mou in both Chien-ning and Chang-chou prefectures was the same size, cannot be answered for lack of evidence, but the prevalence of local measures suggests that the mou was a standard unit: see Perkins, *Agricultural Development,* p. 309, for the argument. In any case, the yield differences are sufficiently large to make it doubtful that they stemmed solely from discrepancies in the size of the mou unit. For a discussion of the comparability of the shih, or picul, see Chapter 2, note 28.

68. See Table 3; also, *Sung-ch'i HC,* 1700 ed., 6.1b.

69. Sun Ching-chih, p. 382.

70. Converted to Ming piculs: see note 23, Chapter Three.

71. *Ku-t'ien HC,* 1606 ed., 4.21a, 4.24a. In this discussion we are of course assuming that the mou unit was constant and that the measures were comparable. See note 67 in this chapter for a discussion.

72. *Hsien-yu HC,* 1558 ed., 3.15b.

73. *Chang-chou FC,* 1573 ed., 11.43b–44b. Amano Motonosuke, *Chūgoku nōgyō-shi,* p. 309.

74. *Shou-ning HC,* 1637 ed., 1.13b.

75. Since irrigation works were often financed by private citizens, they are also a possible outlet for newly acquired wealth. According to the *Chang-chou FC,* 1628 ed., 28.17a–29a, many reservoirs were built during the mid-sixteenth century, and others were repaired. The water supply in many areas of Chang-chou was improved during this period.

76. *Chang-chou FC,* 1573 ed., 11.43b–44b; *Hai-ch'eng HC,* 1633 ed., 4.2a.

77. *Ch'ung-an HC,* 1670 ed., 1.18b–19b. See Amano Motonosuke, *Chūgoku nōgyō-shi,* for an illustration of a well sweep, p. 271.

78. *Shou-ning HC,* 1637 ed., 1.13a.

79. See Chapter Six for a more detailed discussion of this point, using modern data for Fukien.

80. A 50–50 split is cited in the Hai-ch'eng temple lands: *Chang-chou FC,* 1573 ed., 5.53a–b. Areas with the *i-t'ien san-chu* system gave the two landlords a total of 60 per cent of the crop. *Chang-*

chou FC, 1573 ed., 5.7a. In the interior, the landlord retained 70 per cent and sometimes 80 per cent of the harvest. Fu I-ling, "Fu-chien tien-nung," p. 7.

81. Hsü T'ien-t'ai, "Fu-chien tsu tien chih-tu yen-chiu," *Fu-chien wen-hua chi-k'an,* 1.1:66 (1941), discussed in Chapter Six.

82. Calculated from: (1) interest rates of 3–5 per cent a month, p. 98, in Yang Lien-sheng, *Money and Credit in China* (Cambridge: Harvard University Press, 1952); (2) commercial profit cited in *Hai-ch'eng HC,* 1693 ed., 11.1b–2a. For a discussion of relative rates of return from different forms of investment, based on nineteenth century data from Hunan, see L. S. Yang, *Money and Credit,* pp. 101–103.

83. Rising land prices and constant rents may have provided owner-tillers with an economic incentive for selling their plot and becoming tenants.

84. Sudō Yoshiyuki, "Sōdai kanryōsei to daitochi shoyū," *Shakai kōseishi taikei,* ser. 8 (Tokyo: Nihon hyōron sha, 1950), pp. 9–76.

85. Ho Ping-ti, *The Ladder of Success in Imperial China* (New York: Wiley and Sons, 1964), p. 229, table 29.

86. James Parsons, "The Ming Dynasty Bureaucracy: Aspects of Background Forces," *Monumenta Serica,* 22.2:355 (1963), table 4.

87. Ho Ping-ti, *The Ladder of Success,* p. 246, table 35.

88. *Fu-chien t'ung-chih,* 1943 ed., 5.13a–19b.

89. See notes 26, 31 above. On the social organization of Chang-chou and Ch'üan-chou, see Takanaka Toshie, "Mindai no Sen Shō o chūshin to suru toshi kyōdōtai," *Shigaku kenkyū,* nos. 77–79:469–480 (1960).

90. Ho Ping-ti, *The Ladder of Success,* describes the school system, pp. 171–179. For details on the history and curriculum of the Kuo-tzu-chien, see Tani Mitsutaka, "Mindai kansei no kenkyū," *Shigaku zasshi,* 73.4:58–59 (1964).

91. The proliferation of entrance examinations for sheng-yüan status is described by Miyazaki Ichisada, *Kakyo* (Osaka, 1946), p. 39. Quotas were initially set at 20 sheng-yüan per hsien, 30 per chou, and 40 per prefectural unit. See Ho Ping-ti, *The Ladder of Success,* pp. 172, 175.

92. Ho Ping-ti, *The Ladder of Success,* p. 198.

93. Yang Lien-sheng, "K'o-chü shih-tai ti fu-k'ao shih-fei wen-t'i," *Ch'ing-hua hsüeh-pao,* new ser., 2.2:122,127 (1961).

94. *T'ing-chou FC,* 1637 ed., 9.39a–b. This is based on the minimizing assumption that all the boats were salt junks, taxed at the higher rate. If all the boats were commercial junks, taxed at the lower rate, the annual flow of traffic past this point would have been over 43,000 boats.

95. Cited in Ho Ping-ti, *Studies on the Population of China,* pp. 199–200.

96. With a growth rate of 0.5 per cent a year, the population would have increased by 28 per cent from 1491 to 1541. Of course, out-migration in this period may have resulted in a stagnant or declining population. The records throw no light on this possibility.

97. *Cheng-ho HC,* 1832 ed., 3.16b–17a.

98. Sun Ching-chih, pp. 140–141.

99. *Chien-yang HC,* 1607 ed., 1.83b, refers to Sung developments.

100. In the eighteenth century, du Halde found Chien-ning "a Place of Plentiful Trade, because all Commodities that are carried up and down the River pass through it" (du Halde, pp. 165–166). New cash crops were added to Chien-ning's local products: sugar cane became a popular crop in the seventeenth century and is reported in the following gazetteers: *Chien-yang HC,* 1607 ed., 3.32b; *P'u-ch'eng HC,* 1650 ed., 4.15b–16a; *Ch'ung-an HC,* 1670 ed., 1.18b–19b; *Sung-ch'i HC,* 1700 ed., 6.6a. Tobacco became popular in the eighteenth century: see *Sung-ch'i HC,* 1700 ed., 6.3a; Chapter 3 above, note 61; Robert Fortune, I, 251.

101. *Cheng-ho HC,* 1832 ed., 1.29a; Robert Fortune, I, 298.

102. See Chapter Six for further details. The lack of change in Chien-ning's economy is more surprising when the tremendous expansion of its tea trade in the eighteenth and nineteenth centuries is considered. In 1700, 683 piculs of tea were sold in Canton for the London market: E. H. Pritchard, *The Crucial Years of Early Anglo-Chinese Relations, 1750–1850* (Pullman: Washington State College, 1936), pp. 114–115. By 1867, exports of tea had risen to 1.3 million piculs: H. B. Morse, *The Trade and Administration of China* (London: Longmans, Green, 1920), pp. 318–321. As a leading producer

of black tea, Chien-ning's tea industry flourished with this expansion in trade. Descriptions of the extension of tea cultivation have been gathered by Shigeta Atsushi, "Shin-matsu ni okeru Konan cha no shin tenkai — Chūgoku kindai sangyō-shi no tame no danshō," *Ehime daigaku kiyō,* 7.1:57 (1962). With expansion came specialization and Ch'ung-an became a center where tea grown elsewhere was sent to be processed and sold for shipment to Shanghai or Canton. This is described by Shigeta in the article cited above, pp. 54–55, Maeda Katsutarō, "Min Shin no Fukken," pp. 580–583, and by Robert Fortune, I, 220–221.

The failure of expansion in the tea industry to affect other aspects of the peasant economy may be due to tea's position as a crop grown on marginal land. Tea did not compete with rice for the fertile paddy plots; it did not displace rice as the primary crop, nor did it, by competing with rice, push up overall productivity levels.

In the twentieth century, the decline in tea exports led to deterioration in Chien-ning's economy. See Chapter Six for details.

103. Carlo Cipolla, p. 57.

104. Robert Hartwell, "A Cycle of Economic Change in Imperial China: Coal and Iron in Northwest China, 750–1350," *Journal of the Economic and Social History of the Orient,* 10.1:102–159 (1967).

105. Terada Takanobu, "Mindai ni okeru henshō mondai no ichi sokumen — kyō-un nen-rei gin ni tsuite," *Shimizu hakase tsuitō kinen Mindai-shi ronsō* (Tokyo: Dai-an, 1962), p. 278.

106. See "Mindai ni okeru hokuhen no beika mondai ni tsuite," *Tōyōshi kenkyū,* 26.2:48–70 (1967).

Chapter Five / REGIONAL DIVERSITY IN THE DEVELOPMENT OF HUNAN

1. As in the previous section on Fukien, this chapter does not pretend to be an economic geography. The chapter focuses on Ch'ang-sha prefecture and secondarily the prefecture of Heng-chou, while contrasting developments in these regions with Shao-yang hsien, the seat of Pao-ch'ing prefecture. There have been several important studies of Hunan development. Ho Ping-ti provides an

excellent discussion of the opening up of the Yangtze highlands in chaps. 7 and 8 of *Studies on the Population of China,* and traces migration patterns in this region through *hui-kuan:* see his *Chung-kuo hui-kuan shih-lun* (Taipei, 1966), pp. 67–68, 75–77. Other pioneering articles are: Shigeta Atsushi, "Shin-sho ni okeru Konan kome shijō no ichi kōsatsu," *Tōyō bunka kenkyū-jo kiyō,* 10:427–498 (1956), his subsequent study of Hunan tenancy, "Shin sho ni okeru Konan no jinushi-sei ni tsuite — 'Konan shō rei-sei-an' ni yoru shōron," *Wada hakase koki kinen Tōyōshi ronsō* (Tokyo, 1960), and his study of Hunan tea, "Shin-matsu Konan cha." Hunan's participation in national rice markets is described by Abe Takeo. Morita Akira has also contributed two studies on Hunan, "Shindai Konan ni okeru chisui kangai no tenkai," *Tōhōgaku,* no. 20:63–76 (1960) and a study of periodic markets, "Shindai Konan chihō ni okeru teiki-ichi ni tsuite," *Kyūshū sangyō daigaku shōkei ronsō,* 5.1:49–73 (1964). I have also benefited greatly from an unpublished manuscript by Wang Yeh-chien, "Agricultural Development and Peasant Economy in Hunan during the Ch'ing Period (1644–1911)."

2. Yanagida Setsuko, "Sōdai tochi shoyū-sei ni mirareru futatsu no katachi," *Tōyō bunka kenkyū-jo kiyō,* no. 29:95–130 (1963). But Hunan had already begun marketing its rice surplus outside its own area: see Ch'üan Han-sheng, pp. 403–431.

3. Ho Ping-ti, *Studies on the Population of China,* pp. 143–144.

4. Wang Yeh-chien, "Agricultural Development," p. 3. Described in *Pa-ling HC,* 1685 ed., 9.4b–6b. Yo-chou and Ch'ang-sha were particularly affected, although the battles extended as far south as Pao-ch'ing: *Pao-ch'ing FC,* 1849 ed., 97.1b. The late Ming rebellions are studied in detail by Li Wen-chih, *Wan Ming min-pien* (Shanghai, 1948): pp. 88–89 describe Chang Hsien-chung's incursions into Hunan. See his map, p. 2, for rebel movements.

5. Wang Yeh-chien, "Agricultural Development," pp. 3–4.

6. *Ch'ang-sha FC,* 1685 ed., 1.54a–78b.

7. Described by Wang Yeh-chien, "Agricultural Development," p. 3.

8. From 13,892,400 mou in 1685 to 31,256,100 mou in 1724: Wang Yeh-chien, "Agricultural Development," p. 7, table 2. Government interest in agricultural development continued into the 1740's, and included encouragement of supplementary crops such as

t'ung nuts, sericulture, and wax tree cultivation: see "Urge the people to nurture wax trees and plant bamboo," dated 1743, in *Hunan sheng li ch'eng-an,* 8.2a–5a. In 1745–46 the central government also tried to get peasants to grow two crops of rice a year, but without much success: see *Hunan sheng li ch'eng-an,* 8.6a–25b.

9. *I-yang HC,* 1874 ed., 23.40b–41a prints a record of these deliberations: "Details of an investigation of the difference in the newly cultivated acreage of the hsien, and whether or not they should be liable to taxation," by Shen Hua, who was a *hsien-shih* in the I-yang office.

10. Abe Takeo, p. 521.

11. *Ibid.,* p. 522.

12. Using Abe Takeo's (p. 552) estimate that in 1735 about 4–5 million shih of rice from Szechwan and Hukwang (Hupei and Hunan) were moving to the Yangtze rice markets. Abe says (p. 521) that it was Hunan in particular that produced the rice surpluses for Hukwang.

13. Amano Motonosuke, "Shina ni okeru kome no ryūtsū kikō to sono ryūtsū hiyō," *Tōa keizai sōsho,* 1.1:1–32 (1941).

14. This is derived from Table 14 and supported by Abe, pp. 521–523.

15. Shigeta Atsushi, "Shin-sho Konan kome shijō," pp. 448–449. See the discussion in *Shao-yang HC,* 1877 ed., 1.2a.

16. Shigeta Atsushi, "Shin-sho Konan kome shijō," pp. 441–442.

17. Governor Wang Kuo-tung, writing about 1728, compared Ch'ang-sha and Hsiang-t'an and ascribed Hsiang-t'an's faster growth to its superior harbor facilities: *Chu p'i yü-chih,* ts'e 17, 79b–80a.

18. *Hsiang-t'an HC,* 1781 ed., 14.5b.

19. *Hsiang-t'an HC,* 1818 ed., 19.4a–17a, lists these halls, many built in the commercial districts outside the city walls. The most detailed descriptions of the local specialties brought by these merchants to Hsiang-t'an is provided in the 1889 edition of the hsien gazetteer, 11.2b.

20. In I-yang hsien, periodic markets increased from 1 (1685), to 6 (1747) and to 23 (1874). In the 62 years between 1685–1747, markets increased 500 per cent, or 2.9 per cent a year; from 1747–1874, they increased 283 per cent, or slightly over 5 per cent a year. Morita Akira, "Shindai Konan teiki-ichi," p. 53, shows that there

was a gradual increase of periodic markets in Hunan over the Ch'ing dynasty, and a general decline of these markets in Hupei.

21. *Yo-chou FC,* 1746 ed., 12.1b. The four figures presented in Table 16 are too isolated to be meaningful except as general expressions of a trend described in historical documents; as shown in Ch'üan Han-sheng and Wang Yeh-chien, "Ch'ing Yung-cheng nien-chien (1723–1735) ti mi-chia," *Li-shih yü-yen yen-chiu-so chi-k'an,* 30th Anniversary vol. no. I:174–176 (1959), and *Chu p'i yü-chih,* ts'e 6, 6b–35a, cyclical fluctuations in the market price of rice during any given year were very large, and it is necessary to have precise information on the month for which the price is quoted in order to distinguish between seasonal variations and long-term price movements. Yet another difficulty in the prices cited in Hunan sources is that they are expressed in terms of silver. As Sasaki Masaya has shown in his study of Ningpo, fluctuations in the exchange rate between copper cash, the unit in which rice transactions were conducted, and silver were large enough during the eighteenth century to substantially modify price trends expressed in copper cash. See Sasaki Masaya, "Kanpo ni-nen Gin-ken no kō-ryō bōdō," *Kindai Chūgoku kenkyū,* no. 5:202 (1963), table 2. Without information on the market rate of exchange between copper cash and silver in Hunan during the same period, we cannot know how representative these silver figures are. These prices are presented despite these severe strictures because they do indicate the direction in which rice prices moved during the century, and were cited by local writers to illustrate the point that prices had risen. A variety of sources substantiating this historical trend are presented by Ho Ping-ti, *Studies on the Population of China,* pp. 267–268; the Ch'ien-lung emperor's predecessor, the Yung-cheng emperor, also directed his governor to investigate rising rice prices in Hunan in 1727: *Chu p'i yü-chih,* ts'e 6, 23a. In his reply, dated August 30, 1727, Pu-lan-t'ai said the rise in prices was noted as early as 1703, in the K'ang-hsi reign period, and attributed current price increases to officials from Kwangsi and the lower Yangtze provinces, and private merchants, whose bidding drove up the price of rice in the central markets. Prices in areas which did not sell rice for long distance trade were, in the two citations recorded, less than half the price prevailing in Ch'ang-sha and other central rice markets: ts'e 6, 23a, 23b–24a.

The population spurt of the late seventeenth and early eighteenth centuries, cited by Ho Ping-ti, *Studies on the Population of China,* p. 266, suggests why there was an upward pressure on rice prices during this period. The relationship between population growth and price rises is recognized in a 1743 memorial on the Hunan rice market, cited by Shigeta Atsushi, "Shin-sho Konan kome shijō," p. 471: "The rice produced does not increase, while the areas needing rice increase several-fold. The price of Hunan rice has gradually increased." *Hunan sheng li ch'eng-an,* chüan 34. See note 66 in this chapter for a discussion of whether these prices were part of a general inflationary trend.

22. *Hsiang-yin HC,* 1823 ed., 14.29b. In the following pages, information from different parts of Hunan is collected and compared. In this province as in Fukien, fields were commonly measured not in mou but in the seed sown: see *Hsiang-yin HC,* 1823 ed., 14.30a; *Li-ling HC,* 1870 ed., 1.24b. Variance in local grain measures is discussed in *Ch'ang-sha HC,* 1810 ed., 14.7a; *Hsiang-t'an HC,* 1781 ed., 14.5b. See note 67 in Chapter Four for a discussion of the comparability of mou citations and shih measures under these conditions.

23. *Ibid.,* 17.2b. A rice seed which could be double cropped is described, 18.1a–b. All the other citations (see Wang Yeh-chien, "Agricultural Development," p. 12), are over half a century later in date. It is possible that the Hsiang-t'an region had double cropped rice in the mid-sixteenth century: Ho Ping-ti, "Early Ripening Rice," p. 214, cites a 1553 edition of the hsien gazetteer which listed a late ripening variety capable of being planted after a first rice crop was harvested. The devastations of late Ming and early Ch'ing seem to have stopped the practice: it is not described in the eighteenth century gazetteers from Hsiang-t'an. As shown in Chapter Three, reversion from double to single cropping of rice occurred in other areas at other times: in early Ch'ing times, the land–labor ratios and the need to rebuild irrigation networks may have caused the reversion to less intensive cultivation systems in Hunan. The 1745–46 documents in *Hunan sheng li ch'eng-an,* 8.6a–25b, which describe official attempts to encourage double cropping of rice in some parts of the province, indicate that lack of sufficient water was another negative factor working against double cropping.

24. *Hsiang-t'an HC,* 1781 ed., 14.4b.

25. *Ch'ang-sha HC,* 1810 ed., 14.7b–8b.

26. *Hsiang-yin HC,* 1823 ed., 17.2b also lists areas which alternate rice with beans and grains. According to *I-yang HC,* 1874 ed., 2.6b–7a, areas which do not grow two crops of rice plant buckwheat after the rice harvest. This may represent an intensification of cropping from the pattern noted in notes 24 and 25. Ming sources comparing alternative yields of rice, wheat, and millet (*Ch'ang-sha FC,* 1534 ed., 3.25a–b) indicate that one crop a year was normal in the region. By the late eighteenth century, Ch'ang-sha farmers did not usually allow the land to lie fallow after the rice harvest, but the crops they planted — potatoes, bracken roots — did not require much care. By the late nineteenth century, some farmers were growing two crops of rice, others a winter crop which needed more tillage.

27. Wang Yeh-chien, "Agricultural Development," p. 5, table 1.

28. Although Morita Akira, "Shindai Konan chisui kangai," pp. 69–70, discusses embankments after the mid-eighteenth century, he has relied only on secondary sources for his study of the whole movement, pp. 67–69.

29. Wang Yeh-chien, "Agricultural Development," p. 6, citing Li Cheng-i, *Hunan ti hsi-pei chüeh* (Ch'ang-sha, 1946), p. 105. *Economic Geography of Central China,* p. 265, notes that the rice production of the lake districts and the lower reaches of the Hsiang and Yüan Rivers amounted to more than 45 per cent of total rice production in Hunan in the 1950's.

30. *I-yang HC,* 1874 ed., 2.6b–7a; *Hsiang-t'an HC,* 1818 ed., 4.1a–2a.

31. Reservoirs and ponds are listed in: *Ch'ang-sha FC,* 1685 ed., 4.79a–80b; *Hsiang-t'an HC,* 1781 ed., 10.26a–32b; 1818 ed., 5.14a–20a, 11.14a–18b; *Ch'ang-sha HC,* 1810 ed., 10.61b–66b; *I-yang HC,* 1874 ed., 6.17b–19b; *Heng-yang HC,* 1820 ed., 17.68b–73b; *Shao-yang HC,* 1684 ed., 5.36a–40b; 1877 ed., 4.8a–10a.

32. *Hsiang-t'an HC,* 1818 ed., 10.17b.

33. As put by the *Ning-hsiang HC,* 1867 ed., 24.8a: "Since the drought of 1778–79 (we have) sunk wells, dug ponds and constructed embankments to store water." Wang Yeh-chien, "Agricultural Development," gives references in the following gazetteers, note 12: *Ch'ien-yang HC,* 1789 ed.; *Liu-yang HC,* 1818 and 1873

ed.; *Hsiang-t'an HC,* 1818 ed.; *Ning-hsiang HC,* 1867 ed.; and *Yu HC,* 1871 ed. The 1874 edition of *I-yang HC* also describes various irrigation tools, 2.6b–7a, such as the *chieh-kao* and *t'ung-ch'e.* See Amano Motonosuke, *Chūgoku nōgyō-shi,* pp. 270–271 for illustrations. These irrigation instruments were sometimes described along with other details in lists of public landholdings: an example appears in *I-yang HC,* 6.18b.

34. 4.1a–2a, *shui-li* section.

35. This is a conservative estimate based on *T'ien-kung k'ai-wu.* Amano Motonosuke, *Chūgoku nōgyō-shi,* p. 324, discusses these. By the early nineteenth century, the improved *t'ung-ch'e* may have been capable of watering 200 to 300 mou in the same time: see *Liu-yang HC,* 1873 ed., 14.20b–21a. The *t'ung-ch'e* are also described in *Ning-hsiang HC,* 1867 ed., 24.8a.

36. The term *shui-ch'e* included various sorts of water wheels. See Amano Motonosuke, *Chūgoku nōgyō-shi,* pp. 324, 359, and *Liu-yang HC,* 1873 ed., 14.20b–21a.

37. *Liu-yang HC,* 1733 ed., 4.19a–21b.

38. Amano Motonosuke, *Chūgoku nōgyō-shi,* pp. 383–384. The kind of fertilizer used still varied with location: the 1873 edition of *Yüan-chou FC,* 19.8a–b, reports that "The fields close to the city outskirts use nightsoil, those far away cannot obtain it and use grass." Nineteenth century editions also describe the use of lime as a fertilizer and insecticide: see *Ning-hsiang HC,* 1867 ed., 24.8a–b; *Heng-yang HC,* 1894 ed., 11.5a.

39. Ho Ping-ti, *Studies on the Population of China,* p. 173. Kiangsi *tsao: Ch'ang-sha FC,* 1747 ed., 36.1b; *Ch'ang-sha HC,* 1747 ed., 2.1a–b; 1810 ed., 14.11b; *Hsiang-t'an HC,* 1781 ed., 15.1b; 1818 ed., 39.9b–10a. Yunnan *tsao:* Appears in identical sources noted above. Kwangtung *chan: Ch'ang-sha HC,* 1747 ed., 2.1a–b; 1810 ed., 14.11b; *Hsiang-t'an HC,* 1781 ed., 15.1b; 1818 ed., 39.9b–10a.

40. *Heng-yang HC,* 1872–1874 ed., 11.7a–b.

41. Without a comprehensive survey of contemporary local gazetteers, the transmission of rice seed varieties is usually lost. Examples of "hidden" imports include: (1) *T'uan-ku tsao,* found in *Heng-shan HC,* 1746 ed., 4.16a–b; *Ch'ang-sha FC,* 1747 ed., 36.1b; *Hsiang-t'an HC,* 1781 ed., 15.1b; 1818 ed., 39.9b–10a; *Heng-chou FC,* 1875 ed., 19.1b, probably came from Kiangsi, where it was fre-

quently grown in late Ming and early Ch'ing: Amano Motonosuke, *Chūgoku nōgyō-shi,* p. 343. (2) *Ch'ung-yang* (Ninth Month) Glutinous, found in *Heng-shan HC,* 1746 ed., 4.16a–b; *Ch'ang-sha HC,* 1810 ed., 14.11b, is also found growing in Kiangsi at an earlier date: Amano Motonosuke, *Chūgoku nōgyō-shi,* p. 343. It appears as early as 1541 in Fukien: *Chien-ning FC,* 1541 ed., 13.1a–2a. (3) *Yang-t'iao no* (Willow Branch Glutinous), found in *Heng-shan HC,* 1746 ed., 4.16a–b; *Ch'ang-sha HC,* 1747 ed., 2.1a–b; 1810 ed., 14.11b, was widely grown in the contiguous provinces of Yunnan, Hupei, and Kiangsi in late Ming and early Ch'ing times, according to Amano Motonosuke, *Chūgoku nōgyō-shi,* p. 343.

42. *T'ieh-chiao* tsao is cited in *Ch'ang-sha FC,* 1747 ed., 36.1b; *Ch'ang-sha HC,* 1747 ed., 2.1a–b; 1810 ed., 14.11b; *Hsiang-t'an HC,* 1781 ed., 15.1b; 1818 ed., 39.9b–10a; *Hsiang-yin HC,* 1823 ed., 18.1a–b; *Heng-chou FC,* 1875 ed., 19.1b. Kwangtung *chan* in *Ch'ang-sha HC,* 1747 ed., 2.1a–b; 1810 ed., 14.11b; *Hsiang-t'an HC,* 1781 ed., 15.1b; 1818 ed., 39.9b–10a.

43. *Mao-chan: Ch'ang-sha FC,* 1747 ed., 36.1b; *Ch'ang-sha HC,* 1810 ed., 14.11b; *Hsiang-t'an HC,* 1818 ed., 39.9b–10a; *Hsiang-yin HC,* 1823 ed., 18.1a–b. *Huang tsao: Hsiang-yin HC,* 1823 ed., 18.1a–b.

44. *Hsiang-yin HC,* 1823 ed., 18.1a–b. On rainfall, see *Economic Geography of Central China,* pp. 204–205.

45. *Hsiang-yin HC,* 1823 ed., 18.1a–b.

46. *Hsiang-t'an HC,* 1818 ed., 39.2a–b.

47. *I-yang HC,* 1874 ed., 2.6b–7a. At the same time, however, other areas of the prefecture continued on the older calendar: see *Ch'ang-sha HC,* 1871 ed., 16.11a–b.

48. *Li-ling HC,* 1870 ed., 1.24a. It must be stressed that double-cropping was not adopted everywhere. As the 1868 edition of *Wu-ling HC,* 28.1a, put it: "Where the land is level and there is water, two crops of rice can be grown. Hilly land can grow only one crop (of rice)." One crop of rice and a second leguminous or grain crop is reported in *Yu HC,* 1871 ed., 18.2a–3a, and an older three year rotation cycle of tobacco; sweet potatoes, millet, or buckwheat; and sesame is described for hilly fields in the 1867 edition, *Ning-hsiang HC,* 24.8a–b."

49. In more mountainous parts of Hunan, there seems to have

been more continuity between Ming and Ch'ing: for example, the large landowners named Teng who held "several hundred *ch'ing*" of land in Kuei-yang hsien (southeast Hunan) in the early Ch'ing. Li Wen-chih, p. 609. 1 *ch'ing* = 100 mou.

50. *Ch'ang-sha FC,* 1747 ed., 14.6a–7a.

51. Wang Yeh-chien, "Agricultural Development," p. 20.

52. *Hsiang-t'an HC,* 1781 ed., 14.6a.

53. Wang Yeh-chien, "Agricultural Development," p. 20, citing Liu Ta-chün, *Wo kuo tien-nung ching-chi chuang-k'uang* (Shanghai, 1929). J. L. Buck, *Land Utilization,* III, 58–59, Table 22, survey done in Heng-yang hsien, Heng-chou prefecture.

54. Wang Yeh-chien, "Agricultural Development," pp. 16–17, has a table of land prices in various parts of Hunan. This can be supplemented with the following items: 1751, 12.27 liang/mou, *Heng-yang HC,* 1820 ed., 17.80b; 1773–75, 8 liang/mou, *Hsiang-t'an HC,* 1781 ed., 1.32a; and 1854, 11.6 liang/mou, *Shao-yang HC,* 1877 ed., 4.9a. The combined list yields only four items of information on land prices in Ch'ang-sha prefecture. If these are compared with rice prices during the same period, it seems that there was an increase in land prices, both absolutely and relative to the price of rice, but this increase did not occur until the nineteenth century.

Year	Land price (silver liang/mou)	Index	Rice price (silver liang/shih)	Index
1734/35	17[a]	100	0.3737	100
1781	8	47	0.6001	161
1803	32	188	0.8113	217
1906	100	588	1.4528	389

[a] Average of two citations

These figures are of little value, for the following reasons: (1) there are not enough citations; (2) none of the citations come from the same county; and (3) there is no indication of the quality of the land, and these quality variations may account for part of the price difference. Rice prices from P'eng Hsin-wei, II, 850.

55. Wang Yeh-chien, "Agricultural Development," concludes that increases in rent and rent deposits and reductions of farm size were stronger than favorable trends such as expansion of cultivated land

and introduction of secondary crops. Hence, "the peasants in this province were reduced to an economic position even inferior to those in other regions where no comparable increase in agricultural output occurred," p. 40. Shigeta Atsushi, "Shin-sho Konan no jinushisei," tries to set up two contrasting tenancy situations in Ch'ing Hunan: an "oppressed tenancy" in the mountainous frontier areas, and a "strong tenancy" in the advanced economic areas. The conclusions drawn by these two scholars are diametrically opposed: Wang regards the economic development of Ch'ing times as having ultimately been unfavorable to the well-being of the peasant, while Shigeta contends that market developments strengthened the tenant's position. For a general statement of the Marxist position, which stresses the economic pressure resulting from land concentrations and increased tenancy as the force driving peasants into subsidiary industries, see Hsü Ta-ling, II,932–935. There is no dispute about the effects of rising rice prices and productivity, discussed below, on the peasant who owned the land he farmed. The debate centers on the effect of commercialization on tenant welfare, which is therefore the object of our scrutiny. Our contention that the income of tenant farmers in Ch'ang-sha tended to rise during the eighteenth century does not imply that tenants were better off than peasants who owned their own land.

56. Wang Yeh-chien, "Agricultural Development," p. 30. Share rent was still practiced in areas around Lake Tung-t'ing in the nineteenth century. It is cited, for example, in *Pao-ch'ing FC,* 1849 ed., 143.13b–14a.

57. Reported by Morita Akira, "Shindai Konan chisui kangai," p. 74, from *Min shih hsi-kuan ta-chuan.* Tenants who improved the plots paid a larger rent deposit but were then on a fixed rent system, while the other tenants paid the landlord 40 per cent of the harvest.

58. Calculations of rent deposits: rents are based on rice prices in the 1740's, Table 16, and rents, Table 17. The first citation appears in the 1747 edition of *Ch'ang-sha FC,* 14.6a–7a, contemporary with the citation found by Wang Yeh-chien, "Agricultural Development," p. 35, in the 1746 edition of *Yo-chou FC.* It subsequently appears in the 1756 edition of *Hsiang-t'an HC,* 13.6a, and 1781 edition, 14.6a.

59. *Hsiang-t'an HC,* 1818 ed., 39.2a–b.

60. *Pao-ch'ing FC,* 1849 ed., 143.13b–14a; Wang Yeh-chien, "Agricultural Development," pp. 36–38. *Ning-hsiang, HC,* 1867 ed., 24.8b. Although, as Wang Yeh-chien, "The Impact of the Taiping Rebellion," has noted in tables 11, 12, pp. 37–38, many sources suggest an increase in rent deposits, this was not a universal trend. See the 1873 edition of *Pa-ling HC,* 11.8b: "Now the tenants here are better off than elsewhere. Many are people from Ch'ang-sha, Hsiang-t'an, and Liu-yang who have come to be tenants; many do not have rent deposits (to pay) or the sums are very small."

61. L. S. Yang, *Money and Credit,* pp. 101–103.

62. *Economic Geography of Central China,* p. 265.

63. The rent in 1755 of 1.5 shih/mou reported in Hsiang-yin: Wang Yeh-chien, "Agricultural Development," p. 54, table 16. In Hsiang-t'an the rent was 1–1.05 shih/mou, see Table 16.

64. *Hsiang-yin HC,* 1823 ed., 14.29b.

65. Taking the trend in Hsiang-t'an hsien, Table 17, as a guide to what was occurring in Hsiang-yin.

66. *Hsiang-yin HC,* 1823 ed., 14.29b. See note 21 in this chapter for an evaluation of the price figures used. It is very difficult to determine whether the rice prices recorded in the eighteenth century were indicative of an increase in the price of rice relative to other commodities, or whether they were merely part of a general inflationary trend, since the only price lists available for this period are for rice. If the latter alternative is true, the peasant benefited from fixed rents because of rising yields in the century, but not from price movements. The qualitative evidence suggests that rice prices increased relative to other commodities: see Ho Ping-ti, *Studies on the Population of China,* pp. 267–268, and other materials cited in note 21, in which case the effects discussed in the text are pertinent.

67. Before: Landlord's share: 1 shih valued at 0.5 liang = money value 0.5 liang. Tenant's share: 1 shih valued at 0.5 liang = money value 0.5 liang. After: Landlord's share 2 shih valued at 1.5 liang/shih = money value 3 liang, or a 500 per cent increase in money income/mou. Tenant's share: 3–4 shih @ 1.5 liang = 4.5–6 liang, or an 800 to 1,100 per cent increase in money value of harvest/mou. Although the calculations cited above have all been phrased in terms of silver, the rice market actually operated at the lowest level in terms of copper cash; see *Li-ling HC,* 1870 ed., 3.17a. The copper-

silver ratios during the eighteenth century are important in evaluating the effect of rising silver prices on rice sellers. It is possible, for example, to think of a situation where copper prices of rice would be declining while silver prices rose: this would take place if copper were appreciating relative to silver during the period. In such a case, peasants might suffer while landlords, selling on a larger scale for silver, could gain.

P'eng Hsin-wei (1965 ed.), p. 823, has a table showing exchange rates between silver and copper for the eighteenth century, but there are no Hunan citations. Ch'en Chao-nan, *Yung-cheng, Ch'ien-lung nien-chien ti yin-ch'ien pi-chia pien-tung* (Economic Monographs 4, Institute of Economics, Academia Sinica, Taipei, 1966), pp. 11–12, table 10, has two Hunan citations, neither for the late eighteenth century. However, there are two reasons for believing that the terms of exchange between copper and silver remained fairly steady during 1730–1800: (1) Ch'en, graph 1, with data drawn from many regions, shows no discernible downward trend in the copper cash exchanged for one silver tael in this period. (2) P'eng's table, pp. 824–825, of rice prices phrased in copper cash collected from various regions in China, shows prices increasing 226 per cent between 1731 and 1800. This suggests that copper cash rice prices rose as much or more than silver rice prices during this period, and the conclusions in the text are applicable to tenants and landlords who were selling rice.

Farm size is another important factor in evaluating the effect of rising market prices and increasing productivity on tenants in this period. The comparison of Ch'ang-sha and Shao-yang in this chapter indicated that there was probably a decline in farm size in Ch'ang-sha over the eighteenth century. A very large decline in farm size could negate all the benefits of rising prices and productivity. In the absence of information for the period 1730–1790, we are unable to evaluate the degree to which shrinking farm size may have offset higher prices and yields.

68. Tobacco was grown in Heng-chou and the hills of Yo-chou: Shigeta Atsushi, "Shin-sho Konan kome shijō" pp. 460–461, but remained of minor importance. Cotton, grown in the south and the lake districts (Shigeta Atsushi, "Shin-sho Konan no jinushi-sei," p. 461; *Pao-ch'ing FC,* 1685 ed., 13.35a–b; *I-yang HC,* 1874 ed.,

2.12a), continued to be planted in sandy soils along the lake in the 1950's (*Economic Geography of Central China,* p. 262) but never developed into a crop of major importance, p. 279. Elsewhere, soybeans were important: the 1894 edition of *Heng-yang HC,* 11.4b, reports that soybeans were grown within 30 to 40 li of the city and were used to make soy sauce.

69. *Ch'en-chou FC,* 1685 ed., 7.16a–37b.

70. Shigeta Atsushi, "Shin-sho Konan kome shijō," p. 448. The distinctiveness of the rice producing areas in Hunan is described in Abe, pp. 521–523. In Ching-chou, according to the 1885 provincial gazetteer, 40.30b, slash-and-burn agriculture was still being practiced.

71. Shigeta Atsushi, "Shin-sho Konan kome shijō," p. 464 cites an eighteenth century edition of *Ch'ien-yang HC,* chüan 9. This cropping pattern continued to prevail into the 1950's: *Economic Geography of Central China,* p. 263.

72. Amano Motonosure, *Chūgoku nōgyō-shi,* p. 384.

73. *Ibid.*

74. *Yung-chou FC,* 1867 ed., 12b–13a of chüan 5, part 1: "Of the fields in the district only 30 per cent are paddy. The areas where obtaining water is difficult only plant 'husks' (*pao-ku*) and dry land grains (*tsa-liang*)." *Economic Geography of Central China,* p. 260, shows the regional disparity in irrigation facilities. Yields: *Ching-chou chih,* 1879 ed., 5.6a–7a, taking highest rents and assuming they represented half the total yield.

75. Shigeta Atsushi, "Shin-sho Konan kome shijō," pp. 457–462.

76. *Shao-yang HC,* 1877 ed., 1.2a.

77. *Pao-ch'ing FC,* 1567 ed., 3.86a–b for Ming seeds. Amano Motonosuke, *Chūgoku nōgyō-shi,* p. 343, notes Shao-yang's large number of rice varieties. These are listed in the 1684 edition of *Shao-yang HC,* 6.8b–9b.

78. *Economic Geography of Central China,* p. 265.

79. *Pao-ch'ing FC,* 1849 ed., 143.13b–14a.

80. *Ibid.*

81. *Shao-yang HC,* 1684 ed., 6.10b–11a.

82. *Pao-ch'ing FC,* 1849 ed., 97.1b. On rice prices see *Shao-yang HC,* 1684 ed., 6.10b–11a.

83. *Shao-yang HC,* 1877 ed., 4.6b, 1693 entry. See discussion in

note 22, Chapter Five and note 67, Chapter Four on the comparability of mou and shih from different parts of Hunan.

84. Wang Yeh-chien, "Agricultural Development," p. 18, citing 1818 edition of *Liu-yang HC.*

85. C. K. Yang, p. 37.

86. Wang Yeh-chien, "Agricultural Development," p. 18, citing 1870 edition of *Li-ling HC.*

87. To the evidence of the rent figures in Table 19 is added the fact that Shao-yang is still not a major double cropping area: *Economic Geography of Central China,* pp. 269, 321–322. Nor was it one of the traditional double cropping areas cited in this work.

88. *Ibid.*

89. *Hsiang-yin HC,* 1823 ed., 17.2b; *Liu-yang HC,* 1873 ed., 14.20b, as well as the 1818 edition cited by Wang Yeh-chien, "Agricultural Development," note 17; *Li-ling HC,* 1870 ed., 1.24a, also cited by Wang. These and Yu hsien are among those listed as traditional double cropping areas in *Economic Geography of Central China,* pp. 269, 322. As noted in an earlier section, both interplanting and successive planting methods were used. There is no direct information in the gazetteers on the yields obtained with double cropping. In the 1930's, the average annual yield for double cropped land was 6.75 shih (of unhusked rice) per mou, according to Kanda Masao, *Konan shō sōran* (Tokyo: Kai-gai sha, 1937), p. 521. Single crop yields in Liu-yang hsien, for example, varied from 4 to 5.8 shih/mou: 1873 *hsien-chih,* 8.24b–25a.

90. Shigeta Atsushi, "Shin-matsu Konan cha," pp. 53–61. According to H. B. Morse, p. 251, 300,000 piculs of tea a year were moving to Hankow in 1920.

91. *Economic Geography of Central China,* pp. 216–217; no definite date for rice exports given. An 1872–1874 gazetteer of Heng-yang hsien, 11.3b, states that foreign cash was being used in its marketplaces. Morse, p. 521, estimates that "over a million piculs" of rice was being exported annually in 1920.

92. *Economic Geography of Central China,* pp. 265, 324–325.

93. *Ibid.*, p. 391.

94. *Heng-yang HC,* 1872–1874 ed., 9.10a, describes reservoirs, called *nien-t'ang,* capable of watering 2,000 mou.

95. *Economic Geography of Central China,* p. 271. The impor-

tance of water in rice cultivation has been treated in earlier chapters; see notes 23 and 48 in this chapter.

96. *Ibid.*

97. As in Fukien, half of the counties in the province had had none or just one *chin-shih* in the 146 year period.

98. In the sixteenth century, before civil war disrupted the economy, these four prefectures produced 60 per cent of the *chin-shih* in the province: data collected from the 1499–1601 examination results, printed in *Hunan t'ung-chih,* 1934 reprint, pp. 2715–2718, show that of the 223 *chin-shih* in the period, Ch'ang-sha produced 61, Heng-chou 23, Ch'ang-te 20, and Yo-chou 36.

99. But not for a province in Ch'ing China: see Ho Ping-ti, *The Ladder of Success,* pp. 233, 235, for a discussion of how the sliding provincial *chin-shih* quotas set after 1702 affected the academic success of Hunan.

Chapter Six / AGRICULTURAL CHANGE AND THE PEASANT ECONOMY

1. Jan Myrdal, *Report from a Chinese Village* (London: Heinemann, Ltd., 1965), pp. 48, 65–66. Over time, barring large-scale shifts in population from one region to another, farm size in any given region would of course decrease. Ramon Myers discusses this trend in Hopei and Shantung in the period 1870–1930, pp. 137–140.

2. Fei and Chang, pp. 298–299, table 49.

3. Per capita acreage was one sixth of an acre: C. K. Yang, p. 14, but, p. 35, "the majority of farms were from 5 to 10 mou," or 0.83–1.66 acres.

4. Crops requiring the highest labor inputs were cotton (a cash crop) and barley: Sidney D. Gamble, *Ting Hsien: A North China Rural Community* (New York: Institute of Pacific Relations, 1954), p. 240. In Shantung, where wheat was the principal crop, the crops requiring most labor were peanuts, which were difficult to harvest, and sweet potatoes: Martin Yang, *A Chinese Village: Taitou, Shantung Province* (New York: Columbia University Press, 1945), pp. 19–20.

5. Martin Yang, p. 22.

6. Fei Hsiao-t'ung, p. 164.

7. Fei and Chang, pp. 143–144.

8. See Dwight Perkins, *Agricultural Development,* chaps. 3 and 4.

9. The Sung shih was converted at the rate of 1 = 102 modern catties. These figures are in husked rice and taken from the following sources: Sung data from Sudō Yoshiyuki, *Sōdai keizai-shi,* p. 122; the seventeenth century figure from Ch'en Heng-li, pp. 31, 32. These are not average yields, but the highest yields recorded. For Sung developments in Soochow, see Sudō Yoshiyuki, *Sōdai keizai-shi,* pp. 73–206.

10. Ch'en Heng-li, p. 32. Again, this is the highest yield, not an average. This figure can be compared with the best double cropped yield, 796 catties per mou, reported by Li Hsün in his experiments on Soochow plots with the seeds sent by the K'ang-hsi emperor: *Wen-hsien ts'ung-pien,* II, 896, report for August 6, 1717. On this experimental effort, see Jonathan Spence, *Ts'ao Yin and the K'ang-hsi Emperor* (New Haven: Yale University Press, 1966), pp. 278–279.

11. *Economic Geography of East China,* p. 59.

12. Denis Twitchett, *Land Tenure, and the Social Order in T'ang and Sung China* (University of London, 1962).

13. C. K. Yang, p. 29: "The heavy investment in fertilizer, labor, and additional equipment . . . raised the cost of vegetable production above that of rice." In other areas, vegetables were tended with less capital and more care than rice: see Jack Potter's study of a village in the New Territories, *Capitalism and the Chinese Peasant: Social and Economic Change in a Hong Kong Village* (Berkeley: University of California Press, 1968), pp. 86–87. Fei and Chang also comment (p. 216) on the high labor requirements of vegetable farming in Yunnan. Like rice, vegetables responded to increased labor inputs with increased yields; Fei and Chang note that the difference in yield between a well tended plot and a neglected one could mean 7 or 8 times more profit for the first, p. 220. C. K. Yang, p. 29, estimates that vegetable yields were over twice rice yields; Potter, pp. 86–87, calculated that the net profit from growing vegetables in the New Territories in the early 1960's was almost 20 times that for growing rice.

14. C. K. Yang, p. 62; Jack Potter, pp. 86–87. Bernard Gallin,

studying a Taiwan village in 1957–1958, found that vegetable farmers sought news of market conditions on the radio as well as by word of mouth, to determine what vegetables to grow. Gallin, *Hsin Hsing, Taiwan: A Chinese Village in Change* (Berkeley: University of California Press, 1966), p. 63.

15. Fei and Chang, pp. 298–299, table 49, comparing size of vegetable and paddy plots; Jack Potter, pp. 86–87. Perhaps the final stage in this process of agricultural change is represented by the migration of large numbers of villagers to cities for employment, described by Gallin, p. 121, and even found in the 1930's in villages a short distance from Peking: Sidney Gamble, *North China Villages: Social, Political, and Economic Activities before 1933* (Berkeley: University of California Press, 1963), pp. 175–212.

16. Fei and Chang, pp. 143–144.

17. C. K. Yang, pp. 34–35.

18. See Gallin and Potter studies cited earlier. In the modern context, and to a lesser degree before the twentieth century, there was yet another alternative open to a peasant household, that of sending some of the family members out of the village to the town to earn income to supplement receipts from farming. Ramon Myers describes the migration of peasant labor to work in north China towns in the 1930's, and notes (p. 53) that peasants "carefully allocated labor between farming and working outside the village to earn whichever income was the greatest." This is of course a development which is not unique to China; for a description of the same phenomenon in Japan, see Otoyori Tahara, "Class Differentiation of Farmers and Social Structure of Farming Communities in Postwar Japan," p. 51, in Paul Halmos, ed., Sociological Review Monograph 10, *Japanese Sociological Studies* (Keele, Eng.: University of Keele, 1966). In postwar Japan, however, the more important trend has been one following the American pattern, toward the wage or salary earner who resides on a farm and commutes to an off-farm job: the development of part-time farming is discussed by Takeo Misawa in "An Analysis of Part-time Farming in the Postwar Period," in Kazushi Ohkawa, Bruce F. Johnston and Hiromitsu Kaneda, eds., *Agriculture and Economic Growth: Japan's Experience* (Tokyo: University of Tokyo and Princeton University Press, 1970), pp. 250–269.

19. As contrasted to north China: in his Ting hsien study, Sidney Gamble (p. 11) found that less than 5 per cent of the village households were full tenants, and over 92 per cent of the families surveyed owned some land. This is supported by information from other parts of north China: see Gamble's *North China Villages,* p. 24. For an exposition and evaluation of what Ramon Myers calls the "distribution theory" of Chinese agrarian problems, see his book, pp. 14–18, 23–24.

20. Dwight Perkins, *Agricultural Development,* pp. 102–106. For data on the relationship of reduction in farm size to tenancy for Hopei and Shantung, see Myers, table 24, pp. 144–150. In these provinces despite reduced farm size there was no great increase in a landless peasantry; furthermore (pp. 212–213) an increase in farm output occurred, along with (p. 207) increased farm income from the cultivation of new cash crops and supplementary nonfarm activities.

21. Although it is true that these findings were based on evidence from public lands, which may have been slower to raise rents than private landlords, some of the modern village studies also cite cases of landlords who did not raise rents on plots growing higher-yielding vegetables: Fei and Chang, p. 220; Potter, p. 83; but in Sheung Shui, the New Territories, the rent was raised, according to Hugh D. Baker, *A Chinese Lineage Village: Sheung Shui* (London: Frank Cass and Co., 1968), pp. 204–214.

22. *Ch'ang-sha FC,* 1747 ed., 14.6a–7a; *Hsiang-t'an HC,* 1781 ed., 14.6a; 1818 ed., 39.2a–b; *Pao-ch'ing FC,* 1849 ed., 143.13b–14a. Shigeta Atsushi, "Shin-sho Konan no jinushi-sei," builds a hypothesis of historical progression on the basis of evidence concerning a strong body of tenant–cultivators in the rice growing areas of Hunan.

23. Rent bursaries were entrusted with the responsibility for rent collection and tax payment by private landlords, who paid a commission to the bursary for this service. See Muramatsu Yūji, "Nijū seiki shotō ni okeru Soshū kinbō no ichi sosan to sono kosaku seidō — Kōso-shō Go-ken Hi-shi kyō-ju-san kankei 'Soseki ben-sa' satsu no kenkyū," *Kindai Chūgoku kenkyū,* no. 5:149 (1963).

24. Muramatsu Yūji, "A Documentary study of Chinese Landlordism in the Late Ch'ing and the Early Republican Kiangnan,"

Bulletin of the School of Oriental and African Studies, 29.3:591 (1966).

25. Muramatsu Yūji, "Nijū seiki Soshū no ichi sosan," pp. 168–169. Wu Yüan-chang, the erring rent collector, did not even lose his position. In the pre-1911 period, rent collectors were sometimes wives of tenants, p. 141.

26. The practice of giving a discount for prompt payment is described by Muramatsu Yūji, "Nijū seiki Soshū no ichi sosan," p. 22. Examples presented by Muramatsu on pp. 95–96 and discussed on p. 97 give a discount of 30.8 per cent but in the example presented on p. 97 and discussed on p. 98, the tenant received a discount of 44.6 per cent.

27. Ch'en Hsiao-lin and Wang San-yüan's discounted rates for long overdue payment are compared by Muramatsu Yūji with the smaller discount received by Chang Hung-fa for prompt payment: "Nijū seiki Soshū no ichi sosan," pp. 105–107; see also the case of Ch'en Ching-lan, p. 109.

28. Muramatsu Yūji, "Nijū seiki Soshū no ichi sosan," pp. 111–112.

29. Amano Motonosuke, *Shina nōson zakki* (Tokyo: Seikatsusha, 1942), pp. 126–134.

30. The per capita acreage in northwest Fukien was 7 mou: Sun Ching-chih, pp. 113–114. On primitive agriculture, see pp. 140–141.

31. In the 1950's, using chemical fertilizer, yields of 1,000 to 2,000 catties per mou were achieved in this region, almost ten times the yields obtained in northwest Fukien. *Ibid.,* pp. 141, 144.

32. Hsü T'ien-t'ai, pp. 59–80.

33. In Hui-an, Hsien-yu and Chin-men, over 50 per cent of the tenants paid in cash: Hsü T'ien-t'ai, p. 68.

34. Where only 3 per cent of payments fell into this category: Hsü T'ien-t'ai, p. 66.

35. In Yung-an hsien 80 per cent; an itemized list is presented by Hsü T'ien-t'ai, p. 66.

36. Hsü T'ien-t'ai, p. 67. Rent on the best paddy land in Shih-ma, an area in Chang-chou prefecture, was 600 catties per mou (shih catties, paid in unhusked rice).

37. The average fixed rent on middle-grade paddy for the province was 211 catties/mou, about 60 per cent of the average provincial rice yield of 361 catties/mou.

38. Hung Fu, p. 25, converted from kilograms/hectare to catties/mou.

39. Table 11, pp. 215–220, in *Fukken shō tōkei jihō* (Taipei: Minami Shina chōsa shiryō, Nan-yō Kyōkai Taiwan shi-bu, 1937); despite some peculiarities in the table, the information on yields in northwest Fukien accords with information for the 1950's that the average yield in this region was only 200–250 catties/mou: Sun Ching-chih, pp. 140–141.

40. Hung Fu, p. 26. These figures were for localities in a single cropping rice region; in the double cropping area of south Fukien, yields were probably much higher.

41. If fixed rents were 60 per cent of the yield, the 150 catties per mou rent in Ch'ung-an hsien indicates a crop of 250 catties, while the 600 catties/mou rent in Shih-ma (Chang-chou) indicates a total yield of 1,000 catties. The Ch'ung-an peasant was left with 100 catties of rice after paying rent, or one-fourth the rice retained by the Shih-ma tenant after rent. This comparison may prompt some to argue that the difference in yield stems from better land quality on the coast and from nothing else, but we have seen in Chapters Two and Three that land quality in rice cultivation is not a phenomenon of nature, but can be created, or maintained, by human effort and destroyed by human negligence. It, too, is a "man-made" factor.

42. Cash rents for the best land (1937) were 8.4 yüan; for middle grade land, 6 yüan, and for poor land, 4 yüan. Hsü T'ien-t'ai, p. 76, quotes a market price of 2.8 yüan for 100 catties of new rice (unhusked). Cash rents were converted into rice equivalents by using this market price. Cash rents were then equivalent to 300, 214, and 143 catties/mou for the best to the poorest quality land. These rents were only slightly higher than the provincial average fixed rent, while the yield in an area such as Hsing-hua was about 800 catties.

43. The fixed rent for the best land in Hsien-yu hsien, Hsing-hua prefecture, was 400 catties/mou: Hsü T'ien-t'ai, p. 67. This was a county where half of the rents were paid in cash, p. 68.

44. With some exceptions. In Chien-yang hsien, Chien-ning pre-

fecture, it was apparently so difficult to attract tenants that landlords offered land at rents amounting to only 30 per cent of the crop: Hsü T'ien-t'ai, p. 66.

45. There is little information on farm size in the interior vs. the coast. Figures for coastal hsien on average farm size, produced by Buck's farm survey, were: Lung-ch'i (Chang-chou), 15.7 mou; P'u-t'ien (Hsing-hua), 7 mou; and Hui-an (Ch'üan-chou), 6.3 mou. Buck, *Land Utilization,* III, 60, table 28. Hectare figures were converted to mou. These figures generally agree with those reported in *Chien-she yüeh-k'an,* 3.6, cited in the 1934 *Chung-kuo ching-chi nien-chien,* p. F-53: in coastal Hai-ch'eng hsien, 88 per cent of the farms were smaller than 10 mou. In near-by Hsien-yu county, 75 per cent of the farms were over 10 mou in size. It is possible that farms in some parts of northwest Fukien were as large as 30 to 35 mou: assuming an average family size of 5.0, the per capita figure of 7 mou reported in the 1950's would represent a farm of 35 mou. Sun Ching-chih, pp. 113–114.

46. Evidence for the 1950's, *ibid.,* pp. 140–141, 142–146, is supported by evidence for the 1930's, in Hung Fu, pp. 42–44, figs. 10, 11, 12, which shows that most areas in the northwest did not grow winter wheat.

47. In some coastal villages, fishing was an important supplementary source of income for the rural population: *Fukken shō tōkei jihō,* p. 18. In *Emigrant Communities in South China: A Study of Overseas Migration and Its Influence on Standards of Living and Social Change* (Shanghai: Kelly and Walsh, Ltd., 1939), p. 87, Chen Ta noted that "the farmer does not, as is popularly believed, derive his income from a single source but from several." The study covered villages in south Fukien and east Kwangtung.

48. *Hunan nien-chien, 1935,* published by the Secretariat, Hunan Provincial Government (Ch'ang-sha, 1935), pp. 45–46.

49. *Ibid.*

50. *Ibid.* Area figures converted to square kilometers from those presented in p. 8 were used together with the population figures presented on pp. 45–46.

51. *Chung-kuo ching-chi nien-chien, 1934,* pp. F1–2 for agricultural population. The investigations of the Shanghai Research Department of the South Manchurian Railroad provide detailed evi-

dence on the Kiangsu village economy. The citation here is from their study of Ch'ang-shu hsien: *Kōso-shō Jōjuku-ken nōson jittai chōsa hōkokusho* (1939), p. 23, table 10.

52. Hunan information from Heng-yang hsien: Buck, *Land Utilization,* III, 58–59; the Soochow figures are from Amano Motonosuke, *Shina nōson,* p. 127.

53. Regional differences in weights and measures between southern Kiangsu and central Hunan are not large enough to affect the comparison. If we calculate the variance of land and weight measures in these regions from the standard mou and catty, using information collected by Buck, *Land Utilization,* III, 473, the effect of the combined variance of these two measures would have been a slight overstatement of yields in both areas. If a standard catty/standard mou is taken as = 100, the southern Kiangsu yields would be between 96–112, and the Hunan yields would have been 104.

54. The only available information is for I-yang hsien, where 94 per cent of the rents were paid in rice: Buck, *Land Utilization,* III, 61.

55. Dwight Perkins, *Agricultural Development,* p. 105.

56. Cash rents were collected by the Kung-shou bursary in Wu hsien: Muramatsu Yūji, "Nijū seiki Soshū no ichi sosan," whose records extend from 1906–1929, and by the She-ching bursary of the Wu clan, records from 1893–1928: Muramatsu Yūji, "Shinmatsu Min-sho no Kōnan ni okeru hōran kankei no jittai to sono kessan hōkoku — Soshū Go-shi yo-keisan 'Hōshō kaku-gō-bi-sa' satsu no kenkyū," *Kindai Chūgoku kenkyū,* 6:1–66 (1964). They were also found in some of the rent bills, dated 1920–1930, held by the Harvard-Yenching Library: Muramatsu Yūji, "Saikin gūmoku shita jakkan no Chūgoku jinushi-sei kankei bunsho ni tsuite — Harvard-Yenching kenkyū-jo shūzō no soyo sono ta," *Tōyōgakuhō,* 46.4:1–33 (1964).

57. Amano Motonosuke, *Shina nōson,* p. 131.

58. In Muramatsu Yūji, "Nijū seiki Soshū no ichi sosan," p. 118, table 13, and p. 119, table 14, the titular average rents were close to 1 shih/mou. *Chung-kuo ching-chi nien-chien,* p. 169, cites 1 shih/mou as the prevailing rent on the best land in Wu hsien. Muramatsu Yūji, "Shin-matsu Soshū fukin no ichi sosan ni okeru jinushi shoyūchi no chōzei kosaku kankei — Kōso-shō Go-ken Ma Rin issan chichō

sōryō kankei bosatsu ni tsuite," (Hitotsubashi) *Keizaigaku kenkyū,* 6:217–218 (1962), suggests that there was a reduction in rent levels after the Taiping Rebellion which is reflected in the Soochow bursary accounts. According to Wang Yeh-chien, "The Impact of the Taiping Rebellion on Population in Southern Kiangsu," *Papers on China,* 19:121, 128, 129, 131 (1965), however, the rebellion did not really adversely affect Soochow; its population swelled to accommodate refugees and its trade prospered, while agricultural yields remained stable. There was thus no economic reason why the Taiping Rebellion should have brought lower rents to Soochow.

59. Amano Motonosuke, *Shina nōson,* p. 131.

60. Muramatsu Yūji, "Nijū seiki Soshū no ichi sosan," pp. 117, 121–122.

61. Muramatsu Yūji, "Shin-matsu Min-sho no Kōnan," pp. 48–49; also Muramatsu's "Nijū seiki Soshū no ichi sosan," pp. 112–113.

62. Dwight Perkins, *Agricultural Development,* p. 106, note 34.

63. Costs in the early 1930's for shipping rice from Soochow to Shanghai were: by traditional junk, taking 2–5 days, 0.2 yüan per picul; by steamboat, in 20 hours, 0.195 yüan per picul; by train, taking 4 hours, 0.161 yüan per picul. Minami Manshū tetsudō kabushiki gaisha, Shanhai jimusho, Shina shokuhin sōsho dai jūroku shū: *Kome: Shanhai kome shijō chōsa* (Shanghai, 1940), p. 94, Table 30.

64. The calculations were based on the assumption that the Soochow rice price was 90 per cent of the Shanghai price. There is no direct information on Soochow prices, but the rice price in Wu-hsi, to the west of Soochow (and hence farther away from Shanghai), was 78 per cent of the Shanghai price: Amano Motonosuke, "Shina kome no ryūtsū," p. 31. The Wu-hsi rice measure was 88 or 90 per cent of the Shanghai measure, as was Soochow's: see Shanghai shang-yeh ch'u-hsü yin-hang, comp., *Shang-p'in tiao-ch'a ts'ung-k'an,* I, 94–95 (Shanghai, 1931). This means that the Wu-hsi price of a Shanghai picul would be about 88 per cent of the Shanghai price; since Soochow is closer to Shanghai, it was assumed that its rice price would be higher, 90 per cent of the Shanghai price.

Suppose a peasant in Soochow rents 1 mou of land at a rent in kind of 1 shih. According to Table 27, this rent, when commuted, normally comes to only 60 per cent of the Shanghai market price.

Suppose the price of 1 shih of rice in Shanghai were 1 yüan. The peasant, in order to pay his landlord 0.6 yüan (the commuted money rent), takes the rice (1 shih) to sell in Soochow for 90 per cent of the Shanghai price, or 0.9 yüan a shih. He is left with 0.3 yüan after paying the landlord, and has retained 30 per cent of the landlord's contractual share at Soochow rice prices.

65. Although wartime conditions may have been primarily responsible for this phenomenon, the relative disadvantages of being a landlord in this region may have contributed to the fact that bottom soil rights were much cheaper than the topsoil (cultivation) right in Soochow about 1938. The bottom soil right cost 30 to 70 yüan/mou, while the cultivation right cost 70 to 100 yüan: Amano Motonosuke, *Shina nōson,* p. 127.

66. We can compare the average rice price on the Ch'ang-sha market with the Shanghai market price for 1912, 1922, and 1923:

	a. Ch'ang-sha price	b. Shanghai price	*a* as percentage of *b*
1912	4 yüan	7.94 yüan	50.4
1922	9.13	11.26	81.1
1923	5.49	11.20	49.0

All data in terms of 1 picul of husked rice. Ch'ang-sha prices: 1912, p. 88, and 1922–1923 prices, pp. 112–113, table 36, *Konan no kokubei,* comp. Chang Jen-chia, Shina keizai shiryō 14 (Tokyo: Seikatsu-sha, 1940). Shanghai prices from Muramatsu Yūji, "Shinmatsu Min-sho no Kōnan," p. 48, table 15. This discussion is not meant to imply that the total income of a Hunan peasant was smaller than that of a Soochow peasant; information on farm size, which we do not possess, would be needed before a comparison of total incomes could be made. J. L. Buck's 1937 study does not include farm size figures for Soochow, but information for the 1950's suggests that land–man ratios were comparable at this date. Per capita cultivated acreage for the farming population in the regions of Kiangsu along the Yangtze was over one mou; for eastern Hunan, 1.5 mou. *Economic Geography of East China,* p. 53; *Economic Geography of Central China,* p. 321.

67. Buck, *Land Utilization,* III, 311, table 7 on "Percentage of net income from other than farm sources by region" ("all farm" average): in I-yang hsien, Ch'ang-sha, this was only 4 per cent of

farm income, while in parts of Kiangsu (Ch'ang-shu hsien, Wu-hsi) it constituted 34 and 40 per cent of farm income respectively. A later study conducted by a South Manchurian Railroad survey team in Ch'ang-shu disclosed that less than 20 per cent of total income of interviewed households came from agriculture: *Kōso-shō Jōjuku-ken,* appendix, table 13.

68. Japanese interpretations of the Sung landholding system fall into two broadly conflicting schools of thought, whose debate on this topic represents only part of a larger disagreement on the periodization of Chinese history. The Kyoto school, at present headed by Miyazaki Ichisada, continues the schema formulated by Naitō Torajirō: the history of this school has been described by Miyakawa Hisayuki, "An Outline of the Naitō Hypothesis and Its Effects on Japanese Studies of China," *Far Eastern Quarterly,* 14.4:533–552 (1955). The Tokyo school, formerly led by Niida Noboru and Sudō Yoshiyuki, among others, worked within a Marxist-inspired framework. For a brief survey of the academic debates, see *Recent Trends of East Asian Studies in Japan* (Tokyo: Centre for East Asian Studies, 1962), and Shiba Yoshinobu, "Sōdai nōson-shi kenkyū o meguru shomondai," *Shakai keizai shigaku,* 31.1–5:256–269 (1966). A provocative attempt to reconcile these opposing views is Yanagida Setsuko's "Sōdai tochi shoyū-sei ni mirareru futatsu no katachi," *Tōyō bunka kenkyū-jo kiyō,* no. 29:95–130 (1963). Her conclusions point to the need for further detailed analysis of regional variance.

Appendix / FUKIEN'S POPULATION IN THE MING PERIOD

1. An undated list, found in *Pa Min t'ung-chih,* 20.2a–6a, was identified as a 1482 record for the following reasons: (1) the gazetteer itself has a preface dated Hung-chih 4 (1491–1492), but the existence of very different totals for 1492–1493 in *Chien-ning FC,* 1541 ed., 12.1b–9a, suggests an earlier dating for the *Pa Min t'ung-chih* figures; (2) totals for 1482 recorded in six hsien gazetteers were identical with those in *Pa Min t'ung-chih,* so the 1482 date seems plausible. *Chiang-lo HC,* 1585 ed., 6.2a–3a; *Yu-ch'i HC,*

1636 ed., 3.1b–13b; *Sha HC,* 1545 ed., 4.1b–4b; *Ku-t'ien HC,* 1606 ed., 4.2a–4b; *Lo-yüan HC,* 1641 ed., 3.1b–2a; *Kuei-hua HC,* 1614 ed., 4.1a–3b.

2. Ho Ping-ti, *Studies on the Population of China,* p. 8.

3. Figures for 1393 and 1578 in *Min shu,* 39.3b–4a. 1393: 3,-916,806 *k'ou.* 1578: 1,738,793 *k'ou.*

4. *Hsing-hua FC,* 1575 ed., 4.6b; *Ch'üan-chou FC,* 1612 ed., 6.3a–b; *Fu-chou FC,* 1613 ed., 26.4b; *Fu-ch'ing HC,* chüan 2; *Lung-yen HC,* 1558 ed., 1.45b; *Shou-ning HC,* 1637 ed., 1.14a–16a. Gazetteers recording fiscal populations (fractional mouths and adult males): *Kuei-hua HC,* 1614 ed., 4.3b; *Fu-ning chou-chih,* 1593 ed., 4.2b; *Fu-an HC,* 1597 ed., 3.2a–b; and the *Hsing-hua FC,* cited above.

5. Sex ratio of 107 females per 100 males in *Chien-yang HC,* 1607 ed., 3.1b; sex ratio of 130 in *Fu-an HC,* 1597 ed., 3.2a.

6. In eight hsien the sex ratio declined; in three hsien it remained constant; and in four hsien it increased, contrary to Ho's prediction that the sex ratio in the southeast rose sharply (Ho, *Studies on the Population of China,* pp. 11–12). The hsien showing a declining sex ratio were: Lung-ch'i, Lung-yen, Ch'ang-t'ai, Chang-p'ing, and Ning-yang (*Chang-chou FC,* 1628 ed., 8.15b–17a), Yu-ch'i (*Yu-ch'i HC,* 1636 ed., 3.1b–13b), Fu-ning chou (*Fu-ning chou-chih,* 1593 ed., 3.1a–3a and 1614 ed., 7.1b–4b), and Ning-te hsien (*Ning-te HC,* 1591 ed., 2.26a). Those with constant sex ratios were: Shou-ning hsien (*Shou-ning HC,* 1637 ed., 1.14a–16a), Nan-ching hsien, and Hai-ch'eng hsien (last two in *Chang-chou FC,* already cited). Hsien showing increases in the sex ratio were Chien-yang (*Chien-yang HC,* 1607 ed., 3.1b–3a), Chang-p'u, P'ing-ho (last two in *Chang-chou FC*) and Fu-an hsien (*Fu-an HC,* 1597 ed., 3.2a–b).

7. Information in *Fu-ning chou-chih,* 1593 ed., 4.2a, and *Fu-an HC,* 1597 ed., 3.2a–b. The 40 per cent figure is based on a 1953 age distribution table for China, which showed that 35.9 per cent of the population was in ages 0–14, and 7.3 per cent in ages above 60: John S. Aird, "Population Growth and Distribution in Mainland China," II, 364 in *An Economic Profile of Mainland China,* Studies Prepared for the Joint Economic Committee, U.S. 90th Congress (Washington: U.S. Government Printing Office, 1967).

8. Dwight Perkins, *Agricultural Development,* p. 24.

9. John D. Durand, "The Population Statistics of China, A.D. 2–1953," *Population Studies,* 13.2:254 (1960), table A-3.

10. G. W. Skinner, "A Study in Miniature of Chinese Population," *Population Studies,* 5.2:91–103 (1951); also Chao Ch'eng-hsin, "Familism as a Factor in the Chinese Population Balance," *Yenching Journal of Social Studies,* 3.1:1–21 (1940).

11. *Ch'üan-chou FC,* 1612 ed., 6.3a–4b.

12. Durand, p. 254, table A-3.

13. In 1482, Ch'ang-t'ai's average household size was 10.55; *Pa Min t'ung-chih,* 20.2a–6a. By 1612, it was well over 11; *Ch'üan-chou FC,* 1612 ed., 8.15b–17a.

14. As in one explanation of the dynastic cycle: Wang Yü-ch'üan, "The Rise of Land Tax and the Fall of Dynasties in Chinese History," *Pacific Affairs,* 9.2:201–220 (1936).

15. On Fukien's academic success in Ming times, see p. 227, table 27 in Ho Ping-ti, *The Ladder of Success.* The three coastal prefectures of Fu-chou, Ch'üan-chou, and Hsing-hua were among those producing the highest number of chin-shih in Ming times: see his table 35, p. 246.

16. It is possible to correct for the under-reporting of household members by assuming a "true" average household size, then raising the total of individuals reported to bring the recorded household size up to this average. The remaining downward bias can be blamed on the flight of households from the registers. Without more information on amalgamation practices, however, it is not possible to correct for the distortion introduced by the combination of nonkin families, and by the selective reporting of a small fraction of the total number of individuals in the combined household. Ignorance on points such as how many families normally participated in such fiscal combinations, and what percentage of their members were reported for tax purposes, prevents our selection of a method to correct for these evasive practices.

17. *Min shu,* 39.13b; *Pa Min t'ung-chih,* 21.12a–16a.

18. If there were significant differences between the size of landholdings in the interior and on the coast, our method of applying a provincial average for per capita acreage would introduce a serious distortion into the estimates in Column A, Table A.3. For example, if per capita acreage were highest in the interior and lowest on the

coast, applying a provincial average would under-estimate coastal population and overestimate the population of the interior. To test the possibility that such a distortion existed, gazetteers were scanned for 1391 acreage totals. Put together with population figures for 1391, the following hsien per capita acreage averages emerged. They are arranged below to facilitate comparison:

Interior		*Coast*	
1. Chien-yang hsien	4.94 mou	1. Fu-ning chou	3.9 mou
2. Shao-wu	4.42	2. Fu-an hsien	4.8
3. Kuang-tse	4.64	3. Ning-te	5.3
4. T'ai-ning	3.32	4. Ku-t'ien	6.8
5. Chien-ning	4.91	5. Lung-yen	3.2
6. Sha	1.70		
7. Yu-ch'i	3.81		
Median	4.42 mou	Median	4.8 mou

The conclusion suggested by this brief survey is that there was no appreciable difference in the size of landholdings between the coastal and interior hsien. In reality, the coast may have successfully concealed more of its population and emerged with artificially high per capita landholdings, but it is not possible to explore this possibility. It seems that there is no alternative to using the provincial average. *Chien-yang HC,* 1607 ed., 3.5a, 3.1b; *Shao-wu FC,* 1623 ed., 18.2b, 18.10a–b; *Sha HC,* 1545 ed., 4.4b, 4.1b; *Yu-ch'i HC,* 1636 ed., 3.6b, 3.1b; *Fu-ning chou-chih,* 1593 ed., 4.4a, 4.11b, 4.13b, 4.1a–3b; *Ku-t'ien HC,* 1606 ed., 4.6b, 4.2a–4b; *Lung-yen HC,* 1558 ed., 2.51a, 1.44b.

19. Although the percentages would change if the 1482 totals were compared with estimates of 1482 population, based on a 0.5 per cent annual growth rate, the relative rankings of the hsien in under-reporting would remain the same.

BIBLIOGRAPHY

PRIMARY SOURCES

Abbreviations

CC chou-chih 州志 (chou gazetteer)
FC fu-chih 府志 (prefectural gazetteer)
HC hsien-chih 縣志 (hsien gazetteer)
KK Kokuritsu Kokkai toshokan 國立國會圖書館 (National Diet Library), Tokyo
NK Naikaku bunko 內閣文庫 (Cabinet Library), Tokyo
SK Sonkeikaku bunko 尊經閣文庫 (Marquis Maeda Library), Tokyo
TYBK Tōyō bunko 東洋文庫 (Oriental Library), Tokyo
TYBKK Tōyō bunka kenkyū-jo 東洋文化研究所 (Institute of Oriental Culture), University of Tokyo

An-ch'i HC 安溪. 1757 ed. TYBK.
Chang-chou FC 漳州. 1573 ed., reprinted as no. 15–2 in series Chung-kuo shih-hsüeh ts'ung-shu. 中國史學叢書 (Collected works of Chinese history) Taipei: Hsüeh-sheng shu-chü.
Chang-chou FC 漳州. 1628 ed. NK.
Chang-chou FC 漳州. 1877–1878 ed. KK.
Chang-p'u HC 漳浦. 1700 ed. NK, TYBK.
Ch'a-ling CC 茶陵. 1695 ed.
Ch'ang-ning HC 常寧. 1870 ed.
Ch'ang-sha FC 長沙. 1534 ed. KK.
Ch'ang-sha FC 長沙. 1685 ed. NK.
Ch'ang-sha FC 長沙. 1747 ed. KK.
Ch'ang-sha HC 長沙. 1747 ed. NK.
Ch'ang-sha HC 長沙. 1810 ed. TYBK.
Ch'ang-sha HC 長沙. 1871 ed.

Ch'ang-te FC 常德府志. 1813 ed.
Che-chiang t'ung-chih 浙江通志 (Chekiang provincial gazetteer). 1934 photo-reprint of 1899 ed. Commercial Press.
Ch'en-chou FC 辰州. 1685 ed. NK.
Ch'en Fu-liang 陳傅良. *Chih-chai hsien-sheng wen-chi* 止齋先生文集 (Collected writings of Ch'en Fu-liang, 1137–1203). Ssu-pu ts'ung-k'an ed.
Cheng-ho HC 政和. 1832 ed. TYBK.
Chia-ching shih-ssu-nien chin-shih teng-k'o lu 嘉靖拾肆年進士登科錄 (List of successful chin-shih candidates in 1535). NK.
Chia-li chien-i 家禮簡儀 (An abridged household almanac). Full title: *Fan yeh fa-k'an shih min pien-yung chia-li chien-i* 范爺發刊士民便用家禮簡儀 (Mr. Yeh's abridged household almanac for the convenience of literati and the people). 1607 ed. SK.
Chiang-lo HC 將樂. 1585 ed. KK.
Chien-an HC 建安. 1713 ed. KK.
Chien-ning FC 建寧. 1541 ed. SK.
Chien-ning FC 建寧. 1693 ed. Harvard-Yenching Library.
Chien-yang HC 建陽. 1607 ed. KK.
Chien-yang HC 建陽. 1929 ed.
Ch'ien-yu HC 遷遊. 1771 ed., reprinted in 1873. TYBK.
Chin-chiang HC 晉江. 1765 ed. TYBK.
Ching CC 靖. 1879 ed. KK.
Ching-chou hsiang-t'u chih 靖州鄉土志 (Ching-chou gazetteer). 1908 ed.
Chu-p'i yü-chih 硃批諭旨 (The Vermilion Rescripts). 1738.
Ch'üan-chou FC 泉州. 1612 ed. KK.
Ch'üan-nan tsa-chih 泉南雜志 (Ch'üan-chou gazetteer). NK.
Ch'ung-an HC 崇安. 1670 ed. KK, NK.
Fu-an HC 福安. 1597 ed. SK.
Fu-chien t'ung-chih 福建通志 (Fukien provincial gazetteer). 1943 ed.
Fu-ch'ing HC 福清. Undated. KK.
Fu-chou FC 福州. 1596 ed. NK.
Fu-chou FC 福州. 1613 ed. NK.
Fu-ning CC 福寧. 1593 ed. NK, KK.
Fu-ning CC 福寧. 1616 ed. SK.
Hai-ch'eng HC 海澄. 1633 ed. KK.
Hai-ch'eng HC 海澄. 1693 ed. NK.

Heng-chou FC 衡州. 1593 ed. KK.
Heng-chou FC 衡州. 1875 ed. KK.
Heng-shan HC 衡山. 1746 ed. KK.
Heng-yang HC 衡陽. 1820 ed. TYBK.
Heng-yang HC 衡陽. 1872–1874 ed. KK, TYBK.
Hsiang-hsiang HC 湘鄉. 1874 ed. KK.
Hsiang-t'an HC 湘潭. 1756 ed.
Hsiang-t'an HC 湘潭. 1781 ed. NK.
Hsiang-t'an HC 湘潭. 1818 ed. KK, TYBK.
Hsiang-t'an HC 湘潭. 1889 ed. KK.
Hsiang-yin HC 湘陰. 1565 ed. KK.
Hsiang-yin HC 湘陰. 1823 ed. TYBK.
Hsiang-yin t'u-chih 湘陰圖志 (Hsiang-yin gazetteer). 1880 ed.
Hsien-yu HC 仙遊. 1558 ed. SK.
Hsing-hua FC 興化. 1503 ed. KK, TYBK.
Hsing-hua FC 興化. 1575 ed. NK.
Huang Ming chih-fang t'u 皇明職方圖 (The administrative areas of the Ming empire).
Huang Ming kung-chü k'ao 皇明貢學考 (An investigation of the Ming examination system), comp. Wang Ch'i 王圻. 1596 preface. NK.
Hui-an hsien hsü-chih 惠安縣續志 (Rev. ed. of the Hui-an hsien gazetteer). 1612 ed. KK, TYBK.
Hu-nan sheng li ch'eng-an 湖南省例成案 (Administrative precedents for Hunan province). TYBKK.
Hu-nan t'ung-chih 湖南通志 (Hunan provincial gazetteer). 1885 ed. KK.
I-t'ung lu-ch'eng t'u-chi 一統路程圖記 (Maps and records of the itineraries in the empire), comp. Huang Pien 黃汴. 1570 ed. NK.
I-yang HC 益陽. 1874 ed. KK, TYBK.
Ku-t'ien HC 古田. 1606 ed. KK.
Kuang huang yü k'ao 廣皇輿考 (Geography of the empire), comp. Chang T'ien-fu 張天復. c. 1627 ed. NK.
Kuei-hua HC 歸化. 1614 ed. KK.
Kuo-ch'ao tien-hui 國朝典彙 (Imperial statutes). Hsü Hsüeh-chü 徐學聚. NK.
Li CC 澧. 1874 ed.
Li Hsün 李煦. "Su-chou chih-tsao Li Hsün tsou-che," 蘇州織造李煦奏摺 (Memorials of Su-chou Textile Commissioner Li Hsün) in

Wen-hsien ts'ung-pien 文獻叢編 (Collected records), vol. 2. Taipei, Palace Museum, 1964.
Li-ling HC 醴陵. 1871 ed. KK, TYBK.
Lin-hsiang HC 臨湘. 1872 ed.
Ling HC 酃. 1873 ed.
Ling-ling HC 零陵. 1876 ed.
Liu-yang HC 瀏陽. 1733 ed. TYBK.
Liu-yang HC 瀏陽. 1873 ed. KK, TYBK.
Lo-yüan HC 羅源. 1614 ed. KK.
Lung-ch'i HC 龍溪. 1762 ed., reprinted in 1879. TYBK.
Lung-yen HC 龍巖. 1558 ed. KK.
Lung-yen HC 龍巖. 1689 ed. NK.
Min shu 閩書. 1631 ed. NK.
Ning-hsiang HC 寧鄉. 1867 ed.
Ning-te HC 寧德. 1591 ed. TYBK.
Ning-yang HC 寧洋. 1692 ed. NK, TYBK.
O-ning HC 甌寧. 1694 ed. NK, TYBK.
Pa-ling HC 巴陵. 1685 ed. NK.
Pa-ling HC 巴陵. 1873 ed.
Pa Min t'ung-chih 八閩通志 (Fukien provincial gazetteer). 1491 ed. NK.
Pao-ch'ing FC 寶慶. 1567 ed. KK.
Pao-ch'ing FC 寶慶. 1685 ed. NK.
Pao-ch'ing FC 寶慶. 1849 ed. KK.
P'i yü chi 甓餘集. Full title: *Chu chung-ch'eng p'i yü chi* 朱中丞甓康集 (Chu Wan's collected writings). NK.
P'u-ch'eng HC 浦城. 1650 ed. NK.
P'u t'ien HC 浦田. 1758 ed. TYBK.
San shan chih 三山志 (Fu-chou gazetteer). NK.
Sha HC 沙. 1545 ed. KK.
Shan-hua HC 善化. 1877 ed.
Shang ch'eng i-lan 商程一覽 (Survey of commercial routes). NK.
Shao-wu FC 邵武. 1601 ed. SK.
Shao-wu FC 邵武. 1623 ed. NK.
Shao-yang HC 邵陽. 1684 ed. NK.
Shao-yang HC 邵陽. 1877 ed. KK.
Shao-yang hsien hsiang-t'u chih 邵陽縣鄉土志 (Shao-yang hsien gazetteer). 1907 ed.
Shih cheng lu 實政錄 (A record of true government). Full title: *Lu*

Fu-an shih cheng lu 陸福安實政錄 (A record of true government in Fu-an hsien). c. 1595–1596. NK.
Shou-ning HC 壽寧. 1637 ed. KK.
Shou-ning HC 壽寧. 1686 ed. NK.
Shui-lu lu-ch'eng 水陸路程 (Itinerary of water and overland routes). SK.
Sung-ch'i HC 松溪. 1700 ed. NK.
Ta-t'ien HC 大田. c. 1612. KK.
T'ao-yüan HC 桃源. 1576 ed. SK.
T'ao-yüan HC 桃源. 1892 ed.
Te-hua HC 德化. 1687 ed. NK.
T'ing-chou FC 汀州. 1637 ed. NK.
Wan-yung cheng-tsung 萬用正宗 (A multi-purpose "how to do it" guide). NK.
Wu-ling HC 武陵. 1868 ed.
Yen-p'ing FC 延平. 1660 ed. NK.
Yin-shih shu 飲食書 (On food and drink). Sung Kung-wang 宋公王. NK.
Yo-chou FC 岳州. 1746 ed. TYBK.
Yu HC 攸. 1871 ed.
Yu-ch'i HC 尤溪. 1636 ed. KK.
Yüan-chou FC 沅州. 1873 ed.
Yung-an HC 永安. 1594 ed. KK.
Yung-an HC 永安. 1723 ed. TYBK.
Yung-chou FC 永州. 1495 ed. KK.
Yung-chou FC 永州. 1867 ed.
Yung-fu HC 永福. 1612 ed. KK.
Yung-shun FC 永順. 1793 ed.

SECONDARY SOURCES

Abe Takeo 安部健夫. "Beikoku jukyū no kenkyū: 'Yōseishi' no isshō to shite mita" 米穀需給の研究—「雍正史」の一章としてみた (A study of the supply and demand for staple grains as a chapter in the history of the Yung-cheng reign, 1723–1735), *Tōyōshi kenkyū* 東洋史研究 (Studies in Oriental history) 15.4: 484–577 (1957).
Agrarian China. Chicago, Institute of Pacific Relations, 1938.

Aird, John S. "Population Growth and Distribution in Mainland China," *An Economic Profile of Mainland China*, Studies prepared for the Joint Economic Committee, U.S. 90th Congress, vol. 2. Washington, U.S. Government Printing Office, 1967.

Amano Motonosuke 天野元之助. "Shina ni okeru kome no ryūtsū kikō to sono ryūtsū hiyō 支那に於ける米の流通機構とその流通費用 (The organization and cost of rice flows in China), *Tōa keizai sōsho* 東亞經濟叢書 (Papers on East Asian economy) 1.1: 1–32 (1941).

——— *Shina nōson zakki* 支那農村襍記 (Notes on Chinese agriculture). Tokyo, Seikatsu-sha, 1942.

——— "Chin Fu no nōsho to sui-tōsaku gijutsu no tenkai" 陳旉の農書と水稻作技術の展開 (Ch'en Fu's Nung shu and the development of rice cultivation techniques), *Tōhōgakuhō* 東方學報 (Journal of Oriental studies), no. 19: 23–64 (1950), no. 21: 37–133 (1952).

——— "Mindai nōgyō no tenkai" 明代農業の展開 (The development of Ming agriculture), *Shakai keizai shigaku* 社會經濟史學 (Social and economic history) 23.5–6: 19–40 (1958).

——— *Chūgoku nōgyō-shi kenkyū* 中國農業史研究 (A history of Chinese agriculture). Tokyo, Ochanomizu Shobō, 1962.

Bailey, Liberty Hyde. *The Standard Cyclopedia of Horticulture*. New York, Macmillan, 1929.

Baker, Hugh D. *A Chinese Lineage Village: Sheung Shui*. London, Frank Cass and Co., 1968.

Ball, Samuel. *An Account of the Cultivation and Manufacture of Tea in China*. London, Longman, Brown, Green and Longman, 1848.

Beardsley, Richard, John W. Hall, and Robert E. Ward. *Village Japan*. Chicago, University of Chicago Press, 1959.

Bielenstein, Hans. "The Chinese Colonization of Fukien until the End of T'ang," *Studia Serica Bernhard Karlgren Dedicata*. Copenhagen, Ejnar Munksgaard, 1959.

Blair, Emma H. and James A. Robertson. *The Philippine Islands, 1492–1898*. 3 vols. Cleveland, Arthur H. Clark Co., 1903.

Boserup, Ester. *The Conditions of Agricultural Growth: The Economics of Agrarian Change under Population Pressure*. Chicago, Aldine, 1965.

Boxer, C. R. *Fidalgos in the Far East, 1550–1770*. The Hague, Martinus Nijhoff, 1948.

——— "The Manila Galleon, 1565–1815," *History Today* 8.8: 538–547 (1958).

——— ed. *South China in the Sixteenth Century*. London, Hakluyt Society, 1953.

Brown, Delmer. *Money Economy in Medieval Japan*. New Haven, Far Eastern Association, 1951.

Buck, John Lossing. *Farm Ownership and Tenancy in China*. Shanghai, National Christian Council, undated.

——— *Land Utilization in China*. 3 vols. Nanking, University of Nanking, 1937.

Chang T'ien-tse. *Sino-Portuguese Trade from 1514 to 1644*. Leiden, Brill, 1934.

Chao Ch'eng-hsin. "Familism as a Factor in the Chinese Population Balance," *Yenching Journal of Social Studies* 3.1: 1–21 (1940).

Chao Ch'üan-ch'eng. "A Ship's Voyage from Luzon to China in the Eighteenth Century," in E-tu Zen Sun and John de Francis, trs., *Chinese Social History*. Washington, American Council of Learned Societies, 1956.

Chao Yüan-jen. "Languages and Dialects in China," *Geographical Journal* 102.2: 63–67 (1943).

Ch'en Chao-nan 陳昭南. *Yung-cheng Ch'ien-lung nien-chien ti yin ch'ien pi-chia pien-tung* 雍正乾隆年間的銀錢比價變動 (Changes in the relative price of silver and copper cash in the Yung-cheng and Ch'ien-lung reign periods). Economic Monographs no. 4, Institute of Economics, Academia Sinica. Taipei, 1966.

Ch'en Chen-han 陳振漢. "Ming-mo Ch'ing-ch'u (1620-1720) Chung-kuo ti nung-yeh lao-tung sheng-ch'an-lü, ti-tsu ho t'u-ti chi-chung" 明末清初 (1620–1720) 中國的農業勞動生產率, 地租和土地集中 (Chinese agricultural labor productivity, rent, and land concentration in the late Ming and early Ch'ing, 1620–1720), *Chung-kuo tzu-pen-chu-i meng-ya wen-t'i t'ao-lun chi* 中國資本主義萌芽問題討論集 (Collected papers on the issue of sprouts of capitalism in China), vol. I. Peking, San-lien shu-tien 三聯書店, 1957.

Ch'en Heng-li 陳恆力, comp. *Pu nung shu yen-chiu* 補農書研究 (Research on the Pu nung shu). Shanghai, Chung-hua shu-chü 中華書局, 1958.

Chen Ta. *Emigrant Communities in South China: A Study of Overseas Migration and Its Influence on Standards of Living and Social*

Change. Shanghai, Kelly and Walsh, 1939.

China Imperial Maritime Customs. (From 1911 on, The Maritime Customs). *Returns of Trade and Trade Reports*. Shanghai, Inspector General of Customs.

The China Yearbook. Published annually in Tientsin by the Tientsin Press.

Chou Ch'i-chung 周其忠. "Ti-chu chieh-chi ti lien-ho tsu-chih—'P'ing-hu tsu-chan lien-ho pan-shih ch'u' ti chi chien tsui-cheng" 地主階級的聯合組織—「平湖租棧聯合辦事處」的几件罪証 (A cooperative organization of the landlord class: several heinous items from the "P'ing-hu rent bursary cooperative management cases"), *Wen-wu* (Literature), no. 3: 6–7, 11 (1965).

Chung-kuo ching-chi nien-chien, 1934 中國經濟年鑑 (Chinese economic yearbook, 1934). 2 vols. Shanghai, Commercial Press, 1934.

Ch'ü T'ung-tsu. *Local Government in China under the Ch'ing*. Cambridge, Harvard University Press, 1962.

Ch'üan Han-sheng 全漢昇. "Nan Sung t'ao-mi ti sheng-ch'an yü yün-hsiao" 南宋稻米的生產與運銷 (Rice production and marketing in the Southern Sung), *Li-shih yü-yen yen-chiu so chi-k'an* 歷史語言研究所集刊 (Bulletin of the Institute of History and Philology, Academia Sinica) 10: 403–431 (1942).

——— and Wang Yeh-chien 王業鍵. "Ch'ing Yung-cheng nien-chien (1723–1735) ti mi-chia" 清雍正年間(1723–35)的米價 (Rice prices in the Yung-cheng reign period, 1723–1735), *Li-shih yü-yen yen-chiu so chi-k'an*, 30th Anniversary volume, no. 1: 157–185 (1959).

Cipolla, Carlo. *Money, Prices, and Civilization in the Mediterranean World: Fifth to Seventeenth Century*. Princeton, Princeton University Press, 1956.

"Conference report: the origins of the Industrial Revolution," *Past and Present*, no. 17: 71–81 (1960).

Cressey, George. *Land of the 500 Million*. New York, McGraw-Hill, 1955.

Deane, Phyllis and W. A. Cole. *British Economic Growth, 1688–1959, Trends and Structures*. Cambridge, England, Department of Applied Economics Monographs no. 8, 1962.

Dovring, Folke. "The Transformation of European Agriculture," The Cambridge Economic History of Europe." Vol. VI. *The Industrial*

Revolutions and After: Incomes, Population and Technological Change (II). Ed. H. J. Habakkuk and M. Postan. Cambridge, University of Cambridge Press, 1966.

Durand, John D. "The Population Statistics of China, A.D. 2–1953," *Population Studies* 13.2: 209–256 (1960).

Duyvendak, J. J. L. "The True Dates of the Chinese Maritime Expeditions in the Early Fifteenth Century," *T'oung Pao* 34: 341–412 (1939).

Economic Geography of Central China, ed. Sun Ching-chih. Joint Publications Research Service tr. Washington, 1960.

Economic Geography of East China, ed. Sun Ching-chih. Joint Publications Research Service tr. Washington, 1961.

Fei Hsiao-t'ung. *Peasant Life in China: A Field Study of Country Life in the Yangtze Valley*. London, Routledge & Kegan Paul, 1939.

——— and Chang Chih-i. *Earthbound China: A Study of Rural Economy in Yunnan*. London, Routledge and Kegan Paul, 1949.

Feuerwerker, Albert. "China's Modern Economic History in Communist Chinese Historiography," *The China Quarterly*, no. 22: 31–61 (1965).

Fortune, Robert. *The Tea-Districts of China and India*. 2 vols. London, John Murray, 1853.

Freedman, Maurice. *Chinese Lineage and Society: Fukien and Kwangtung*. London School of Economics Monographs on Social Anthropology no. 33. New York, Humanities Press, 1966.

Fu I-ling 傅衣凌. "Ming Ch'ing shih-tai Fu-chien tien-nung feng-ch'ao k'ao-lüeh" 明清時代福建佃農風潮考略 (A brief examination of tenant movements in Ming and Ch'ing Fukien), *Fu-chien wen-hua chi-k'an* 福建文化季刊 (Fukien cultural quarterly) 1.1: 9–16 (1941).

——— "Fu-chien tien-nung ching-chi shih ts'ung-k'ao" 福建佃農經濟史叢考 (An inquiry into historical materials on the tenant economy of Fukien), *Fu-chien hsieh-ho ta-hsüeh wen shih ts'ung-k'an* 福建協和大學文史叢刊 (Fukien Christian University literary and historical gazette), no. 2: 3–34 (1944).

——— "Ming-tai Chiang-nan ti-chu ching-chi hsin chan ti ch'u pu yen-chiu" 明代江南地主經濟新展的初步研究 (Research on the first steps in the new development of the landlord economy of Ming Chiang-nan), *Hsia-men ta-hsüeh hsüeh-pao* 廈門大學學報

(Amoy University review), no. 5: 117–126 (1954).

——— *Ming Ch'ing shih-tai shang-jen chi shang-yeh tzu-pen* 明清時代商人及商業資本 (Merchants and mercantile capital in Ming and Ch'ing times). Peking, Jen-min ch'u-pan she, 1956.

——— "Ming-tai Su-chou chih-kung, Chiangsi t'ao-kung fan feng-chien tou-cheng shih-liao lei-chi" 明代蘇州織工, 江西陶工反封建鬪爭史料類輯 (Materials on the anti-feudal struggle of Su-chou textile weavers and Kiangsi potters in Ming times), *Chung-kuo tzu-pen-chu-i meng-ya wen-t'i t'ao-lun chi*, vol. I. Peking, San-lien shu-tien, 1957.

——— "Ming-tai Chiang-nan fu-hu ti fen-hsi" 明代江南富戸的分析 (An analysis of the wealthy households in Ming Chiang-nan), *Chung-kuo tzu-pen-chu-i meng-ya wen-t'i t'ao-lun chi*, vol. I. Peking, San-lien shu-tien, 1957.

——— *Ming Ch'ing nung-ts'un she-hui ching-chi* 明清農村社會經濟 (Peasant society and economy in Ming and Ch'ing). Peking, San-lien shu-tien, 1961.

Fujii Hiroshi 藤井宏. "Shin-an shōnin no kenkyū" 新安商人の研究 (The Hsin-an merchants), *Tōyōgakuhō* 東洋學報 (Journal of Oriental studies) 36.1–4: 1–44, 32–60, 65–118, 115–145 (1953–1954).

Fukken-shō tōkei jihō 福建省統計時報 (Fukien statistical journal). Taipei, 1937.

Fukutake, Tadashi. *Japanese Rural Society*, tr. R. P. Dore, London, Oxford University Press, 1967.

Furushima Kazuo 古島和雄. "Min-matsu Chōkō deruta ni okeru jinushi keiei—Chin-shi nōsho no ichi kōsatsu" 明末長江デルタに於ける地主經營—沈氏農書の一考察 (The landlord economy of the Yangtze delta in late Ming: an examination of Mr. Shen's nung shu), *Rekishigaku kenkyū* 歷史學研究 (Historical studies), no. 148: 11–23 (1950).

Gallagher, Louis J. *China in the Sixteenth Century: The Journals of Matthew Ricci, 1585–1610*. New York, Random House, 1953.

Gallin, Bernard. *Hsin Hsing, Taiwan: A Chinese Village in Change*. Berkeley, University of California Press, 1966.

Gamble, Sidney D. *Ting Hsien: A North China Rural Community*. New York, Institute of Pacific Relations, 1954.

——— *North China Villages: Social, Political, and Economic Activities*

Before 1933. Berkeley, University of California Press, 1963.

Geertz, Clifford. *Agricultural Involution: The Process of Ecological Change in Indonesia*. Berkeley, University of California Press, 1966.

Grist, D. H. *Rice*. London, Longmans, Green, 1959.

du Halde, J. B. *Description Geographique, Chronologique, Politique et Physique de l'Empire de la Chine et de la Tartarie Chinoise*. 2 vols. London, 1736, 1741.

Han Ta-ch'eng 韓大成. "Ming tai shang-p'in ching-chi ti fa-chan yü tzu-pen-chu-i ti meng-ya" 明代商品經濟的發展與資本主義的萌芽 (The development of a commercial economy in Ming times and sprouts of capitalism), *Ming Ch'ing she-hui ching-chi hsing-t'ai ti yen-chiu* 明清社會經濟形態的研究 (Research on Ming and Ch'ing society and economy), comp. Chung-kuo jen-min ta-hsüeh Chung-kuo li-shih chiao yen shih 中國人民大學中國歷史教研室 (Seminar on Chinese history at the People's University). Shanghai, 1957.

Hanley, Susan B. and Kozo Yamamura, "A Quiet Transformation in Tokugawa Economic History," *Journal of Asian Studies*, 30.2: 373–384 (1971).

Hartwell, Robert. "A Cycle of Economic Change in Imperial China: Coal and Iron in Northwest China, 750–1350," *Journal of the Economic and Social History of the Orient* 10.1: 102–159 (1967).

Hayashida Seizo and Gakuji Hasebe. *Chinese Ceramics*, tr. Charles A. Pomeroy. Tokyo, Tuttle, 1966.

Hibino Takeo 日比野丈夫. "Tō Sō jidai ni okeru Fukken no kaihatsu" 唐宋時代に於ける福建の開發 (Fukien's development in T'ang and Sung times), *Tōyōshi kenkyū* 4.3: 1–27 (1939).

Ho Ping-ti. "Early Ripening Rice in Chinese History," *Economic History Review*, 2nd ser. 9.2: 200–218 (1956).

——— *Studies on the Population of China, 1368–1953*. Cambridge, Harvard University Press, 1959.

——— *The Ladder of Success in Imperial China: Aspects of Social Mobility, 1368–1911*. Science Editions. New York, John Wiley and Sons, 1964.

——— "The Introduction of American Food Plants into China," *American Anthropologist*, 57.2: 191–201 (1965).

——— 何炳棣. *Chung-kuo hui-kuan shih-lun* 中國會館史論 (A historical survey of Landsmannschaften in China). Taipei, 1966.

——— *Huang-t'u yü Chung-kuo nung-yeh ti ch'i-yüan* 黃土與中國農業的起源 (The yellow earth and the origins of Chinese agriculture). Chinese University of Hong Kong, 1969.

Hoang, Pierre. *Notions techniques sur la propriété en Chine avec un choix d'actes et de documents officiels*. Variétés Sinologiques, no. 11. Shanghai, 1897.

Hoskins, W. G. "English Agriculture in the 17th and 18th Centuries," 10th Congresso Internazionale di scienze storiche (1955), *Relazioni*, vol. IV, *Storia Moderna*. Florence, 1955.

Hsü Ta-ling 許大齡. "Shih-liu shih-chi, shih-ch'i shih-chi ch'u-chi Chung-kuo feng-chien she-hui nei-pu tzu-pen-chu-i ti meng-ya" 十六世紀十七世紀初期中國封建社會內部資本主義的萌芽 (Sprouts of capitalism within China's feudal society in the sixteenth and early seventeenth centuries), *Chung-kuo tzu-pen-chu-i meng-ya wen-t'i t'ao-lun chi*, vol. II. Peking, San-lien shu-tien, 1957.

Hsü T'ien-t'ai 徐天胎. "Fu-chien tsu tien chih-tu yen-chiu" 福建租佃制度研究 (A study of rent and tenurial systems in Fukien), *Fu-chien wen-hua chi-k'an* 1.1: 59–80 (1941).

Hughes, George. *Amoy and the Surrounding Districts*. Hong Kong, de Souza, 1872.

Hunan nien-chien, 1935 湖南年鑑 (Hunan yearbook for 1935). Changsha, Secretariat, Hunan Provincial Government, 1935.

Hung Fu. "Land Utilization Maps of Fukien Province with Notes on the Physical Environment in Its Bearing upon Land-use and the Distribution of Population," *Tsing-hua University Science Reports*. Ser. C: Geological and Geographical series. 1.1: 17–53 (1936).

Hung Huan-ch'un 洪煥椿. "Lun shih-wu, shih-liu shih-chi Chiang-nan ti-ch'ü tzu-pen-chu-i sheng-ch'an kuan-hsi ti meng-ya" 論十五十六世紀江南地區資本主義生產關係的萌芽 (The sprouting of capitalistic production relationships in the Chiang-nan area in the fifteenth and sixteenth centuries), *Chung-kuo tzu-pen-chu-i meng-ya wen-t'i t'ao-lun chi hsü-pien* 中國資本主義萌芽問題討論集續編 (Sequel to collected papers on the issue of sprouts of capitalism in China). Peking, San-lien shu-tien, 1960.

Hurlbut, Floy. *The Fukienese: A Study in Human Geography*. Ph. D. diss., University of Nebraska. Published by the author, May 1930.

Imabori Seiji 今堀誠二. "Shindai ni okeru kosaku seido ni tsuite" 清代における小作制度について (On the tenancy system in

Ch'ing), *Tōyō bunka* 東洋文化 (Oriental culture) 42: 57–86 (1967).

Ipponsugi Reiko 一本杉玲子. "Tō-sei—Min-matsu Shin-sho no Fukken ni okeru" 冬牲・明末清初の福建に於ける (The winter sacrifices in Fukien during late Ming and early Ch'ing times), *Shiron* 史論 (History) 1: 36–49 (1953).

Iwao Seiichi. "Li Tan, Chief of the Chinese Residents at Hirado, Japan in the Last Days of the Ming Dynasty," *Memoirs of the Research Department of the Tōyō Bunko*, no. 17: 26–83 (1958).

Kanda Masao 神田正雄. *Konan-shō sōran* 湖南省綜覽 (Hunan handbook). Tokyo, Kai-gai sha 海外社, 1937.

Kann, Eduard. *The Currencies of China*. Shanghai, Kelly and Walsh, 1927.

Kataoka Shibako 片岡芝子. "Min-matsu Shin-sho no Kahoku ni okeru nōka keiei" 明末清初の華北に於ける農家經營 (The peasant economy of North China in late Ming and early Ch'ing), *Shakai keizai shigaku* 25.2–3: 77–100 (1959).

——— "Fukken no ichiden ryōshu sei ni tsuite" 福建の一田兩主制について (On the system of two levels of land ownership in Fukien), *Rekishigaku kenkyū*, no. 294: 42–49 (1964).

Katayama Seijirō 片山誠二郎. "Mindai kaijō mitsu-bōeki to enkai chihō gōshinsō—'Chu Wan' no kai-kin seisaku kyōkō to sono zasetsu no katei o tōshite no ichi kōsatsu" 明代海上密貿易と沿海地方郷紳層—朱紈の海禁政策強行とその挫折の過程を通しての一考察 (Ming illegal sea trade and the coastal gentry—Chu Wan's enforcement of the sea ban and the course of its failure), *Rekishigaku kenkyū* 164: 23–32 (1953).

——— "Gekkō 'nijū-shi shō' no han-ran" 月港「二十四將」の反亂 (The rebellion of the 24 leaders in Yüeh-kang), *Shimizu hakase tsuitō kinen Mindai shiron-sō* 清水博士追悼記念明代史論叢 (Studies in Ming history in honor of the late Dr. Shimizu). Tokyo, Daian, 1962.

Katō Shigeshi 加藤繁. "Keizai-shi jō yori mitaru Kita Shina to Minami Shina" 經濟史上より觀たる北支那と南支那 (North and South China from the perspective of economic history), *Shakai keizai shigaku* 12.11–12: 1–13 (1943).

——— *Shina keizai-shi kōshō* 支那經濟史考證 (Studies in Chinese economic history). 2 vols. Tokyo, Tōyō bunko, 1953.

Kiangsu sheng nung-yeh tiao-ch'a lu 江蘇省農業調查錄 (A survey of

Kiangsu agriculture), comp. Agricultural Department, Tung-nan University, 1925.

King, Frank H. H. *Money and Monetary Policy in China*. Cambridge, Harvard University Press, 1965.

Kitayama Yasuo 北山康夫. "Tō Sō jidai ni okeru Fukken shō no kaihatsu ni kansuru ichi kōsatsu" 唐宋時代に於ける福建省の開發に關する一考察 (A look at the development of Fukien in T'ang and Sung times), *Shirin* 史林 (History) 24.3: 91–100 (1939).

Kobata Atsushi 小葉田淳. "Nihon no kin gin gaikoku bōeki ni kansuru kenkyū—sakoku izen ni okeru" 日本の金銀外國貿易に關する研究—鎖國以前に於ける (Research on Japan's foreign trade before the policy of excluding foreigners), *Shigaku zasshi* 史學雜誌 (Journal of history) 44.10: 1280–1318 and 44.11: 1381–1434 (1933).

——— "Mindai Shō Sen-nin no kai-gai tsūshō hatten, toku ni Kai-chō no shōzei-sei to Nichi-Min bōeki ni tsuite" 明代漳泉人の海外通商發展, 特に海澄の餉稅制と日明貿易に就いて (The development of overseas trade by persons from Chang-chou and Ch'üan-chou in Ming times, with special reference to the Hai-ch'eng military supplies tax system and Sino-Japanese trade), *Tōa ronsō* 東亞論叢 (Papers on East Asia) 4: 125–169 (1941).

——— *Nihon to Minami Shina* 日本と南支那 (Japan and China). Taipei, 1942.

——— "The Production and Uses of Gold and Silver in 16th and 17th Century Japan," tr. W. D. Burton, *Economic History Review*, second series 18.2: 245–266 (1965).

Konan no kokubei 湖南の穀米 (Hunan rice), Comp. Chang Jen-chia 張人价. Shina keizai shiryō 14 支那經濟史料 (Chinese economy materials, 14). Tokyo, Seikatsu-sha, 1940.

Ku Ching-yen 賈敬顔. "Ming tai tz'u-ch'i ti hai-wai mao-i" 明代瓷器的海外貿易 (Foreign trade in porcelain in the Ming period), *Chung-kuo tzu-pen-chu-i meng-ya wen-t'i t'ao-lun chi*, vol. I. Peking, San-lien shu-tien, 1957.

Kuwabara Jitsuzō. "On P'u Shou-keng, a Man of the Western Regions who was the Superintendent of the Trading Ships Office in Ch'üan-chou towards the end of the Sung dynasty, together with a general sketch of (the) trade of the Arabs in China during the T'ang and Sung eras," *Memoirs of the Research Department of the Tōyō Bunko*, no. 2: 1–79 (1928) and no. 7: 1–102 (1935).

Ley, Charles D., ed. *Portuguese Voyages, 1498–1663.* New York, Dutton, 1947.

Li Kuang-pi 李光璧. "Ming tai shou-kung-yeh ti fa-chan" 明代手工業的發展 (The development of handicraft industries in the Ming period), *Chung-kuo tzu-pen-chu-i meng-ya wen-t'i t'ao-lun chi*, vol. I. Peking, San-lien shu-tien, 1957.

Li Wen-chih 李文治. *Wan Ming min-pien* 晚明民變 (Popular rebellions in the late Ming). Shanghai, 1948.

——— "Ch'ing tai Ya-p'ien chan-cheng ch'ien ti ti-tsu, shang-yeh tzu-pen kao-li tai yü nung-min sheng-huo" 淸代鴉片戰爭前的地租, 商業資本, 高利貸與農民生活 (Land rent, commercial capital, usury and peasant life in Ch'ing times before the Opium War), *Chung-kuo tzu-pen-chu-i meng-ya wen-t'i t'ao-lun chi*, vol. II. Peking, San-lien shu-tien, 1957.

Liang Fang-chung 梁方仲. "Ming tai hu-k'ou t'ien-ti chi t'ien-fu t'ung-chi" 明代戶口田地及田賦統計 (Figures on Ming population, acreage and land taxes), *Chung-kuo she-hui ching-chi shih chi-k'an* 中國社會經濟史季刊 (Chinese social and economic history) 3.1: 75–129 (1935).

——— Bibliographical review section, on *Wan-li k'uai-chi lu* 萬歷會計錄 (Statistical records for the Wan-li reign period), *Chung-kuo chin-tai ching-chi shih yen-chiu chi-k'an* 中國近代經濟史研究集刊 (Journal of modern Chinese economic history) 3.2: 292–299 (1935).

——— "Ming tai yin-k'uang k'ao" 明代銀鑛考 (Silver mining in the Ming period), *Chung-kuo she-hui ching-chi shih chi-k'an* 中國社會經濟史集刊 (Chinese social and economic history) 6.1: 65–112 (1939).

——— "Ming tai kuo-chi mao-i yü yin ti shu ch'u-ju" 明代國際貿易與銀的輸出入 (Ming international trade and silver flows), *Chung-kuo she-hui ching-chi shih chi-k'an* 6.2: 267–324 (1939).

——— *The Single-Whip Method of Taxation in China*, tr. Wang Yü-ch'üan. Cambridge, Harvard University Press, 1956.

Lieu, D. K. "Land Tenure Systems in China," *Chinese Economic Journal* 2.6: 457–474 (1928).

Lin Yüeh-hwa. *The Golden Wing: A Sociological Study of Chinese Familism.* London, Kegan Paul, Trench, Trubner, 1948.

Liu Ta-chung and Yeh Kung-chia. *The Economy of the Chinese Mainland: National Income and Economic Development, 1933–1959.*

Princeton, Princeton University Press, 1965.

Maeda Katsutarō 前田勝太郎. "Min Shin no Fukken ni okeru nōka fukugyō" 明清の福建における農家副業 (On the subsidiary industries of peasant households in Fukien during Ming), *Suzuki Shun kyōju kanreki kinen Tōyōshi ronsō* 鈴木俊教授還歴記念東洋史論叢 (Collected articles on Far Eastern history commemorating Professor Suzuki Shun's 61st birthday). Tokyo, San-yō sha, 1964.

——— "Mindai chūki ikō no Fukken ni okeru suiri kikō no hembō ni tsuite" 明代中期以降の福建における水利機構の變貌について (Changes in irrigation organizations in Fukien since mid-Ming), *Tōhōgaku* 東方學 (Oriental studies), no. 32: 88–101 (1966).

Medley, Margaret. "Ching-te-chen and the Problem of the 'Imperial Kilns,'" *Bulletin of the School of Oriental and African Studies* 39.2: 326–338 (1966).

Meilink-Roelofsz, M. A. P. *Asian Trade and European Influence in the Indonesian Archipelago between 1500 and about 1630*. The Hague, Martinus Nijhoff, 1962.

Meskill, John, tr. *Ch'oe P'u's Diary: A Record of Drifting across the Sea*. Tucson, Association for Asian Studies, 1965.

Minami Manshū tetsudō kabushiki gaisha, Shanhai jimusho. Shiryō 34 南滿洲鐵道株式會社, 上海事務所 (South Manchurian Railroad Company, Shanghai office, no. 34). *Kōso-shō Jōjuku-ken nōson jittai chōsa hōkokusho* 江蘇省常熟縣農村實態調査報告書 (Report of an agricultural survey of Ch'ang-shu hsien, Kiangsu province). Shanghai, 1939.

Minami Manshū tetsudō kabushiki gaisha, Shanhai jimusho. 南滿洲鐵道株式會社, 上海事務所 (South Manchurian Company, Shanghai office). Shina shōhin sōsho dai jū-roku shū 支那商品叢書第16輯 (Chinese commodities no. 16), *Kome—Shanhai komeshijō chōsa* 米—上海米市場調査 (Rice: a survey of the Shanghai rice market). Shanghai, 1940.

Misawa, Takeo, "An Analysis of Part-time Farming in the Postwar Period," in Kazushi Ohkawa, Bruce F. Johnston and Hiromitsu Kaneda (ed.), *Agriculture and Economic Growth: Japan's Experience*. Tokyo: University of Tokyo and Princeton University Press, 1970.

Miyakawa Hisayuki. "An Outline of the Naitō Hypothesis and Its

Effects on Japanese Studies of China," *Far Eastern Quarterly*, 14.4: 533–552 (1955).

Miyazaki Ichisada 宮崎市定. *Kakyo* 科擧 (The examination system). Osaka, 1946.

——— "Chūgoku kinsei no nōmin bōdō—toku ni To Mo-shichi no ran ni tsuite" 中國近世の農民暴動—特に鄧茂七の亂について (Peasant uprisings in modern China: the Teng Mao-ch'i rebellion), *Tōyōshi kenkyū* 30.1: 1–13 (1947).

——— *Tōyōteki kinsei* 東洋的近世 (The modern period in the Far East). Osaka, Kyōiku Times, 1950.

——— "Mindai So-Shō chihō no shi-dai-fu to min-shū—Mindai shi so-byō no kokoromi" 明代蘇松地方の士大夫と民衆—明代史素描の試み (The gentry and populace of Ming Su-chou and Sung-chiang: an attempt at a rough sketch of Ming history), *Shirin* 37.3: 1–33 (1954).

——— *Ajia shi kenkyū* アジア史研究 (Asian history), vol. III. Kyoto, Nakamura Press, 1963.

Morita Akira 森田明. "Shindai Konan ni okeru chisui kangai no tenkai" 清代湖南における治水灌漑の展開 (The development of water control and irrigation in Ch'ing Hunan), *Tōhōgaku*, no. 20: 63–76 (1960).

——— "Shindai Konan chihō ni okeru teiki-ichi ni tsuite" 清代湖南地方における定期市について (On the periodic markets in Ch'ing Hunan), *Kyūshū sangyō daigaku shōkei ronsō* 九州產業大學商經論叢 (Business and economic papers of Kyūshū Industrial University) 5.1: 49–73 (1964).

Morse, Hosea Ballou. *The Trade and Administration of China*. London, Longmans, Green, 1920.

Muramatsu Yūji 村松祐次. "Shin-matsu Soshū fukin no ichi sosan ni okeru jinushi shoyūchi no chōzei kosaku kankei—Kōso-shō Go-ken Ma Rin issan chichō sōryō kankei bosatsu ni tsuite" 清末蘇州附近の一租棧における地主所有地の徵稅・小作關係—江蘇省吳縣馮林一棧地丁漕糧關係簿冊について (Tax collection and tenants on landlord owned lands in a rent bursary near Suchou in late Ch'ing—tax records of the Feng Lin bursary, Wu hsien, Kiangsu province), (*Hitotsubashi*) *Keizaigaku kenkyū* 經濟學研究 (Hitotsubashi economic review) 6: 133–383 (1962).

——— "Kokuritsu Kokkai toshokan shūzō no 'Gyorin satsu' ni

tsuite" 國立國會圖書館收藏の「魚鱗册」について (The "Fish Scale" books in the National Diet Library), (*Hitotsubashi*) *Keizaigaku kenkyū* 7: 247–325 (1963).

——— "Nijū seiki shotō ni okeru Soshū kinbō no ichi sosan to sono kosaku seido—Kōso-shō Go-ken Hi-shi kyōju-san kankei 'soseki bensa' satsu no kenkyū 二十世紀初頭における蘇州近傍の一租棧とその小作制度—江蘇省吳縣費氏恭壽棧關係「租籍便查」册の研究 (An early twentieth century rent bursary near Su-chou and the tenancy system: a study of the "Handy rent reference" of the Fei "Respecting longevity" bursary of Wu hsien, Kiangsu), *Kindai Chūgoku kenkyū* 近代中國研究 (Studies on modern China) 5: 1–184 (1963).

——— "Shin-matsu no Kōnan ni okeru kosaku jōken to kosaku ryō ni tsuite—Kōso-shō Go-ken Han shi gisō, onajiku Go-shi Yo-kei-san no 'shōyu,' 'shōran,' 'soyu,' 'jijō,' 'sekkyaku,' oyobi 'shussetsu bisa' satsu no kenkyū" 清末の江南における小作條件と小作料について—江蘇省吳縣范氏義莊同吳氏畬經棧の「召由」・「承攬」, 「租由」, 「字條」・「切脚」および「出切備査」册の研究 (Tenant conditions and tenant fees in late Ch'ing Chiang-nan—research on the documents of the Fan charitable estate, Wu hsien, Kiangsu province, and the Wu bursary documents dealing with the terms *chao-yu*, *ch'eng-lan*, *tsu-yu*, *tsu-t'iao*, *ch'ieh chiao* and *ch'u ch'ieh pei-ch'a*), (*Hitotsubashi daigaku*) *Shakaigaku kenkyū* 社會學研究 (Hitotsubashi sociological review), no. 5: 129–208 (1963).

——— "Saikin gūmoku shita jakkan no Chūgoku jinushi-sei kankei bunsho ni tsuite—Harvard-Yenching kenkyū-jo shūzō no soyo sono ta" 最近遇目した若干の中國地主制關係文書について—哈佛燕京研究所收藏の租繇その他 (Recently examined documents dealing with the Chinese landlord system: rent documents in the collection of the Harvard-Yenching Library), *Tōyōgakuhō* 46.4: 1–33 (1964).

——— "Shin-matsu Min-sho no Kōnan ni okeru hōran kankei no jittai to sono kessan hōkoku—Soshū Go-shi yo-keisan 'Hōshō kaku-gō bi-sa' satsu no kenkyū 清末民初の江南における包攬關係の實態とその決算報告—蘇州吳氏畬經棧「報銷各号備查」册の研究 (The real conditions of tax farming in late Ch'ing and early Republican Chiangnan and reports of settlements: the "Report of accounts of various sub-branches" of the Wu bursary, Suchou),

Kindai Chūgoku kenkyū 6: 1–66 (1964).

——— "A Documentary Study of Chinese Landlordism in the Late Ch'ing and the Early Republican Kiangnan," *Bulletin of the School of Oriental and African Studies* 29.3: 566–599 (1966).

——— "Kindai Chūgoku no tochi bunsho ni tsuite—sono shurui to seishitsu" 近代中國の土地文書について—その種類と性質 (Modern Chinese land documents—different categories and their characteristics), (*Hitotsubashi*) *Keizaigaku kenkyū* 10: 1–50 (1966).

Myrdal, Jan. *Report from a Chinese Village*. London, Heinemann, 1965.

Nakane Chie. *Kinship and Economic Organization in Rural Japan*. New York, Humanities Press, 1967.

Niida Noboru 仁井田陞. "Shina kinsei no ichi-den ryō-shu kankō to sono seiritsu" 支那近世の一田兩主慣行と其の成立 (The practice of two lords to a field in modern China and its establishment), *Hōgaku kyōkai zasshi* 法學協會雜誌 (Law Association review) 64.3: 129–154 and 64.4: 241–261 (1946).

——— "Gen Min jidai no mura no kiyaku to kosaku shōsho nado—Nichiyō hyakka-zensho no rui nijū shu no naka kara" 元明時代の村の規約と小作證書など—日用百科全書の類二十種の中から (Yüan and Ming regulations of villages and tenant bonds—from 20 encyclopedia of daily use), *Tōyō bunka kenkyū-jo kiyō* 東洋文化研究所紀要 (Papers from the Research Center for Oriental Culture) 8: 123–166 (1956).

——— *Chūgoku hōsei-shi kenkyū: Tochi-hō torihiki-hō* 中國法制史研究：土地法取引法 (Chinese legal history: the laws concerning land and transactions). Tokyo, Tokyo University Press, 1960.

——— *Chūgoku hōsei-shi kenkyū: dorei nōdo-hō, kazoku sonraku-hō* 中國法制史研究：奴隷農奴法，家族村落法 (Chinese legal history: laws concerning slaves, households and villages). Tokyo, Tokyo University Press, 1962.

Nishijima Sadao 西嶋定生. "Shina shoki mengyō shijō no kōsatsu" 支那初期棉業市場の考察 (An investigation of early cotton markets in China), *Tōyōgakuhō* 31.2: 122–148 (1947).

——— "Mindai ni okeru momen no fukyū ni tsuite" 明代に於ける木棉の普及について (On the distribution of cotton in Ming), *Shigaku zasshi* 57.4: 1–22 and 57.5: 18–47 (1948).

Nishio Keijirō 西尾銈次郎. "Kodai ni okeru kōzan gijutsu no kenkyū"

古代に於ける鑛山技術の研究 (Research on ancient mining techniques), *Nihon kōgyō kaishi* 日本鑛業會誌 (Japanese Mining Association journal), no. 452: 682–685 (1922).

Ochse, J. J., M. J. Soule, Jr., M. J. Dijkman, and C. Wehlburg. *Tropical and Subtropical Agriculture*. New York, Macmillan, 1961.

Parsons, James. "The Ming Dynasty Bureaucracy: Aspects of Background Forces," *Monumenta Serica* 22.2: 343–406 (1963).

P'eng Hsin-wei 彭信威. *Chung-kuo huo-pi shih* 中國貨幣史 (A history of Chinese money). 2 vols. in the 1954 ed.; 1 vol. in the 1965 ed. Shanghai, Jen-min ch'u-pan she.

Perkins, Dwight. "Government as an Obstacle to Industrialization: The Case of Nineteenth-Century China," *The Journal of Economic History* 27.4: 478–492 (1967).

——— *Agricultural Development in China, 1368–1968*. Chicago, Aldine, 1969.

Postan, M. M. and E. E. Rich, eds. *The Cambridge Economic History*, vol. II. *Trade and Industry in the Middle Ages*. Cambridge, Cambridge University Press, 1952.

Potter, Jack M. *Capitalism and the Chinese Peasant: Social and Economic Change in a Hong Kong Village*. Berkeley, University of California Press, 1968.

Price, Ernest B. "Transportation and Public Works," in *Fukien: A Study of a Province in China*. Shanghai, Presbyterian Mission Press, 1925.

Pritchard, E. H. *The Crucial Years of Early Anglo-Chinese Relations, 1750–1850*. Pullman, Washington State College, 1936.

Saeki Yūichi 佐伯有一. "Mindai shōyaku-sei no hōkai to toshi kinu orimono-gyō ryūtsū shijō no tenkai" 明代匠役制の崩壞と都市絹織物業流通市場の展開 (The decline of the Ming artisan system and the development of urban textile flows to markets), *Tōyō bunka kenkyū-jo kiyō* 10: 359–426 (1956).

Sakai Tadao 酒井忠夫. "Mindai no nichiyō ruisho to shomin kyōiku" 明代の日用類書と庶民教育 (Ming encyclopedia of daily use and popular education) in Hayashi Tomoharu 林友春 ed., *Kinsei Chūgoku kyōiku-shi kenkyū* 近世中國教育史研究 (The history of modern Chinese education). Tokyo, 1958.

Sakakida, Evelyn. "Fukien in the Mid-Sixteenth Century: A Socio-Economic Study." Ph.D. diss., Harvard University, 1967.

Sakuma Shigeo 佐久間重男. "Mindai kai-gai shi-bōeki no rekishiteki haikei—Fukken-shō o chūshin to shite" 明代海外私貿易の歷史的背景—福建省を中心として (The historical background of illegal foreign trade in Ming with focus on Fukien), *Shigaku zasshi* 62.1: 1–25 (1953).

——— "Min-chō no kai-kin seisaku" 明朝の海禁政策 (The Ming sea ban policy), *Tōhōgaku*, no. 6: 42–51 (1953).

Sasaki Masaya 佐々木正哉. "Kanpo ni-nen Gin-ken no kō-ryō bōdō" 咸豐二年鄞縣の抗糧暴動 (The anti-tax riot in Yin hsien in 1852), *Kindai Chūgoku kenkyū* 5:187–299 (1963).

Shanghai shang-yeh ch'u-hsü yin-hang 上海商業儲蓄銀行 comp. *Shang-p'in tiao-ch'a ts'ung-k'an* 商品調查叢刊 vol. I. Shanghai, 1931.

Shiba Yoshinobu 斯波義信. "Nan Sō kome shijō no bunseki" 南宋米市場の分析 (An analysis of Southern Sung rice markets), Tōyōgakuhō 39.3: 31–66 (1956).

——— "Sōdai Kōnan no mura-ichi to byō-ichi" 宋代江南の村市と廟市 (Markets and fairs in Sung Chiangnan), *Tōyōgakuhō* 44.1: 41–76 and 44.2: 89–97 (1961).

——— "Sōdai ni okeru Fukken shōnin to sono shakai keizai teki haikei" 宋代における福建商人とその社會經濟的背景 (Fukien merchants in the Sung and their socio-economic background) in *Wada hakase koki kinen Tōyōshi ronsō* 和田博士古稀記念東洋史論叢 (Studies in Oriental history in honor of the 70th birthday of Dr. Wada). Tokyo, Kodansha, 1960.

——— "Sōdai nōson shi kenkyū o meguru shomondai" 宋代農村史研究をめぐる諸問題 (Topics on the history of Sung agriculture), *Shakai keizai shigaku* 31.1–5: 256–269 (1966).

——— *Sōdai shōgyō shi kenkyū* 宋代商業史研究 (Research on Sung commercial history). Tokyo, Kazama Shobō, 1968.

——— "Sōdai shōgyō shi kenkyū no tame no oboegaki" 宋代商業史研究のための覺書 (A note on research concerning Sung commercial history), *Shigaku zasshi* 72.6: 49–69 (1963).

Shigeta Atsushi 重田德. "Shin-sho ni okeru Konan komeshijō no ichi kōsatsu" 清初における湖南米市場の一考察 (An investigation of early Ch'ing rice markets in Hunan), *Tōyō bunka kenkyū-jo kiyō* 10: 427–498 (1956).

——— "Shin-sho ni okeru Konan no jinushi-sei ni tsuite—'Konan-shō rei sei-an' ni yoru shōron" 清初における湖南の地主制について「湖南省例成案」による小論 (Notes on the early Ch'ing landlord system in Hunan, based on "Administrative Precedents for Hunan province"), *Wada hakase koki kinen Tōyōshi ronsō*. Tokyo, Kodansha, 1960.

——— "Shin-matsu ni okeru Konan cha no shin tenkai—Chūgoku kindai sangyō-shi no tame no danshō" 清末における湖南茶の新展開—中國近代產業史のための斷章 (New developments in Hunan tea in the late Ch'ing: a brief study in the history of modern enterprises in China), *Ehime daigaku kiyō* 愛媛大學紀要 (Ehime University papers), 7.1: 47–62 (1962).

Shimizu Taiji 清水泰次. "Mindai Fukken no nōka keizai—toku ni ichi-den san-shu no kankō ni tsuite" 明代福建の農家經濟—特に一田三主の慣行について (The peasant economy of Ming Fukien —the custom of three lords to a field), *Shigaku zasshi* 63.7: 1–21 (1954).

Singer, Charles, E. J. Holmyard, A. R. Hall, and Trevor I. Williams, eds. *A History of Technology, Volume III: From the Renaissance to the Industrial Revolution, c. 1500–c. 1750*. Oxford, Clarendon Press, 1957.

Skinner, G. William. "A Study in Miniature of Chinese Population," *Population Studies* 5.2: 91–103 (1951).

——— "Marketing and Social Structure in Rural China," *Journal of Asian Studies* 24.1: 1–43 (1964), 24.2: 195–228 and 24.3: 363–399 (1965).

Spence, Jonathan. *Ts'ao Yin and the K'ang-hsi Emperor, Bondservant and Master*. New Haven, Yale University Press, 1966.

Sudō Yoshiyuki 周藤吉之. "Sōdai kanryōsei to daitochi shoyū" 宋代官僚制と大土地所有 (Sung bureaucracy and large land ownership), *Shakai kōsei-shi taikei* 社會構成史大系 (A comprehensive history of social structure), series 8. Tokyo, Nihon hyōron sha, 1950.

——— "Nan Sō no denkotsu, ya-kotsu, en-kotsu ni tsuite—toku ni 'kai-ten shū-bai' to no kankei," 南宋の田骨・屋骨・園骨について—特に「改典就賣」との關係 (The Southern Sung terms *t'ien-ku, ya-ku, yüan-ku* and their relationship to mortgaging practices), *Tōhōgaku*, no. 21: 73–86 (1961).

——— *Sōdai keizai-shi kenkyū* 宋代經濟史研究 (Sung economic

history). Tokyo, Tokyo University press, 1962.

Sun Ching-chih 孫敬之, ed. *Hua-nan ti-ch'ü ching-chi ti-li* 華南地區經濟地理 (Economic geography of South China). Peking, 1959.

Sun, E-tu and Shiou-chuan Sun, trs. *T'ien-kung k'ai-wu: Chinese Technology in the Seventeenth Century*. University Park, Pa., Pennsylvania State University Press, 1966.

Takanaka Toshie 高中利惠. "Mindai no Sen Shō o chūshin to suru toshi kyōdōtai" 明代の泉・漳を中心とする都市共同體 (Urban groupings in Ming with emphasis on Ch'üan-chou and Chang-chou), *Shigaku kenkyū* 史學研究 (Historical studies), nos. 77–79: 469–480 (1960).

Tani Mitsutaka 谷光隆. "Mindai kansei no kenkyū" 明代監生の研究 (Research on Imperial Academy students in Ming times), *Shigaku zasshi* 73.4: 56–81 and 73.6: 69–82 (1964).

——— "Mindai sensei-shi josetsu" 明代銓政史序說 (Introduction to the history of civil service recruitment under the Ming), *Tōyōshi kenkyū* 23.2: 77–93 (1964).

Tahara, Otoyori. "Class Differentiation of Farmers and Social Structure of Farming Communities in Postwar Japan," in Paul Halmos (ed.), Sociological Review monograph #10: *Japanese Sociological Studies*. Keele: University of Keele, 1966.

Tawney, R. H. *Land and Labor in China*. London, Allen & Unwin, 1932.

Terada Takanobu 寺田隆信. "Mindai Soshū heiya no nōka keizai ni tsuite" 明代蘇州平野の農家經濟について (On the peasant economy in the Suchou plain during the Ming), *Tōyōshi kenkyū* 16.1: 1–26 (1957).

——— "So Shū chihō ni okeru toshi no mengyō shōnin ni tsuite" 蘇・松地方に於ける都市の棉業商人について (Cotton merchants in urban markets in Suchou and Sungchiang), *Shirin* 41.6: 52–69 (1958).

———"'Mindai ni okeru henshō mondai no ichi sokumen—kyō-un nen-rei gin ni tsuite" 明代における邊餉問題の一側面—京運年例銀について (An aspect of border supply problems in Ming: the capital transport silver levy), *Shimizu hakase tsuitō kinen Mindai-shi ronso* 清水博士追悼記念明代史論叢 (Studies in Ming history in honor of the late Shimizu Taiji). Tokyo, Dai-an, 1962.

——— "Mindai ni okeru hokuhen no beika mondai ni tsuite" 明代

における北邊の米價問題について (Rice prices in Ming on the northern borders), *Tōyōshi kenkyū* 26.2: 48–70 (1967).

Ts'ao Yung-ho. "Chinese Overseas Trade in the late Ming Period," *Proceedings of the Second Biennial Conference of the International Association of Historians of Asia*. Taipei, 1962.

Wang Chung-lo 王仲犖. "Ming tai Su Sung Chia Hu ssu-fu ti tsu-o ho Chiang-nan fang-chih yeh" 明代蘇·松·嘉·湖四府的租額和江南紡織業 (Rents in the four Ming prefectures of Su-chou, Sung-chiang, Chia-hsing, and Hu-chou, and Chiangnan textiles), *Chung-kuo tzu-pen-chu-i meng-ya wen-t'i t'ao-lun chi*, vol. I. Peking, San-lien shu-tien, 1957.

Wang Yeh-chien. "Agricultural Development and Peasant Economy in Hunan during the Ch'ing Period (1644–1911)." Unpub. ms.

——— "The Impact of the Taiping Rebellion on Population in Southern Kiangsu," *Papers on China* 19: 120–158 (1965).

Wang Yü-ch'üan. "The Rise of Land Tax and the Fall of Dynasties in Chinese History," *Pacific Affairs* 9.2: 201–220 (1936).

Wickberg, Edgar. *The Chinese in Philippine Life, 1850–1898*. New Haven, Yale University Press, 1965.

Worcester, G. *The Junks and Sampans of the Yangtze*. 2 vols. Shanghai, Inspectorate General of Customs, 1947.

Wright, Stanley. *Kiangsi Native Trade and Its Taxation*. Shanghai, 1920.

Wu Ch'eng-lo 吳承洛. *Chung-kuo tu-liang-heng shih* 中國度量衡史 (A history of Chinese weights and measures). Chung-kuo wen-hua shih ts'ung-shu 中國文化史叢書 (Collected history of Chinese culture), ed. Wang Yün-wu 王雲五 and Fu Wei-p'ing 傅緯平, vol. VII. Shanghai, Commercial Press, 1937.

Wu Chi-hua 吳緝華. *Ming tai hai-yün chi yün-ho ti yen-chiu* 明代海運及運河的硏究 (Research on sea transport and the Grand Canal in Ming). Taipei, Institute of History and Philology, Academia Sinica, 1961.

Wu Ching-hong. "The Rise and Decline of Ch'üan-chou's International Trade and Its Relation to the Philippine Islands," *Proceedings of the Second Biennial Conference of the International Association of Historians of Asia*. Taipei, 1962.

Wu Han 吳晗. *Tu shih cha-chi* 讀史劄記 (Detailed records of historical studies). Peking, San-lien shu-tien, 1956.

——— "Ming ch'u she-hui sheng-ch'an-li ti fa-chan" 明初社會生產力

的發展 (The development of social productive capacity in early Ming), *Chung-kuo tzu-pen-chu-i meng-ya wen-t'i t'ao-lun chi*, vol. I. Peking, San-lien shu-tien, 1957.

Wu Kuang-ch'ing. "Ming Printing and Printers," *Harvard Journal of Asiatic Studies* 7.3: 203–260 (1943).

Yabuuchi Kiyoshi 藪内清, ed. *Ten-kō kaibutsu no kenkyū* 天工開物の研究 (Studies of *T'ien-kung k'ai-wu*). Tokyo, 1953.

Yanagida Setsuko 柳田節子. "Sōdai tochi shoyū-sei ni mirareru futatsu no katachi" 宋代土地所有制にみられる二つの型 (Two models found in landowning systems during the Sung), *Tōyō bunka kenkyū-jo kiyō* 29: 95–130 (1963).

Yang, C. K. *A Chinese Village in Early Communist Transition*. Cambridge, Massachusetts Institute of Technology Press, 1959.

Yang Lien-sheng. *Money and Credit in China*. Cambridge, Harvard University Press, 1952.

——— 楊聯陞. "K'o-chü shih-tai ti fu-k'ao shih-fei wen-t'i" 科擧時代的赴考旅費問題 (On grants to cover the expenses of traveling to the examinations), *Ch'ing-hua hsüeh-pao* 清華學報 (The Ts'ing-hua University journal), new series 2.2: 116–128 (1961).

Yang, Martin C. *A Chinese Village: Taitou, Shantung Province*. New York, Columbia University Press, 1945.

Yule, Henry. *The Book of Ser Marco Polo*. New York, Charles Scribner's Sons, 1903.

GLOSSARY

An-ch'i 安溪
An-fu 安福
An-hsiang 安鄉
An-hua 安化
An-jen 安仁

Ch'a-ling 茶陵
Chan-ch'eng 占城
Chang-chou fu 漳州府
Chang Hsien-chung 張獻忠
Chang Hung-fa 張洪法
Chang-p'ing 漳平
Chang-p'u 漳浦
Ch'ang-chou hsien 長洲縣
Ch'ang-lo 長樂
Ch'ang-ning 常寧
Ch'ang-sha 長沙
Ch'ang-t'ai 長泰
Ch'ang-t'ing 長汀
Ch'ang-te 常德
Chao-an 詔安
Ch'ao-chou 潮州
Chen-tse 震澤
Ch'en-ch'i 辰谿
Ch'en Ching-lan 陳靜蘭
Ch'en-chou 辰州
Ch'en Fu-liang 陳傅良
Ch'en Hsiao-lin 陳少林
Cheng-ho 正和
Cheng Jo-ts'eng 鄭若曾
Ch'eng-pu 城步
Chi hao 祭號
Ch'i-chung 寄種
Ch'i-yang 祁陽
Chia-ho 嘉禾
Chiang-hua 江華
Chiangnan 江南
chieh kao 桔槔
Chien-ning 建甯
Chien-shan 藍山
Chien-yang 建陽
Ch'ien-lung 乾隆
Ch'ien-yang 黔陽
Ch'ien-yu 僊遊
Chih-chiang 芷江
chih-ch'ien 制錢
chin 金
Chin 蘄
Chin-chiang 晉江
Chin-chou 金州
chin-chuang 進莊
Chin-men 金門
chin-shih 進士
Ching-chou 靖州
ch'ing 頃
ch'ing-liu 淸流
ch'iu 坵
chou t'ien 洲田

Chu Wan 朱紈
Ch'ung-an 崇安
Ch'ung-chen 崇禎
Ch'ung-yang 重陽
Chüan 涓
Ch'üan-chou 泉州

Erh-shou 二牧

Fan-tzu 翻子
Fen-ch'ih tsao 分遲早
fen-t'u yin 糞土銀
feng-shui 風水
Fo-lang-chi 佛郎機
Fu-an 福安
Fu-ch'ing 福淸
Fu-chou 福州
Fu-ning chou 福寗州

Hai-ch'eng 海澄
Hai k'e lung, Ch'ang ho 海客壠, 長盌
hai-t'ien 海田
Hankow 漢口
Heng-chou 衡州
Heng-shan 衡山
Heng-t'ang 横塘
Heng-yang 衡陽
ho 合
Hou-kuan 侯官
Hsi pien 西邊
hsi-t'un 牲頓
Hsiang 湘
Hsiang-hsiang 湘鄉
Hsiang-t'an 湘潭
Hsiang-yin 湘陰
hsiao-hsieh 小寫
hsiao-tsu 小租

hsien 秈
hsien 縣
hsien-shih 縣事
Hsien-yu 仙遊
Hsin-hua 新化
Hsin-ning 新寗
Hsin-t'ien 新田
Hsing-hua 興化
Hsing-ning 興寗
Hsü-p'u 溆浦
hsün-ts'ao 熏草
hu 斛
Hua-jung 華容
Huai-an 懐安
Huang-chu tsao 黃竹早
Huang ho 黃禾
Huang-li hsiang 黃歷鄉
huang-liao-li 黃料釐
Huang-mang 黃芒
huang-pi-shih 黃幣峙
Huang tsao 黃早
Hui-an 惠安
Hui-chou 徽州府
hui-kuan 會館
hui-tsu-chü 會租據
Hui-t'ung 會同
Hukwang 湖廣
Hung-chih 弘治

I-chang 宜章
i-hsüeh 義學
i-t'ien liang-chu 一田兩主
i-t'ien san-chu 一田三主
I-t'ung lu-ch'eng t'u-chi 一統路程圖記
I-yang 益陽

Kan-chou 乾州

K'ang-hsi 康熙
keng t'ao 粳(秔)稻
Kiangsi tsao 江西早
Kiulung 九龍
k'ou 口
ku 谷
Ku-t'ien 古田
Kuang huang yü k'ao 廣皇輿考
Kuang-tse 光澤
Kuei-hua 歸化
Kuei-tung 桂東
Kuei-yang 桂陽
Kung hao 公號
Kung Kuang-liu 龔光六
Kuo-tzu-chien 國子監
Kwangtung chan 廣東粘

lan-na hu 攬納戶
Lei-yang 耒陽
li 里
Li-chou 澧州
Li-ling 醴陵
Li Tzu-ch'eng 李自成
liang 兩
Lien-ch'eng 連城
Lien-chiang 連江
Lien shui 漣水
Lin-hsiang 臨湘
Lin-wu 臨武
Ling 酃
Ling-ling 零陵
Liu Han-tien 劉漢典
Liu-yang 劉陽
lo 籮
lo-liao-li 羅料釐
Lo-yüan 羅源
Lu-ch'i 瀘溪
Lung-ch'i 龍溪
Lung-shan 龍山
Lung-yang 龍陽
Lung-yen 龍巖
lung-yen 龍眼
lychee 荔枝

ma-t'ou 馬頭
Ma-yang 麻陽
Mao chan 毛粘
Min 閩
Min-ch'ing 閩清
mou 畝

Nan-an 南安
Nan-ching 南靖
Nan-p'ing 南平
Ning-hua 寧化
Ning po 寧波
Ning-te 寧德
Ning-yang 寧洋
Ning-yüan 寧遠

O-ning 甌寧

Pa-ling 巴陵
pai-tui 白兌
Pao-ching 保靖
Pao-ch'ing 寶慶
pao-ku 苞穀
pao-tien yin 保佃銀
Pei Chihli 北直隸
p'ei-chu 賠主
p'ei-t'ien 賠田
p'eng-min 棚民
p'i 坡
p'ing 秤
P'ing-chiang 平江
P'ing-ho 平和

Pu-lan-t'ai 布蘭泰
P'u-ch'eng 浦城
P'u-t'ien 莆田

Sang-chih 桑植
sao-chou 掃箒
Sha 沙
Shan-hua 善化
Shang-ch'eng i-lan 商程一覽
Shang-hang 上杭
shang-shui 商稅
shao-p'eng 梢篷
Shao-wu 邵武
Shao-yang 邵陽
she-hsüeh 社學
She t'ao 畲稻
sheng 升
sheng-yüan 生員
shih 市
shih 石
shih-hsi 食牲
Shih-ma 石碼
Shih-men 石門
Shou-ning 壽甯
shui-ch'e 水車
Shui-chien ke, Huo kuan lung 水梘隔, 火管壠
Shui chien (keng) ke 水梘(梗)隔
shui-li 水利
Shui-lu lu-ch'eng 水陸路程
Shun-ch'ang 順昌
So-ching tsao 縮頸早
Soochow (Su-chou) 蘇州
Ssu men shou yen ch'eng 寺門首庵埕
su 粟
Sui-ning 綏甯
Sung-ch'i 松溪
ta-hsieh 大寫
ta-tsu 大租
Ta-tung 大冬
Ta-yang-o ch'i-chung lung-hou keng 大洋尾溪中壠后坑
ta-yang yüan 大洋元
tai-t'ien 埭田
T'ai-ning 泰甯
tan 擔
tan-pa-ku 淡芭菰
tang-pa 盪耙
t'ang 塘
Tao-chou 道州
T'ao-yüan 桃源
Te-hua 德化
T'ieh-chiao tsao 鐵脚早
tien 店
tien-t'ou yin 佃頭銀
T'ien-ch'i 天啓
t'ien-hsi 田牲
t'ien-hsiang tsao 天降早
t'ien ken 田根
t'ien ku 田骨
t'ien mien 田面
t'ien p'i 田皮
Ting 定
T'ing-chou 汀州
tou 斗
tsa-liang 雜糧
tsao 早
tsung 總
tu 都
T'u-ch'un 突脣
T'u-lun 土稐
T'uan-ku tsao 團谷早
Tung-an 東安
tung-hsi 冬牲
Tung pien, Ma wan ke 東邊,

馬巒隔
Tung-t'ing 洞庭
t'ung (tree) 桐
T'ung-an 同安
t'ung-ch'e 筒車
T'ung-tao 通道
Tzu 資
Tz'u-ch'i 慈谿
Tz'u-li 慈利

wan 晩
Wan-li 萬歷
Wan-yung cheng-tsung 萬用正宗
Wang San-yüan 王三元
Wang Shih-mao 王世懋
wen 文
Wo t'ou, Chi lung 齋頭, 基壠
Wu-chiang 吳江
Wuhsi 無錫
Wu hsien 吳縣
Wu-hsü 浯嶼
Wu-i-shan 武夷山
Wu-kang chou 武岡州
Wu-ling 武陵
Wu-mang 烏芒
Wu-p'ing 武平
Wu San-kuei 吳三桂
Wu Yüan-chang 吳元章

Ya-ho 亞禾
Yang-chou 揚州
Yang-t'iao no 柳條糯
Yenan 延安
Yen-p'ing 延平
Yo-chou 岳州
Yu-ch'i 尤溪
Yu hsien 攸縣
Yung-an 永安
Yung-cheng 雍正
Yung-chou 永州
Yung-ch'un 永春
Yung-fu 永福
Yung-hsing 永興
Yung-ming 永明
Yung-shun 永順
Yung-ting 永定
Yüan 元
Yüan 沅
Yüan-chiang 沅江
Yüan-chou 沅州
Yüan-ho 元和
Yüan-ling 沅陵
Yüeh-kang 月港
Yünnan tsao 雲南早

Index

Harvard East Asian Series

1. *China's Early Industrialization: Sheng Hsuan-huai (1884–1916) and Mandarin Enterprise.* By Albert Feuerwerker.
2. *Intellectual Trends in the Ch'ing Period.* By Liang Ch'i-ch'ao. Translated by Immanuel C. Y. Hsü.
3. *Reform in Sung China: Wang An-shih (1021–1086) and His New Policies.* By James T. C. Liu.
4. *Studies on the Population of China, 1368–1953.* By Ping-ti Ho.
5. *China's Entrance into the Family of Nations: The Diplomatic Phase, 1858–1880.* By Immanuel C. Y. Hsü.
6. *The May Fourth Movement: Intellectual Revolution in Modern China.* By Chow Tse-tsung.
7. *Ch'ing Administrative Terms: A Translation of the Terminology of the Six Boards with Explanatory Notes.* Translated and edited by E-tu Zen Sun.
8. *Anglo-American Steamship Rivalry in China, 1862–1874.* By Kwang-Ching Liu.
9. *Local Government in China under the Ch'ing.* By T'ung-tsu Ch'ü
10. *Communist China, 1955–1959: Policy Documents with Analysis.* With a foreword by Robert R. Bowie and John K. Fairbank. (Prepared at Harvard University under the joint auspices of the Center for International Affairs and the East Asian Research Center.)
11. *China and Christianity: The Missionary Movement and the Growth of Chinese Antiforeignism, 1860–1870.* By Paul A. Cohen.
12. *China and the Helping Hand, 1937–1945.* By Arthur N. Young.
13. *Research Guide to the May Fourth Movement: Intellectual Revolution in Modern China, 1915–1924.* By Chow Tse-tsung.
14. *The United States and the Far Eastern Crises of 1933–1938: From the Manchurian Incident through the Initial Stage of the Undeclared Sino-Japanese War.* By Dorothy Borg.
15. *China and the West, 1858–1861: The Origins of the Tsungli Yamen.* By Masataka Banno.
16. *In Search of Wealth and Power: Yen Fu and the West.* By Benjamin Schwartz.

17. *The Origins of Entrepreneurship in Meiji Japan.* By Johannes Hirschmeier, S.V.D.
18. *Commissioner Lin and the Opium War.* By Hsin-pao Chang.
19. *Money and Monetary Policy in China, 1845–1895.* By Frank H. H. King.
20. *China's Wartime Finance and Inflation, 1937–1945.* By Arthur N. Young.
21. *Foreign Investment and Economic Development in China, 1840–1937.* By Chi-ming Hou.
22. *After Imperialism: The Search for a New Order in the Far East, 1921–1931.* By Akira Iriye.
23. *Foundations of Constitutional Government in Modern Japan, 1868–1900.* By George Akita.
24. *Political Thought in Early Meiji Japan, 1868–1889.* By Joseph Pittau, S.J.
25. *China's Struggle for Naval Development, 1839–1895.* By John L. Rawlinson.
26. *The Practice of Buddhism in China, 1900–1950.* By Holmes Welch.
27. *Li Ta-chao and the Origin's of Chinese Marxism.* By Maurice Meisner.
28. *Pa Chin and His Writings: Chinese Youth Between the Two Revolutions.* By Olga Lang.
29. *Literary Dissent in Communist China.* By Merle Goldman.
30. *Politics in the Tokugawa Bakufu, 1600–1843.* By Conrad Totman.
31. *Hara Kei in the Politics of Compromise, 1905–1915.* By Tetsuo Najita.
32. *The Chinese World Order: Traditional China's Foreign Relations.* Edited by John K. Fairbank.
33. *The Buddhist Revival in China.* By Holmes Welch.
34. *Traditional Medicine in Modern China: Science, Nationalism, and the Tensions of Cultural Change.* By Ralph C. Croizier.
35. *Party Rivalry and Political Change in Taishō Japan.* By Peter Duus.
36. *The Rhetoric of Empire: American China Policy, 1895–1901.* By Marilyn B. Young.
37. *Radical Nationalist in Japan: Kita Ikki, 1883–1937.* By George M. Wilson.
38. *While China Faced West: American Reformers in Nationalist China, 1928–1937.* By James C. Thomson Jr.

39. *The Failure of Freedom: A Portrait of Modern Japanese Intellectuals.* By Tatsuo Arima.
40. *Asian Ideas of East and West: Tagore and His Critics in Japan, China, and India.* By Stephen N. Hay.
41. *Canton under Communism: Programs and Politics in a Provincial Capital, 1949–1968.* By Ezra F. Vogel.
42. *Ting Wen-chiang: Science and China's New Culture.* By Charlotte Furth.
43. *The Manchurian Frontier in Ch'ing History.* By Robert H. G. Lee.
44. *Motoori Norinaga, 1730–1801.* By Shigeru Matsumoto.
45. *The Comprador in Nineteenth Century China: Bridge between East and West.* By Yen-p'ing Hao.
46. *Hu Shih and the Chinese Renaissance: Liberalism in the Chinese Revolution, 1917–1937.* By Jerome B. Grieder.
47. *The Chinese Peasant Economy: Agricultural Development in Hopei and Shantung, 1890–1949.* By Ramon H. Myers.
48. *Japanese Tradition and Western Law: Emperor, State, and Law in the Thought of Hozumi Yatsuka.* By Richard H. Minear.
49. *Rebellion and Its Enemies in Late Imperial China: Militarization and Social Structure, 1796–1864.* By Philip A. Kuhn.
50. *Early Chinese Revolutionaries: Radical Intellectuals in Shanghai and Chekiang, 1902–1911.* By Mary Backus Rankin.
51. *Communication and Imperial Control in China: Evolution of the Palace Memorial System, 1693–1735.* By Silas H. L. Wu.
52. *Vietnam and the Chinese Model: A Comparative Study of Nguyễn and Ch'ing Civil Government in the First Half of the Nineteenth Century.* By Alexander Barton Woodside.
53. *The Modernization of the Chinese Salt Administration, 1900–1920.* By S. A. M. Adshead.
54. *Chang Chih-tung and Educational Reform in China.* By William Ayers.
55. *Kuo Mo-jo: The Early Years.* By David Tod Roy.
56. *Social Reformers in Urban China: The Chinese Y.M.C.A., 1895–1926.* By Shirley S. Garrett.
57. *Biographic Dictionary of Chinese Communism, 1921–1965.* By Donald W. Klein and Anne B. Clark.
58. *Imperialism and Chinese Nationalism: Germany in Shantung.* By John E. Schrecker.
59. *Monarchy in the Emperor's Eyes: Image and Reality in the Ch'ien-lung Reign.* By Harold L. Kahn.

60. *Yamagata Aritomo in the Rise of Modern Japan, 1838–1922.* By Roger F. Hackett.
61. *Russia and China: Their Diplomatic Relations to 1728.* By Mark Mancall.
62. *The Yenan Way in Revolutionary China.* By Mark Selden.
63. *The Mississippi Chinese: Between Black and White.* By James W. Loewen.
64. *Liang Ch'i-ch'ao and Intellectual Transition in China, 1890–1907.* By Hao Chang.
65. *A Korean Village: Between Farm and Sea.* By Vincent S. R. Brandt.
66. *Agricultural Change and the Peasant Economy of South China.* By Evelyn S. Rawski.